Gender Discrimination for Religious Reasons in Islamic Countries and International Human Rights Treaties

Europäische Hochschulschriften Recht

European University Studies in Law

Publications Universitaires Européennes de Droit

Band/Volume 6672

Maryam Mosavi

Gender Discrimination for Religious Reasons in Islamic Countries and International Human Rights Treaties

PETER LANG

Bibliografische Information der Deutschen Nationalbibliothek
Die Deutsche Nationalbibliothek verzeichnet diese Publikation in der Deutschen Nationalbibliografie; detaillierte bibliografische Daten sind im Internet über http://dnb.d-nb.de abrufbar.

Library of Congress Cataloging in Publication Data
A CIP catalog record for this book has been applied for at the Library of Congress.

Zugl.: Osnabrück, Univ., Diss., 2020

D 700
ISSN 0531-7312
ISBN (Print) 978-3-631-84391-8
E-ISBN (E-PDF) 978-3-631-84982-8
E-ISBN (EPUB) 978-3-631-84983-5
E-ISBN (MOBI) 978-3-631-84984-2
DOI 10.3726/b18163

This publication has been peer reviewed.

www.peterlang.com

Acknowledgments

First and foremost, I am obliged to acknowledge my gratitude and appreciation to Prof. Dr. Albrecht Weber for accepting my supervisor and allowing me to carry out my thesis in the Department of Law of the University of Osnabrueck. I want to thank my supervisor for all the knowledge he shared with me, his readiness for scientific discussion, critical comments on written works, supporting me thoroughly to make this thesis possible, and especially his inexhaustible patience throughout my study.

I express my deep sense of thankfulness to Barbara and Dr. Bernd Hartlieb for their unforgettable practical, and emotional support amicably. I owe my gratitude to them, which made my stay in Berlin possible and enjoyable.

Finally, I take this opportunity to express my profound thanks to my parents, especially my beloved mother, who believed me for their love, encouragement, and supporting spiritually and instrumentally.

Abstract

Gender equality and non-discrimination are women's fundamental human rights that are recognized in general and specialized international human rights treaties. They contain the principles of gender equality rights and non-discrimination; thus, bind states to eliminate gender discrimination and promote gender equality rights formally *(de jure)* and in practice *(de facto)*. However, several states have put forth their specific interpretation of gender equality rights due to each state's diverse cultural, religious, traditional, political, and socio-economic aspects. Therefore, the realization of gender equality rights may be hindered under a state's jurisprudence of gender equality rights. Religious reasons might be used as a justification to impose discrimination against women. Islam recognizes as the official religion in the constitutional law of Islamic countries, and religious scholars have the competence to interpret Islamic law, resulting in a series of unequal rights for women based on Islamic law. This form of gender discrimination influences many different aspects of women's rights and often continues in legal structures.

Nevertheless, a majority of Islamic countries have ratified the international human rights treaties but have put reservations in place based on Sharia concerning articles on gender equality rights. In doing so, they circumvent the legal effect of specific provisions in their obligations. The general character of such reservations leads to a broad interpretation of gender equality rights within Sharia. Accordingly, other states parties objected to those reservations on the grounds of the incompatibility with the treaty's object and purpose. Furthermore, the international monitoring mechanisms address the gender issues resulting in their role being essential to the degree by which international law accepts gender discrimination for religious reasons in practice.

Zusammenfassung

Bei der Geschlechtergleichstellung und dem Diskriminierungsverbot handelt es sich um grundlegende Menschenrechte von Frauen, die in allgemeinen und besonderen internationalen Menschenrechtsverträgen anerkannt sind. Diese Verträge enthalten die Grundsätze, die Geschlechtergleichstellung und das Diskriminierungsverbot betreffen, verpflichten also Staaten dazu, geschlechtsspezifische Diskriminierung zu unterbinden und Rechte auf Geschlechtergleichstellung formal und in der Praxis zu fördern. Nichtsdestotrotz haben verschiedene Staaten eigene Deutungen von Geschlechtergleichstellung formuliert, die auf unterschiedliche kulturelle, religiöse, traditionelle, politische und sozio-ökonomische Sachverhalte der einzelnen Staaten Bezug nehmen.

Deshalb kann die Verwirklichung der Rechte auf Geschlechtergleichstellung durch die für solche Rechte einschlägige Rechtsprechung eines Staates behindert werden. Religiöse Gründe können als Rechtfertigung herangezogen werden, um Frauen zu diskriminieren. Der Islam gilt im Verfassungsrecht islamischer Staaten als offizielle Religion, und Religionsgelehrte sind befugt, islamisches Recht zu deuten, was dazu führt, daß eine Vielzahl ungleicher Rechte von Frauen auf der Grundlage islamischen Rechts geschaffen werden. Diese Art der Geschlechterdiskriminierung hat Einfluß auf verschiedene Aspekte der Rechte von Frauen, und findet in formalem Recht oft seine Fortsetzung. Dennoch hat eine Mehrheit der islamischen Länder die internationalen Menschenrechtsverträge ratifiziert, hat aber zugleich hinsichtlich der Artikel über Rechte, die Geschlechtergleichheit betreffen, auf die Scharia gestützte Vorbehalte formuliert.

Auf diese Weise umgehen diese Länder die rechtlichen Wirkungen bestimmter Vorschriften der Dokumente, die sie unterzeichnet haben. Der allgemeine Charakter dieser Vorbehalte führt dazu, daß eine allgemeine Deutung von Geschlechtergleichstellung, wie sie nach der Scharia verstanden werden soll, formuliert wird. Dementsprechend erheben andere Unterzeichnerstaaten zunehmend Einwendungen gegen solche Vorbehalte mit der Begründung, sie seien mit dem Gegenstand und dem Ziel des jeweiligen Vertrags unvereinbar. Außerdem befassen sich internationale Kontrollmechanismen mit geschlechtsspezifischen Fragen des Völkerrechts, die sich auf die Akzeptanz religiös begründeter geschlechtsspezifischer Diskriminierung beziehen.

Table of Contents

Abbreviations

CEDAW	Convention on the Elimination of All Forms of Discrimination against Women
CESCR	The Committee on Economic, Social and Cultural Rights
CSW	The Commission on the Status of Women
ECHR	The European Court of Human Rights
G.C	General Comment
G.R	General Recommendation
HRC	Human Rights Committee
ICCPR	International Covenant on Civil and Political Rights
ICESCR	International Covenant on Economic, Social and Cultural Rights
ICJ	International Court of Justice
OP	Optional Protocol
UDHR	Universal Declaration of Human Rights
UN	United Nations
VCLT	The Vienna Convention on the Law of Treaties

Introduction

The human rights system creates mechanisms to promote and protect fundamental human rights. The first step is to define the fundamental rights as basic human rights that belong to everyone without any discrimination. Second, human rights law obliges states to 'respect, ensure and fulfill' fundamental rights through appropriate measures in their legislation and policies; and the third step contains monitoring mechanisms that determine to which degree states meet their obligations under human rights treaties.

Equality and non-discrimination are fundamental human rights because respect for human rights and fundamental rights will be guaranteed when discrimination is not permitted. However, the right to equality and non-discrimination have two different concepts. Still, in parallel, they promote the right to equality and endeavor to eliminate any and all forms of discrimination. Therefore, in human rights law, this is known as 'the right to equality and non-discrimination', which must be guaranteed in the law (*de jure*) and also in practice (*de facto*).

The concept of discrimination provides a list of 'prohibited grounds'; the particular reference to 'or other status' or 'any kind of discrimination' creates an 'open-ended' situation for the recognition of extending the ambit of a 'prohibited ground'.[1] Gender-based discrimination is one of these and recognizes in general and specialized international human rights treaties; these set forth international gender equality standards.

Although several states recognize the general terms of gender equality and non-discrimination in their national constitution, which does not formulate any detailed framework. Thus, they put forth their specific interpretation of gender equality and non-discrimination that in general, do not comply with legal standards of gender equality and non-discrimination as enshrined in international treaties law. In fact, they justify their limitations on unequal gender rights in culture, religion, traditional, political, and socio-economic aspects. Therefore, the realization of gender equality rights may be hindered under the state's jurisdiction of gender equality rights, while they affirm the legal obligations to "respect, protect and fulfill equal rights" for women.

1 The Equal Rights Trust, Declaration of Principles on Equality: A Contribution to International Human Rights, London, 2008, Principle 5

Religious reasons also might be used to impose serious discrimination against women. In Islamic countries, Islam is recognized as an official religion in their constitution law, so much that they prioritize the Sharia law in their domestic laws. Typically, religious clerics have the competence to interpret Islamic law; that creates a male domination system and often assumes unequal rights for women compared to men. Discrimination against women defers to religious reasons and results in two consequences for women; first, there is legal gender discrimination where women face severe legal obstacles. Second, non-legal gender discrimination is a social-cultural obstacle for religious reasons.

As much as the legal system of Islamic countries is based on Islam, the degree of Islamic law interpretation varies across the spectrum. In other words, the extent of the understanding of Sharia impacts the capacity of women's access to equal rights. These differences are due to social norms, economic factors, and the nature of politics in each Islamic country. For example, in principle, Pakistan and Saudi Arabia are Islamic countries and create gender discrimination based on Sharia. But, in Pakistan, the social and political dynamics have provided areas for women's activities and religious-liberal communities to review Islam's re-interpretation for promoting women's rights as a whole, as far as women access higher government levels or serve as judges in high courts, which indicates the dynamic between Islam and gender issues. Nonetheless, Pakistani women still face discriminatory laws related to inheritance under Islamic jurisprudence. In contrast, Saudi Arabia has a strict interpretation of Islam, restricting women's presence in public decision-making, as well as discriminating against women in family law.

The potential legal gender discrimination based on religion occur more during participation in the public decision-making process and family law, where women have been a significant subject to discrimination. By and large, women's participation in the decision-making processes demonstrates whether they will be politically marginalized or whether their presence in different levels of decision-making positions would seek to promote gender equality laws. Additionally, discrimination in family law often justifies on religious grounds, and women do not have the same rights as men in family matters.

Even though Islamic countries impose their jurisdiction over gender discrimination in domestic laws under Islam's name, the majority of them have ratified international human rights treaties. Islamic countries by ratifying the international human rights treaties show that they are engaging with international mechanisms. Still, they have put in place the 'reservation based on Islam' concerning articles on gender equality rights. Thus far, such reservations create a gap to integrate women's human rights. In doing so, they want to exclude the legal effect of specific provisions in their obligations.

Moreover, such reservations lead to extending a general interpretation of gender equality. In this context, the Human Rights Committee (General Comment No. 24) states that reservations must be 'specific and transparent'; however, these reservations have had a general character, and their meaning is vague. Therefore, according to the Vienna Convention (1969), they are incompatible with 'the object and purpose of the treaty'. Furthermore, for other states parties, such reservations are unacceptable, and they made objections to the reservation on the grounds of the 'compatibility test'. Hence, they call on reserving Islamic states to be soon able to withdraw or modify their reservations based on Islam; in doing so, these states indicate their commitment to comply with international law.

Furthermore, Islamic countries have accepted the various procedures for monitoring within a 'Committee' by the ratification of international human rights treaties. Thus, through monitoring mechanisms will be identified to which degree states parties meet their obligation to gender equality rights, in practice. In this regard, it must add that most Islamic countries have ratified the international human rights treaties, but have not ratified separate their Optional Protocols, which include complaints' procedures. By these procedures, the committees agree to consider the submission of claims by an individual or group of individuals within the jurisdiction of a state that alleged violations must be related to "any of the rights set forth in the relevant Convention".[2] That means Islamic countries have been denied access to a legal instrument for lodging communications against them. As a result, the monitoring mechanisms for Islamic countries limit the consideration of their periodic reports that open 'constructive dialogue', especially about the scope of the reservations based on Islamic law and their justification. Moreover, the Committee makes its interpretation of substantive provisions in the form of general comments/ recommendations.

Nevertheless, there is a fundamental conflict in gender issues between Islamic law and international women's human rights. On the one hand, Islam intertwines in culture, social, legal, and political structures; on the other hand, Islamic countries are not marginalized from the international human rights system. Therefore, the following issues need to address:

---

2 Article 2 of the OP-CEDAW

1) the degree to which international law has accepted gender discrimination for religious reasons in practice, and
2) the future tendency of international law concerning the recognition of this particularity, with regard to the tension between international women's human rights and women's rights in Islamic law.

These questions will be analyzed and discussed in successive Chapters.

Chapter one presents a theoretical overview of the principle of equality and non-discrimination in international law and the term of each concept. Moreover, this chapter briefly defines gender discrimination in international human rights treaties. The general principle of gender discrimination endorses the Universal Declaration of Human Rights (1948), the International Covenant on Economic, Social and Cultural Rights (1966), and the International Covenant on Civil and Political Rights (1966). These international covenants create general terms of gender equality rights, and oblige states parties to implement them 'immediately the substantive equality rights'; however, these articles do not establish a framework for implementation of the prohibition of non-discrimination. Also, the Convention on the Elimination of All Forms of Discrimination against Women (CEDAW) is a specialized treaty addressing women's human rights issues. The CEDAW contains more details of equality rights by 'eliminating any discrimination against women'; in other words, it takes up the structural obstacles that makeup discrimination against women when rooted in culture, religion, traditional, political, and socio-economic aspects. The most crucial point in this chapter will discuss the existing obstacles to realizing equality and non-discrimination concerning diversity in international communities. Several states recognize the general term of non-discrimination, but they set forth their jurisdiction of gender equality in domestic laws. Therefore, there is a conflict between their definition of gender discrimination and the establishment of gender equality as requested in international law, where they do not undertake the legal consequences of violating or ignoring the relevant articles.

Nonetheless, Islamic countries impose a series of legal and public policies discriminating against women based on religion, while claiming a form of legality. In doing so, women face structural barriers that establish in domestic laws. Therefore, chapter two provides essential violations of gender discrimination based on Islamic law, includes women's participation in the public decision-making process and family law. The most important areas for women's participation in public decision-making include political parties, executive branches, national parliaments, and judiciary bodies. In general, the political structure has mobilized the religious scholars (*ulama)* to restrict women's political activity for religious reasons, when they have initiated a process of Islamisation.

On the other hand, the political structure has understood that they need women to embrace in public life for their legitimacy. As a result, today, women participate in decision-making processes under the watch of conservative and religious lines, even at a lower level of participation. Moreover, family law often justifies on religious grounds, and most discrimination against women occurs in matters of divorce, custody of children, and inheritance. It would also be addressed under which conditions reformed some issues in family law if family law amended in some of the Islamic countries.

The first section of chapter three deals with the role of international mechanisms to promote and protect gender equality rights. Mainly, it focuses on the functioning of the CEDAW-Committee as a special women's rights monitoring mechanism. Also, it addresses the evolution of its General Recommendations for the development and elaboration of specific provisions of the CEDAW.

However, what is even more challenging is the general reservation to human rights treaties, a process in which Islamic countries have abused by entering reservations based on Islam to gender issues articles, especially to CEDAW. In this regard, the second section of chapter three considers the reservations based on Islam to key provisions of the CEDAW, which target women's fundamental human rights. Thus, the CEDAW-Committee, the Human Rights Committee, and the CESCR have essential roles in reviewing such reservations, which are maintained to deal with practical problems. On the one hand, the committees (especially the CEDAW-Committee) must have a pragmatic attitude because these reservations are still more religiously based. Developing women's rights under the name of human rights faces stiff opposition from the dominant religious perspectives. On the other hand, the committees maintain the role of bodies of international monitoring mechanisms to promote and protect human rights. Hence, the committees must attend to the compatibility of the state's obligations with the international women's human rights, regardless of any grounding in domestic laws, culture, or religion.

Thus, through the committees' consideration of periodic reports and general comments/recommendations would be indicated the following concerns:

- First, whether Islamic governments take steps to comply with international law, through modifying or withdrawing their reservation, and under which conditions are the reservations modified, or do they remain?

- Second, it would need to clarify that under international law, to which degree the international community is comfortable with gender discrimination for religious reasons in the form of the reservation to human rights treaties?
- Third, are there practical recommendations to balance gender issues between international law and Islamic law?

Chapter 1 The Definition of Gender Discrimination according to International Human Rights Treaties: Historical Introduction

A. The Right to Equality in International Human Rights Law

The human rights system plays an essential role in protecting and promoting fundamental human rights for all people at the regional and international levels. The principle of equality and non-discrimination is also fundamental human rights because respect for human rights and fundamental rights cannot be achieved when discrimination is permitted. Thus, equality and non-discrimination are, without a doubt, a "fundamental rule of international human rights law",[3]which stresses the prohibition of discriminatory acts on grounds and, while doing so, promotes equality.

This part contains two sections. Section A covers the mechanisms of human rights law used to protect and promote fundamental human rights, and Section B addresses the status of equality rights and non-discrimination in international human rights law.

A.1 General Overview of Fundamental Human Rights

A series of human rights treaties is the source of basic rights and fundamental freedoms in the civil, political, economic, social, and cultural context that all human beings should enjoy without discrimination. These fundamental rights are recognized as "inherent, inalienable, interdependent, and indivisible"; this means they cannot be taken away, that the enjoyment of one right affects the enjoyment of others, and that they must all be respected.[4] Human rights law has constructed the following mechanisms to protect fundamental human rights:

---

3 OHCHR, Vienna Declaration and Programme of Action, adopted by the World Conference on Human Rights in 1993. A/CONF.157/23, para. 15

4 OHCHR | International Law, accessed at: http://www.ohchr.org/EN/ProfessionalInterest/Pages/InternationalLaw.aspx.

First, human rights law is self-explanatory and is comprised of a series of fundamental/societal rights that, at their core, protect the dignity of all humans. They are the rights a person has simply by being human, regardless of their nationality, location, sex, national origin or ethnicity, color, religion, language, or any other status. The scope of fundamental human rights encompasses:

- the right to undertake certain activities (travel, expression, religion)
- the freedom from certain conditions (torture, slavery, and inhumane treatments)
- the rights to services (education, health, a fair legal system, and the ability to work)
- the protection of people of vulnerable groups, such as the disabled, children, women, and refugees.[5]

Thus, fundamental rights are defined as basic human rights; they belong to everyone regardless of their situation. The international community "must treat human rights globally in a fair and equal manner, on the same footing, and it is the duty of states, regardless of their political, economic and cultural systems, to promote and protect all human rights and fundamental freedoms".[6] The most important these fundamental rights include the Right to self-determination, the Right to liberty, the Right to Equality, the Right to due process of law, the Right to freedom of movement, the Right to freedom of religion.

Secondly, international human rights create an international standard for how all humans should be treated. Accordingly, human rights treaties oblige states to 'respect, ensure and fulfill' fundamental rights. States should adopt the necessary measures and policies to make sure their domestic laws conform to these treaties' provisions. In this context, the Vienna Declaration talks about "the solemn commitment of all States to fulfill their obligations to promote universal respect for, and observance and protection of, all human rights and fundamental freedoms for all in accordance with the Charter of the United Nations, other instruments relating to human rights, and international law".[7] In general, international human rights treaties are covenants between a state and the international community,

---

5 Southeast Asian Human Rights Studies Network (SEAHRN), Human Rights, Textbook, accessed at: http://shapesea.com/wp-content/uploads/2016/02/HR-Textbook-Ch-1-Fundamentals-Ed-1.pdf. p. 5

6 OHCHR | Vienna Declaration and Programme of Action, para. 5

7 OHCHR | Vienna Declaration and Programme of Action, para. 1

whereby states are required to guarantee that fundamental rights are respected in their territories.[8]

Third, international human rights also contain monitoring mechanisms to ensure that human rights standards are 'respected, implemented and enforced' at the regional and international levels.[9] Through these monitoring mechanisms, the degree to which states have met their obligation under human rights treaties can be measured. Additionally, they ensure that states can be held accountable for violating or ignoring the human rights standard.

To summarize, international human rights do not set merely forth fundamental rights; rather, they seek to protect these rights by imposing obligations and duties on states, through their mechanisms, by monitoring the state's responsibility to respect, protect and fulfill human rights.

A.2 The Right to Equality and Non-Discrimination

Equality and non-discrimination are core elements of international human rights, whereby everyone must be treated equally before the law without any discrimination, such as that based on "race, colour, sex, language, religion, political or other opinion, national or social origin, property, birth or other status".[10] The measures establishing equality provide the means to remove the perpetuation of discrimination. Additionally, the principle of equality serves an interpretive and guidance function for policy/legislative makers, courts, and other human rights bodies when applying and developing human rights standards.[11] Equality rights and non-discrimination guarantees equal circumstances without any distinction or difference with regards to treatment in the law (*de jure*) and also in practice (*de facto*).[12]

---

8 International Justice Resource Center (blog), Overview of the Human Rights Framework, accessed at: http://www.ijrcenter.org/ihr-reading-room/overview-of-the-human-rights-framework/.

9 "OHCHR | International Law," accessed at: http://www.ohchr.org/EN/ProfessionalInterest/Pages/InternationalLaw.aspx.

10 Article 2 of UDHR

11 Farrior, Stephanie, Equality and Non-Discrimination under International Law (Routledge, 2017), p. 27

12 The content of the right to equality includes the following aspects: (i) the right to recognition of the equal worth and equal dignity of each human being; (ii) the right to equality before the law; (iii) the right to equal protection and benefit of the law; (iv) the right to be treated with the same respect and consideration as all others; (v) the right

A.2.1 The Concept of Equality and Discrimination

The concept of equality: The classic form of equality or formal equality refers to people being treated equally as individuals regardless of a group membership. It recognizes in the international human rights context in the phrase 'equality before the law' or 'benefit of the law'. But in recent years, the notion of equality has been translated into realizing equality or substantive equality in international law; hence, equality must go beyond the consistent treatment found in formal equality. In other words, equality not only applies a negative obligation not to discriminate but also imposes obligations to recognize differences between people. So, substantive equality occurs by removing the barriers to the advancement of disadvantaged groups, allowing them to take advantage of available opportunities.[13]

An approximate definition of equality can found in the Declaration of Principles on Equality.[14]

Principle 1 states that "The right to equality is the right of all human beings to be equal in dignity, to be treated with respect and consideration and to participate on an equal basis with others in any area of economic, social, political, cultural or civil life. All human beings are equal before the law and have the right to

---

to participate on an equal basis with others in any area of economic, social, political, cultural or civil life.

See also: The Equal Rights Trust, Declaration of Principles on Equality: A Contribution to International Human Rights, London, 2008, p. 60

13 Farrior, Stephanie, Equality and Non-Discrimination under International Law, Vol. 2, Ashgate, 2015, p. 54-55

14 The Declaration of Principles on Equality adopted 2008, The Equal Rights Trust- which was endorsed by experts and activities on equality and human rights from many countries around the world; to combat discrimination and promote equality as a fundamental human right and a basic principle of social justice. This Declaration consisting of 27 principles on equality are based on legal concepts that have evolved in UN, regional, and national jurisprudence. Although many of the terms employed in the Declaration are sufficiently well established, the resulting conception of equality in its entirety opens a new space for standard development in the international human rights system.

Also this Declaration has been used as the basis for developing anti-discrimination and equality in number of regional and international instrument. For example, in 2009, the UN Committee on Economic, Social and Cultural Rights (CESCR) made use of a number of key concepts from the Declaration in its General Comment 20: Non-discrimination in economic, social and cultural rights.

equal protection and benefit of the law". This definition of equality encompasses both ***formal and substantive equality***. Thus, the main elements of equality are equal enjoyment of all human rights and equal protection and benefit of the law. It also provides equal participation in all areas of life upon which human rights touch. However, in parallel to eliminating all forms of discrimination, substantive equality must be incorporated into policy by lawmakers.[15]

Moreover, the enjoyment of equality requires that ***appropriate measures*** be taken, if necessary, in legislation and policy to guarantee the equality of rights of the persons concerned. In this regard, there may be demands for positive action (affirmative action) to effectuate full equality rights — this form of preference being an exception to the general norms of non-discrimination. Positive action includes "a range of legislative, administrative and policy measures to overcome past disadvantage and to accelerate progress towards equality of particular groups is a necessary element within the right to equality".[16] For example, General Recommendation No. 25 by the Committee on the Elimination of Discrimination against Women calls for the implantation of temporary special measures to execute *de facto* or substantive equality for women to overcome past, targeted discrimination against them.[17]

The concept of discrimination: discrimination and unequal treatment are rooted in prejudice and stigma, which violate individual rights and interests. The concept of discrimination provides a list of 'prohibited grounds' with particular reference to 'or other status' or 'any kind of discrimination'. This open-ended formulation of non-discrimination seeks to cover all such forms of discrimination, allowing for an expansion of the recognized list of 'prohibited grounds'. It can be seen in the ever-expanding list of protected groups as a result of significant factors in society and the subsequent development of international human rights.

---

15 NYU Global Institute for Advanced Study, Article 7: The Equality and Non- Discrimination Provision. Appendix E to the Report of the Global Citizenship Commission. Cambridge, UK: Open Book Publishers, 2016, p. 15

16 Principle 3 of the Declaration of Principles on Equality, p. 61

17 CEDAW, General Recommendation No. 25 states that "should target discriminatory dimensions of past and current societal and cultural contexts which impede women's enjoyment of their human rights and fundamental freedoms. They should aim at the elimination of all forms of discrimination against women, including the elimination of the causes and consequences of their de facto or substantive inequality. Therefore, the application of temporary special measures in accordance with the Convention is one of the means to realize de facto or substantive equality for women, rather than an exception to the norms of non-discrimination and equality."

For example, new areas of equality and non-discrimination are being amplified, such as discrimination based on sexual orientation or health status, which are beyond the historically most egregious forms of discrimination based on race, color, ethnic origin, sex, language, religion, political or other opinions.[18]

In this regard, it must note that some forms of discrimination may have a "reasonable and objective justification." It is often the case that forms of discrimination must be balanced against claims of legitimate state interest, leading to proportional discrimination where the state's interest is strong enough.[19] It has also been recognized in General Comment No. 18, where it acknowledges that "not every differentiation of treatment will constitute discrimination, if the criteria for such differentiation are reasonable and objective and if the aim is to achieve a purpose which is legitimate under the Covenant".[20] Hence, not all forms of discrimination are prohibited.

In most human rights treaties, individual human rights related to equal treatment are acknowledged without any 'distinction, exclusion, resection' or preference associated with a particular group of characteristics.[21] Furthermore, grounds for discrimination should be explicitly referred to in legislation (formal discrimination) — so that states may 'guarantee' that the prohibition of any kind of discrimination will be exercised (substantive discrimination).

A.2.2 The Structure of Equality and Non-Discrimination

The structure of equality and non-discrimination in international human rights treaties has a triple status: it is a general principle, a freestanding right, and an accessory right.

- The right to equality is a general principle of the human rights framework: the right to be equal, as well as the enjoyment of human rights in the law and

18 Principle 5 of the Declaration of Principles on Equality

19 Farrior, Equality and Non-Discrimination under International Law, p. 63

20 CCPR, General Comment No. 18: Non-discrimination, adopted by the Human Rights Committee, 1989, para. 13

21 The Declaration of Principles on Equality, p. 63
The term "characteristic" refers to people who have been subjected to discrimination and is not meant to denote a metaphysical property of the person. Rather, it denotes the perceptions of others as well as the self-description of the ground on which one has been discriminated against. "Characteristic" should be understood to mean a feature that is not necessarily of a permanent or immutable nature, and can sometimes be short-lived or blend into other characteristics.

practice, which states in all human rights instruments. For instance, the Universal Declaration of Human Rights (UNHR) reaffirms that equal rights are the "foundation of freedom, justice, and peace in the world".[22]

- The right to equality is a freestanding right: this is a separate right, unrelated to or dependent upon other rights. Equality before the law and equal protection of the law are also freestanding rights because they are not dependent on or related to the recognition of any other civil, cultural, economic, political, or social rights.[23]
- The right to equality is an accessory right: this continues to "protect individuals from discrimination in the exercise of the other rights protected in the treaty",[24] in which states must respect the right to equality in public and private life; the right to equal liberty and security of the person; and the right to equal freedom of expression.

This structure of equality and non-discrimination plays an essential role in the development of the legal standard for equality rights in international human rights law. The enshrinement of the freestanding right to equality has the practical implementation in some "jurisdictions, [as] a separate, stand-alone right to non-discrimination". Additionally, accessory rights to other rights can strengthen equality in socio-economic life, which the states undertake to recognize as the relevant rights.[25]

A.2.3 The Sources of Equality and Non-Discrimination in International Law

International human rights law recognizes the right to equality and non-discrimination in two distinct ways: through general and specialized treaties.

---

22 In preamble, first recital of the UDHR stated that: "Whereas recognition of the inherent dignity and of the equal and inalienable rights of all members of the human family is the foundation of freedom, justice and peace in the world.

23 The Declaration of Principles on Equality, p. 62
Compare also, NYU Global Institute for Advanced Study, Article 7: The Equality and Non-Discrimination Provision, p. 1-3

24 Icelandic Human Rights Centre, The Right to Equality and Non-Discrimination, accessed, http://www.humanrights.is/en/human-rights-education-project/human-rights-concepts-ideas-and-fora/substantive-human-rights/the-right-to-equality-and-non-discrimination.

25 NYU Global Institute for Advanced Study, Article 7: The Equality and Non-Discrimination Provision, p.2

In general, UNHR, (Article 1, 2, and 7) and the International Covenant on Civil and Political Rights (ICCPR, Article 26) stress "equality before the law and equal protection of the law." Also, the International Covenant on Economic, Social and Cultural Rights (ICESCR, Article 2 (2)) and the ICCPR (Article 2 (1)) explicitly prohibits discrimination on any grounds.

Furthermore, there are specialized treaties for certain groups that may face discriminatory laws. These treaties are aimed at and detailed toward eliminating discrimination and promoting equality rights. They include discrimination against indigenous peoples, migrants, minorities, people with disabilities, discrimination against women, children, racial, religious discrimination, or discrimination based on sexual orientation and gender identity. Both general and specialized treaties set forth monitory provisions to ensure the implementation of equality rights; primarily calling for the creation of an expert committee tasked with creating an observing and reporting process, making general comments or recommendations, and considering individual complaints.

A.3 The Principle of Equality and Non-Discrimination in Practice

The above-stated summary mostly provides a theoretical overview of equality and non-discrimination principles found in international human rights treaties. The extent to which these general principles of equality and non-discrimination enforce by states in practice is mixed, because of existing obstacles to the realization of equality and non-discrimination concerning diversity in international communities.

Most states recognize in their domestic laws, particularly in national constitutions, the concept of equality and non-discrimination. Anti-Discrimination provisions are formulated in general terms of discrimination and do not establish any detailed framework of non-discrimination. Since states have different interpretations of what amounts to discrimination, they accordingly put forth their specific justifications as to why they cannot fully comply with legal standards of equality and non-discrimination as enshrined in international human rights treaties. In this regard, it states that "national equality legislation, whether in the form of one unified, comprehensive Act or a combination of several pieces of legislation covering specific equality strands or areas of activity, should be sufficiently detailed to realize the right to equality".[26]

26 Declaration of Principles on Equality, Equal Rights. p. 67

Thus, due to the diverse definitions of equality and non-discrimination rooted in the culture, religion, traditional, political, and socio-economic aspects of each state; states take different approaches towards unequal conditions. Hence, the realization of equality may hinder because states often seek to preserve their interests in manners that conflict with the establishment of equality and non-discrimination. To overcome this, the monitoring system of human rights is used to identify the barriers to realizing equality and non-discrimination at national, regional, and international levels that should be strengthened.

B. Gender Discrimination in International Human Rights Treaties

The prohibited grounds of discrimination cover an extensive range of issues with gender-based discrimination being one of them. The concept of gender discrimination recognizes major international human rights treaties, including the International Bill of Human Rights, which is generally formulated. The Bill comprises three texts: the Universal Declaration of Human Rights (1948), the International Covenant on Economic, Social and Cultural Rights (1966), and the International Covenant on Civil and Political Rights (1966). Also, the Convention on the Elimination of All Forms of Discrimination against Women (CEDAW), the specialized treaty addressing women's human rights issues, should be included in this discussion.

This section seeks to summarize and consider the concept of gender discrimination under international human rights treaties, including those as mentioned earlier.

B.1 Universal Declaration of Human Rights (UDHR)

With the end of the Second World War and its unspeakable atrocities, the international community swore to never again allow such horrendous violations of fundamental human rights to occur. Therefore, world leaders decided to create a Declaration of human rights that would establish and protect individuals' rights throughout the world, which complemented the Charter of UN protecting certain human rights. Thus, in its first session in 1946, the General Assembly drafted a Declaration placing a particular emphasis on the fundamental and freedoms of human rights. The Assembly tasked the Commission on Human Rights with the formulation of a Declaration that should be "relatively short, inspirational, energizing, and broadly accessible to peoples everywhere".[27] The Commission,

27 Brown, Gordon (ed.), The Universal Declaration of Human Rights in the 21st Cen-

composed of people from various legal, political, cultural, and religious backgrounds from all regions of the world, set out to achieve this goal. The final draft submitted by René Cassin was delivered to the Commission on Human Rights, which was held in Geneva. The draft of the Declaration transmitted to the General Assembly for comments became known as the Geneva draft. Finally, according to its resolution 217 A (III), the Assembly adopted the Universal Declaration of Human Rights (UDHR), comprised of 30 articles, in 1948.[28]

The UDHR was and remains a monumental step in the history of human rights and has become accepted as the foundational document of international human rights law. For the first time, the document created universal fundamental human rights and was also the first international instrument recognizing individual rights in the civil, political, economic, social, and cultural fields. As a practical matter, the Declaration contained two key ethical components, which served as the foundation for freedom, justice, and peace around the world: a commitment to the inherent dignity and a commitment to equality and non-discrimination for every human.[29]

B.1.1 The Nature of Articles Based on Equality and Non-Discrimination

Equality and non-discrimination are also fundamental principles in the UDHR. Some articles of the UDHR refer explicitly or implicitly to an equality right, as is found in the following articles:

Article 1 proclaims that: "All human beings are born free and equal in dignity and rights". There is no doubt that socio-historical aspects influenced the formation of this Article.

About these historical circumstances, Article 1 is seen as a moral principle that is "unobjectionable from the perspectives of otherwise rival cultural, religious and political tradition". The unobjectionable nature of this principle is crucially essential for the promotion of the international human rights process. On the other hand, Article 1 does not help with the question concerning why

tury: A Living Document in a Changing World. Cambridge, UK: Open Book Publishers, 2016, p. 29-30

28 History of the Document , accessed at: http://www.un.org/en/sections/universal-declaration/history-document/index.html.

29 Universal Declaration of Human Rights (UDHR) | 1948, Encyclopedia Britannica accessed at: https://www.britannica.com/topic/Universal-Declaration-of-Human-Rights.

such an entitlement to freedom and equal dignity should prescribe a system of inalienable and equal rights as enumerated in the UDHR.[30]

Article 2 regards as containing the universality provision concerning rights to equality.[31] Article 2 recognizes general protection against discrimination in specific situations.[32] The reference to 'without distinction of any kind' indicates that the broad categories of discrimination are not exhaustive. In other words, this provision is not an exclusive list of rights; rather, it is a point of departure for the designation of rights. While Article 2 includes discrimination based on gender, it is not alone sufficient to achieve gender equality. Instead, it has served as a model for the codification of the general principle of non-discrimination in the other international human rights treaties.[33]

Article 7establishes a general principle of equality before the law as well as equal protection against discrimination.[34] Analyzing the UDHR from an equality perspective reveals the many ways equality is necessary to protect, promote, and fulfill human rights adherence. Article 7 elaborates the principle of non-discrimination with two discernible elements: equality before the law and equal protection of the law in the first sentence, and equal protection in the second.

Although the UDHR represents the general provisions of non-discrimination, it does not codify who is responsible for ensuring all the rights enunciated in the Declaration. The Declaration is silent about who has to secure these rights

30 Ibid, p. 71

31 Article 2 of the UDHR: "Everyone is entitled to all the rights and freedoms set forth in this Declaration, without distinction of any kind, such as race, color, sex, language, religion, political or other opinion, national or social origin, property, birth or other status. Furthermore, no distinction shall be made on the basis of the political, jurisdictional or international status of the country or territory to which a person belongs, whether it be independent, trust, non-self-governing or under any other limitation of sovereignty."

32 Also, there are several other provisions prohibit discrimination in specific fields, for example articles 4 (the anti-slavery provision), 7 (the non-discrimination provision), 10 (the right to a hearing provision), 16 (the marriage and family provision), 18 (the thought and worship provision), 21 (the democracy provision), 23 (the conditions of work provision) and 26 (the education provision).

33 Alfredsson, Eide, The Universal Declaration of Human Rights. p. 87

34 Article 7 of the UDHR: "All are equal before the law and are entitled without any discrimination to equal protection of the law. All are entitled to equal protection against any discrimination in violation of this Declaration and against any incitement to such discrimination."

and assumes that states are the primary bearers of responsibility. Since corresponding legal duties shift to states in which state jurisdiction is an essential role in promoting the purpose of the UDHR.[35]

In this regard, it must note that underlying those articles is an exception that permits states to limit the individual's rights. Article 29 (2) places the burden of proof on anyone who seeks to restrict rights to show that such restrictions are necessary on the grounds of "morality, public order, and the general welfare".[36] Thus, Article 29 (2) opens the door for individual states to offer justifications for human rights derogation.[37] Therefore, it might be said that a gap exists between the purpose of the UDHR to protect human rights and the state's interests that might be used to limit these rights. Alternatively, at the very least, the UDHR seeks to preserve a balance between the realization of rights in the UDHR and the legitimate interests of states.[38]

B.1.2 The Status of the UDHR

The UDHR includes a series of moral imperatives concerning human rights law. On the one hand, the UDHR is a Declaration rather than a treaty; therefore, it has non-binding status, which at the beginning was one of its significant

---

35 Compare also: Brown, Gordon (ed.), The Universal Declaration of Human Rights in the 21st Century, p. 18 and 70-71

36 Article 29 (2) states: "In the exercise of his rights and freedoms, everyone shall be subject only to such limitations as are determined by law solely for the purpose of securing due recognition and respect for the rights and freedoms of others and of meeting the just requirements of morality, public order and the general welfare in a democratic society".

37 Brown, Gordon (ed.), The Universal Declaration of Human Rights in the 21st Century, p. 57-58

38 Alfredsson, Eide, The Universal Declaration of Human Rights, p. 634 and 643
the Commission (The Global Citizenship Commission (GCC)) acknowledged that the following standards should apply: "first, derogations ought to be publicly announced and publicly justified, whenever possible, and organized in the context of a legislative framework that provides for independent supervision and oversight; second, the justification should substantiate that the derogations in question are the minimum required to achieve the stated objectives; third, suitable arrangements should be in place for the supervision of detention, including procedural safeguards; and fourth, derogations should be for a fixed period, with renewal subject to the same conditions."
Brown, Gordon (ed.), The Universal Declaration of Human Rights in the 21st Century, p. 60

weaknesses. On the other hand, such non-binding status has the advantage of promoting human rights because its inherent flexibility provides a dynamic process to develop international human rights law in many legislative initiatives.[39] The UDHR was developed and established through the International Covenant on Civil and Political Rights and the International Covenant on Economic, Social and Cultural Rights, which followed twenty-eight years later. The primary purpose of drafting the covenants was to organize international co-operation for effective enforcement of individual human rights; hence, without monitoring the application of its rights, the Covenants would have "little practical value".[40] These covenants have binding status in international law by imposing legal obligations on states.

B.2 International Covenant on Civil and Political Rights (ICCPR)

Civil and political rights, rooted in classical human rights, are known as 'first generation' rights; in contrast, economic, social, and cultural rights are known as 'the second generation'. Civil rights provide conditions that protect an "individual's physical and mental integrity, life and security", and guarantee the liberal freedom of the individual "from the State." These rights include the rights to protecting the family, rights to liberty, and security of the person, rights to a Fair Trial. Political rights contain participation in civil society and guarantee the democratic freedom of access 'to the State'. These also include the right to vote and to participate in the public life of the state, the freedom of expression and assembly, and the freedom of thought, conscience, and religion.[41]

The International Covenant on Civil and Political Rights (ICCPR) contains the substantive civil and political rights which were adopted by the UN General Assembly in December 1966 and entered into force in March 1976. As of 2017, 169 states became parties to the Covenant.

The Covenant continues the important interpretation of civil and political rights, which the UDHR identified, but there are some differences in this

39 Universal Declaration of Human Rights (UDHR) | 1948, Encyclopedia Britannica, accessed at: https://www.britannica.com/topic/Universal-Declaration-of-Human-Rights.

40 Saul, Ben; Kinley, David H.; Mowbray, Jacqueline, The International Covenant on Economic, Social and Cultural Rights: Cases, Materials, and Commentary (OUP Oxford, 2014). p. 15 and 49

41 Nowak, Manfred, U.N. Covenant on Civil and Political Rights: CCPR Commentary, 2nd, rev. ed. Aufl. (Kehl [u.a.]: Engel, 2005). In Introduction(XX)

area. The ICCPR addresses the substantive civil and political rights explicitly so that these rights are 'immediately binding' upon states parties. Besides, the monitoring-body of the ICCPR (the Human Rights Committee) has an essential role in developing jurisprudence in international law. Hence, the ICCPR is a "universal instrument" that provides the core of the legally binding human rights protection about civil and political rights.[42]

The core provisions related to political and civil rights under the Covenant include; the right to life (Art.6), the right to freedom and security (Art. 9), the respect of privacy (Art. 17), the prohibition of torture and cruel, inhuman or degrading treatments (Art. 7), the freedom of thought, conscience and religion (Art. 18), freedom of movement (Art. 12), freedom of association, including the right to form trade-unions (Art. 22) and the cultural rights of ethnic minorities (Art. 27).

Articles Based on Equality and Non-Discrimination: The Covenant set forth several provisions in the context of equality and non-discrimination. The general provisions of non-discrimination contain in Articles 2 (1) and 26, and Article 3 addresses the prohibition of discrimination in relating to sex.

B.2.1 Article 2 (1): General Principle of Equality and Non-Discrimination-Accessory Character

Article 2 (1) regards the prohibition of discrimination in the exercise of the rights only recognized by the Covenant.[43]

The first part of Article 2 (1) constructs the obligation of a state party related to all 'individuals' within the 'state's territory and subject to its jurisdiction'. According to this phrase in Article 2 (1), the beneficiaries of the ICCPR are 'individual' and not 'collectives of individuals' such as the right of an individual to belong to an ethnic, linguistic, or religious minority. Hence, a state party is responsible only for persons 'within its territory'. In other words, all individuals achieve civil and political rights under ICCPR on equal footing when they are

42 Conte, Alex; Davidson, Scott; Burchill, Richard, Defining civil and political rights: the jurisprudence of the United Nations Human Rights Committee, Repr (Aldershot [u.a.]: Ashgate, 2005), p. 2-3

43 Article 2 (1) of the ICCPR: "Each State Party to the present Covenant undertakes to respect and to ensure to all individuals within its territory and subject to its jurisdiction the rights recognized in the present Covenant, without distinction of any kind, such as race, color, sex, language, religion, political or other opinion, national or social origin, property, birth or other status."

citizens or non-citizens in the state's territory.[44] In this regard, the Human Rights Committee has intended to increase the legal protections of a state within its jurisdictional authority, even when there is a violation of rights situated outside its sovereign territory.

Furthermore, the Committee made the meaning of this provision clarifies that a person who has fled abroad not be prevented by Article 2 (1), from submitting individual communication. Second, states parties are responsible for violation of the Covenant by foreign diplomatic representatives, and also they are responsible for the actions of their agents on foreign territory.[45] Therefore, according to the Committee's jurisprudence, the protection of a person is not limited to the state's territory; rather, it has been developed by case law in this context.

The second part of Article 2 (1) contains the scope of "prohibited grounds" of discrimination as enumerated in Article 2 (1). The bounds of non-discrimination are not exclusive, but they are capable of extension. On the other hand, the reference to 'other status' makes an 'open-ended' situation to extend for the recognition of a further ambit of a 'prohibited ground'. It should mention that discrimination based 'on other status' has been developed by the Committee in "*an ad hoc fashion on a case-by-case basis*".[46]

Regarding discrimination, Article 2 (1), does not define it in the Covenant, but the Committee elucidates the notion of discrimination through General Comment No. 18. The term of discrimination should be understood to imply "any distinction, exclusion, restriction or preference which is based on any ground such as race, color, sex, language, religion, political or other opinion, national or social origin, property, birth or other status, and which has the purpose or effect of nullifying or impairing the recognition, enjoyment or exercise by all persons, on an equal footing, of all rights and freedoms".[47] It seems that the Committee permits no exception; however, the Committee acknowledges that there is a distinction between different classes of persons based on 'objective and reasonable' criteria.[48]

---

44 Ibid, p. 3-4

45 Nowak, U.N. Covenant on Civil and Political Rights, p. 44

46 Conte, Davidson, Burchill, Defining civil and political right, p. 299-300

47 CCPR, General Comment No. 18, para. 7

48 CCPR, General Comment No. 18, para. 13. The Committee states "not every differentiation of treatment will constitute discrimination, if the criteria for such differentiation are reasonable and objective and if the aim is to achieve a purpose which is legitimate under the Covenant."

In general, Article 2 (1) provides fundamental rights of equality and non-discrimination. It creates the 'obligation' of non-discrimination on states parties to implement 'immediately' the substantive rights, which are mentioned in the Covenant. Still, this Article does not establish a framework for implementing the prohibition of non-discrimination. Therefore, the Committee demands states parties "to be informed about legal provisions and administrative measures directed at diminishing or eliminating such discrimination".[49]

B.2.2 Article 3: Discrimination Based on Gender- Accessory Character

Article 3 states that: "the states parties to the present Covenant undertake to ensure the equal right of men and women to the enjoyment of all civil and political rights set forth in the present Covenant". Article 3 'guarantees' equal rights for women and men, which obliges states parties to take a positive obligation with specific measures in practice. In this regard, the HRC completes Article 3, which states that "it must not only adopt measures of protection but also positive measures in all areas so as to achieve the effective and equal empowerment of women".[50]

The HRC has expressed that gender is a more important issue than the enumerated grounds of discrimination in the ICCPR than others.[51] In this regard, the Committee has formulated two General Comments on Article 3, General Comment No. 4, in 1981, and General Comment No. 28, in 2000. These General Comments address more detailed gender equality rights in the enjoyment of civil and political rights. In fact, Article 3 alone does not add increased protection in the framework of gender discrimination, and it must be read in conjunction with other Articles or/ Statements — especially with Article 26, in doing so, it may be doubted whether Article 3 comprises specific claims going beyond this.[52]

---

49 CCPR, General Comment No. 18, para. 9

50 CCPR, General Comment No. 28: Article 3 (The Equality of Rights Between Men and Women), adopted by Human Rights Committee, 2000, para. 3

51 Vandenhole, Wouter, Non-Discrimination and Equality in the View of the UN Human Rights Treaty Bodies (Intersentia nv, 2005), p. 115

52 Nowak, U.N. Covenant on Civil and Political Rights. p. 46

B.2.3 *Article 26: Right to Equality before the Law and Right of Non-Discrimination- Freestanding Character*

Article 26 considerably widens the scope of non-discrimination than does Article 2 (1) and Article 3. [53] The HRC acknowledges that "while Article 2 limits the scope of the rights to be protected against discrimination to those provided for in the Covenant, Article 26 does not specify such limitation, but provides in itself an autonomous right".[54] It seems that Article 26 comprehensively sets forth the prohibition of discrimination and its freestanding character guaranteeing non-discrimination with all rights so that states allow to examine all kinds of complaints outside the scope of the civil and political rights guaranteed under the ICCPR.[55] While Articles 2 and 3 limit the rights' scope as endorsed in the ICCPR to be protected against discrimination. These Articles are necessary to the character because a violation of these provisions can be found "only in conjunction with the concrete exercise of the substantive rights ensured by the Covenant".[56]

The first clause of Article 26 guarantees 'equality before the law' and 'equal protection of the law'. The concept of "equality before the law" is not directed to legislation, preferably to its enforcement of the law. That means judges and administrative branches must not apply legislation in an arbitrary or discriminatory manner. In other words, an arbitrary application of the law itself does not constitute a discriminatory provision; instead, it is a violation of the principle of equality before the law.[57] The concept of 'equal protection of the law' guarantees *de jure* equality through recognition of equality rights by enacting special laws and adequate protection against discrimination. In fact, the keywords of Article

53 Article 26 of the ICCPR states that: "All persons are equal before the law and are entitled without any discrimination to the equal protection of the law. In this respect, the law shall prohibit any discrimination and guarantee to all persons equal and effective protection against discrimination on any ground such as race, color, sex, language, religion, political or other opinion, national or social origin, property, birth or other status."

54 CCPR, General Comment No. 18, para. 12

55 Vandenhole, Non-Discrimination and Equality in the View of the UN Human Rights Treaty Bodies. p. 13

56 Ibid, p. 13

57 Alfredsson, Gudmundur, ed. International Human Rights Monitoring Mechanisms: Essays in Honour of Jakob Th. Möller, The Raoul Wallenberg Institute Human Rights Library : RAWA / Raoul Wallenberg Institutet För Mänskliga Rättigheter Och Humanitär Rätt. - Leiden [U.a.]: Nijhoff, 1997- 7 (The Hague [u.a.]: Nijhoff, 2001), p. 126

26 'equal before the law' and 'equal protection of the law' are used "to add some color to the extent without having a separate meaning".[58] Therefore, the right to equal protection of the law, the prohibition of discrimination, and the right to protection against discrimination in Article 26 form a unit. They have to do with "an obligation on states parties to ensure substantive equality by way of legislation".[59] It also can be concluded that non-discrimination in Article 26 "is a principle above the law", circumscribing the legitimacy of laws themselves.[60]

The second sentence of Article 26 states 'effective protection against discrimination' requires a 'positive obligation' to establish 'effective protection against discrimination'. Thus, it imposes an obligation on states parties to take measures protecting against discrimination 'on any grounds' in their laws. Positive measures of protection are necessary when certain groups of persons have been targeted by discrimination or when they have been subjected to specific matters of discrimination in the private sector. [61] It must add that Article 26 not merely permits positive measures but also requires states' obligation to comply with this Article.[62] However, the absence of extent adequate measures to correct discrimination may lead to violating Article 26.[63]

Article 26 also refers to 'any grounds' in the scope of prohibited discrimination. The issue of 'grounds' relates to "the permissibility or the reasonableness of the impugned distinction". It means that an unreasonable distinction may violate Article 26 regardless of the grounds upon which that distinction is made. Therefore, the regime of 'grounds' remains essential "to the extent that they help establish or disprove reasonability".[64] In this regard, the HRC made clear that

---

58 Ibid, p. 126

59 Nowak, U.N. Covenant on Civil and Political Rights, p. 606-608

60 Joseph, Sarah; Castan, Melissa, The International Covenant on Civil and Political Rights: cases, materials, and commentary, Third Edition, Oxford Univ. Press, 2013, p. 768

61 Nowak, U.N. Covenant on Civil and Political Rights. p. 608

62 Council of Europe, Non-Discrimination: A Human Right, Seminar to mark the entry into force of Protocol No. 12 Strasbourg, 11 October 2005, Council of Europe Publishing, 2006, p. 17
See also General Comment. 18 para. 10, that states: "the principle of equality sometimes requires States parties to take affirmative action in order to diminish or eliminate conditions which cause or help to perpetuate discrimination prohibited by the Covenant .....[H]owever, as long as such action is needed to correct discrimination in fact, it is a case of legitimate differentiation under the Covenant."

63 Nowak, U.N. Covenant on Civil and Political Rights, p. 631

64 Joseph und Castan, The International Covenant on Civil and Political Rights. p. 780

differentiation of treatment is permissible if: (1) the goal is to achieve a legitimate purpose; (2) the criteria for such differentiation are reasonable and objective.[65] However, it must add a reasonable relationship of proportionality between the legitimate aim and the discriminatory measure under review. In other words, "the objective of differentiation must be legitimate, and the means chosen must be appropriate and proportionate to that objective".[66] Therefore, since "the reasonable and objective test" is potentially very subjective, the Committee considers "reasonable and objective" on a case-by-case basis.[67]

It may lead to the conclusion that the principles of equality and non-discrimination have developed through the HRC's jurisprudence. Still, in this regard, the Committee does not use the full potential of the relevant provisions to apply non-discrimination stated in the ICCPR. On the one hand, the relevant provisions of equality and non-discrimination are not narrow or formalistic, but they are modernistic and egalitarian. Therefore, they are used in consideration of contemporary international human rights. They provide the Committee with new opportunities to establish universal equality for all peoples because through these provisions, especially Article 26; they strengthen the dynamic status of the interpretation and application of the principle of equality and non-discrimination.[68] On the other hand, to implement equality, the Committee utilizes a more flexible approach in practice. It means that the Committee addresses "what is to be considered reasonable"; depends on the specific circumstance, therefore considers the political process, financial structure, culture, and religion status within the objective and reasonable criteria;[69] hence, it may be open to challenge before the Committee when applying the principle of non-discrimination and equality. As a result, the Committee may be frustrated in developing the potential of those articles.

Regarding gender discrimination, it should mention that ICCPR has also paid special attention to gender discrimination, which is stated above. Therefore, the Committee has considered a wide range of gender issues in the public and private sectors. Moreover, the Committee has identified the most critical grounds

65 CCPR, General Comment No. 18, para. 13

66 Weiwei, Li, Equality and Non-Discrimination Under International Human Rights Law, The Norwegian Centre for Human Rights, 2004, p. 9

67 Joseph, Castan, The International Covenant on Civil and Political Rights, p. 781

68 Farrior, Equality and Non-Discrimination under International Law, p. 52

69 Nowak, U.N. Covenant on Civil and Political Rights, p. 628

for discrimination, such as traditions, customs, persistent attitudes, and prejudices, which form obstacles for women to enjoy the same rights as men.[70]

B.3 International Covenant on Economic, Social and Cultural Rights (ICESCR)

The International Covenant on Economic, Social and Cultural Rights (ICESC) was adopted by General Assembly Resolution 2200 A (XXI) of 16 December 1966 and came into force on 3 January 1976, after having been ratified by a majority of states. Economic, social, and cultural rights were recognized as essential elements of fundamental human rights granted to humans for their security, happiness, and fulfillment. These rights provide a commitment to "social integration, solidarity and equality" when the protection of ESC rights for everyone is ensured.[71]

The structure of the ICESCR is divided into three significant parts. First, the ICESCR establishes a framework for analysis, interpretation, and enforcement of economic, social and cultural rights, including the right to an adequate standard of living, the right relating to work, the right to education, the right to physical and mental health, the rights to social security such as protection of the family, and participation in cultural life.[72]

Secondly, the Covenant obliges states to adopt measures aimed to achieve ESC rights at the national and international levels. Hence, the ICESCR contains the essential obligations of states to 'respect, protect, and fulfill' ESC rights. The obligation to respect means states are obliged to identify infringements of the ESC rights within the state's jurisdiction to ensure that its legislation is in line with the Covenant obligations. The obligation to protect demands that states prevent their citizens from having ESC rights infringed upon by others. The obligation to fulfill requires states to actively realize ESC rights in the form of legislative, administrative, budgetary, judicial, or other measures.[73] In this regard, the

70 Vandenhole, Non-Discrimination and Equality in the View of the UN Human Rights Treaty Bodies, p. 115-116

71 Mapulanga-Hulston, Jackbeth K, Examining the justiciability of economic, social and cultural rights, International journal of human rights, Volum 6, 2002, p. 34

72 Ssenyonjo, Manisuli, Economic, Social and Cultural Rights in International Law (Bloomsbury Publishing, 2016). p. 3

73 Compare also, Riedel, Eibe; Giacca, Gilles; Golay, Christophe, Economic, Social, and Cultural Rights in International Law: Contemporary Issues and Challenges (OUP Oxford, 2014), p. 18-19

Convenat requires states to abolish or modify any laws, policies, or practices that interfere with the enjoyment of economic, social and cultural rights.[74] Third, it creates the Committee on the Economic, Social and Cultural Rights (CESCR) to monitor the obligations under Covenant within its mechanisms.

Articles Based on Equality and Non-Discrimination under ICESCR: The ICESCR also calls for states to adopt a 'guarantee to non-discrimination', and as well as promote equality rights. States are called upon to eliminate both *de jure* and *de facto* discrimination by taking measures to achieve equality.[75] Article 2 (2) of the present Covenant contains, in general, principles of equality and non-discrimination concerning some individual rights; Article 3 establishes gender equality.

B.3.1 Article 2 (2): The General Principle of Equality and Non-Discrimination — Accessory Character

Article 2 (2) requires state actors "to guarantee that the rights enunciated in the present Covenant will be exercised without discrimination of any kind as to race, colour, sex, language, religion, political or other opinion, national or social origin, property, birth or other status".

---

74 Leckie, Scott; Gallagher, Anne, Economic, Social, and Cultural Rights: A Legal Resource Guide, (University of Pennsylvania Press, 2011), in introduction

75 States parties to "guarantee" that the Covenant rights will be exercised without discrimination of any kind, discrimination must be eliminated both formally and substantively: Formal discrimination: Eliminating formal discrimination requires ensuring that a State's constitution, laws and policy documents do not discriminate on prohibited grounds; for example, laws should not deny equal social security benefits to women on the basis of their marital status;
Substantive discrimination: Merely addressing formal discrimination will not ensure substantive equality as envisaged and defined by article 2, paragraph 2. The effective enjoyment of Covenant rights is often influenced by whether a person is a member of a group characterized by the prohibited grounds of discrimination. Eliminating discrimination in practice requires paying sufficient attention to groups of individuals which suffer historical or persistent prejudice instead of merely comparing the formal treatment of individuals in similar situations. States parties must therefore immediately adopt the necessary measures to prevent, diminish and eliminate the conditions and attitudes which cause or perpetuate substantive or de facto discrimination.
See also, CESCR, General Comment No. 20: Non-Discrimination in Economic, Social and Cultural Rights (Art. 2, Para. 2, of the International Covenant on Economic, Social and Cultural Rights), Forty-Second Session, 2009, para. 8.

There are several significant points worth consideration in the framework of Article 2 (2):

First, the scope of prohibited grounds of discrimination, as stated in the Article is not exhaustive, as is made clear by the inclusion of the words 'and other status'. While it is unclear what 'other status' might include, it is reasonable to conclude that other specific forms of unfair discrimination that negatively affect the enjoyment of the rights within the Covenant, for instance, non-discrimination based on sexual orientation or disability, is one of them.[76] Nevertheless, the reference to discrimination based on 'other status' lends itself to an 'open-ended' debate about what non-discrimination forms are explicitly included. The CESCR has interpreted the scope of the non-discrimination concerning Article 2 (2) through its General Comment No. 20. This provides additional protection against discrimination on health, nationality, disability, poverty, age, and sexual orientation, so far as, it requires state actors to guarantee non-discrimination "in the exercise of each of the economic, social and cultural rights enshrined in the Covenant and can only be applied in conjunction with these rights".[77]

Secondly, according to this Article, non-discrimination is an immediate and cross-cutting obligation under the term of 'guarantee' and imposes obligations that are to be both formally and substantively exercised.[78] Hence, the Committee has stated that non-discrimination is "to be implanted fully and immediately"[79] to all the prohibited grounds of discrimination. In order to practice this, states are granted "a margin of discretion in adopting appropriate measures in complying with this immediate obligation"[80] so long as these states seek "to adopt the necessary measures and as well as positive action to prevent, diminish and eliminate the condition and attitudes which cause or perpetuate substantive or de facto discrimination".[81]

---

76 Farrior, Equality and Non-Discrimination under International Law, p. 120

77 CESCR, General Comment No. 20, para. 7

78 CESCR, General Comment No. 20, para. 7

79 CESCR, General Comment No. 11: Plans of action for primary education, 1999, para. 10

80 CESCR, General Comment No. 16: on the Equal Right of Men and Women to the Enjoyment of All Economic, Social and Cultural Rights, UN Doc. E/C.12/2005/4, 2005, para. 32

81 CESCR, General Comment No. 20, para. 8
See also: "Limburg Principles on the Implementation of the International Covenant on Economic, Social and Cultural Rights," ESCR-Net, accessed:

Third, because of Article 2 (2)'s general wording related to the concept of non-discrimination, the Committee set forth a definition of discrimination using such words as 'any distinction', 'exclusion', and 'restriction'. It has acknowledged that "discrimination constitutes any distinction, exclusion, restriction or preference or other differential treatment that is directly or indirectly based on the prohibited grounds of discrimination and which has the intention or effect of nullifying or impairing the recognition, enjoyment or exercise, on an equal footing, of Covenant rights".[82] Thus, non-discrimination is not an objective standard.

On the other hand, the Committee also permitted restrictions based on objective and reasonable interests in two instances. First, the aim and effects of the measures or omissions are legitimate, compatible with the nature of the Covenant rights, and solely for promoting the general welfare in a democratic society. Secondly, there is a clear and reasonable relationship of proportionality between the aim sought to be realized and the measures or omissions and their effects.[83]

To sum up, Article 2 (2) provides a general framework regarding the principle of equality and non-discrimination for accessing how ESC rights are to be practiced. In fact, Article 2 (2) only prohibits discrimination and shifts its implantation to states without considering whether states violate or ignore the Article. Thus, it is not binding, an all-encompassing tool to eliminate any discrimination. Moreover, any interpretation of Article 2 (2) must link to the Committee's attitude found within General Comments and Concluding Observations; otherwise, Article 2 (2) would be an international tool for reaffirming equality and non-discrimination under the general term of 'guarantee'. It must also acknowledge that the term of 'guarantee' might allow for monitoring mechanisms to measure whether the state has met its obligations.

---

https://www.escr-net.org/resources/limburg-principles-implementation-international-covenant-economic-social-and-cultural, para. 35-40
States' obligation to eliminate discrimination is immediately which is endorsed in the Limburg Principles; measures taken for the sole purpose of securing adequate advancement of certain groups or individuals requiring protection in order to ensure their equal enjoyment of economic, social and cultural rights are not considered discrimination, provided that such measures do not lead to the maintenance of separate rights for different groups and are not continued after their objectives have been achieved.

82 CESCR, General Comment No. 20, para. 7

83 Ibid, para. 13

B.3.2 Article 3: Non-Discrimination Based on Gender- Accessory Character

Article 3 also provides equality rights based on gender that states "the equal right of men and women to the enjoyment of all economic, social and cultural rights."

Article 3 recognizes an equal right for women and men to enjoy the same enjoyment of economic, social, and cultural rights. This Article does not merely state the principle of equality between the sexes but instead obliges states to establish equality effectively in reality; however, it is not enough to factual equality.[84]

The Scope of Gender Discrimination under Article 3: For understanding the scope of gender equality (Article 3) of the ICESCR, one must refer to General Comment No. 16 (2005), which can be viewed as one of the most important statements related to gender discrimination in international human rights law. The General Comment states, "the equal right of men and women to the enjoyment of all human rights is one of the fundamental principles recognized under international law".[85] This General Comment also defined discrimination against women literally as enshrined in Article 1 of CEDAW with reference to "any distinction, exclusion or restriction",[86] which created an absolute non-discrimination between both sexes.

Moreover, the Committee stressed that the realization of gender equality must take place in-laws and practice. The Comment reads, "failure to ensure ***formal*** and ***substantive*** equality in the enjoyment of the specific rights enumerated in the Covenant] constitutes a violation of that right".[87] Importantly, the Committee stressed that the prohibition of discrimination is not to be achieved progressively: it is an obligation of immediate effect.[88] In particular, the right to gender

---

84 Sepúlveda, M. Magdalena, The nature of the obligations under the International Covenant on Economic, Social and Cultural Rights, School of Human Rights Research series / School of Human Rights Research <Utrecht>. - Antwerpen [u.a.] : Intersentia, 1999- ; ZDB-ID: 2017500-0 18 (Antwerpen [u.a.]: Intersentia, 2003), p. 404

85 CESCR, General Comment No. 16, para. 1

86 Ibid, para. 11
Discrimination refer "any distinction, exclusion or restriction on the basis of sex which has the effect or purpose of impairing or nullifying the recognition, enjoyment or exercise by women, irrespective of their marital status, on a basis of equality of men and women, of human rights and fundamental freedoms in the political, economic, social, cultural, civil or any other field".

87 Ibid, para. 41

88 Vandenhole, Non-Discrimination and Equality in the View of the UN Human Rights Treaty Bodies, p. 23

equality is an immediate obligation for treaty parties to ensure that women can enjoy the right to equality concerning ESC rights under Covenant. In this context, the Committee demanded that "every State party has a margin of discretion in adopting ***appropriate measures*** in complying with its primary and immediate obligation to ensure the equal right of men and women to the enjoyment of all their economic, social and cultural rights. Among other things, state parties have to integrate appropriate strategies into national plans of action for human rights to ensure equal rights of men and women to the enjoyment of economic, social and cultural rights".[89] For instance, the adoption of ***temporary special measures*** may be 'necessary' to advance substantive equality for women in the enjoyment of rights under ICESCR and may be possible to improve the *de facto* position of women.[90] Hence, the application of appropriate measures is a tool for accelerating the development of ESC rights under the ICESCR.[91]

The Implementation of Article 3: The implementation of Article 3 must connect with other articles of the Covenant. The combining of Article 3 with Article 2 (2) provides significant legal protection against all forms of discrimination; both articles are integrally related and mutually reinforcing to the equality rights as enshrined in the ICESCR.[92] It is also true when they link with other articles such as Article 11 (1) (housing rights provisions such as inheritance).[93] In this regard, its two significant points should be addressed: the first is that the implementation of Article 3 depends on Article 2 (2) because implementation and interpretation of Article 3 are informed by the implementation and interpretation of Article 2 (2), while concerning Article 3 more details must be taken into account. Secondly, Article 3 adds nothing to the protections found in Article 2 (2) because of the concept of equal rights in Article 3 concerning women's position and nothing more.[94]

---

89 CESCR, General Comment No. 16, para. 32

90 Ibid, para. 35

91 Riedel, Giacca, Golay, Economic, Social, and Cultural Rights in International Law, p. 156

92 Vandenhole, Non-Discrimination and Equality in the View of the UN Human Rights Treaty Bodies, p. 23

93 UN Office of the High Commissioner for Human Rights (OHCHR), Fact Sheet No. 16 (Rev.1), The Committee on Economic, Social and Cultural Rights, May 1996, No. 16 (Rev.1), p. 6
Compare also: Farrior, Equality and Non-Discrimination under International Law, p. 110-111

94 Saul; Kinley; Mowbray, The International Covenant on Economic, Social and Cultural Rights, p. 237

Article 3 seems to reflect the preoccupation of the United Nations at the time concerning gender discrimination.[95] Thus, years later, the Limburg Principles in 1986 endorsed the idea that the implementation of Article 3 should take into consideration the CEDAW and other relevant instruments as well as the activities of the supervisory Committee (CEDAW).[96] In particular, the principle of substantive equality articulated by CEDAW and echoed by ICESCR is also integral to establishing women's ESC rights[97] because using the CEDAW Committee may strengthen recommendations and approaches related to women's ESC rights. On the other hand, it is crucial that in the implementation of the principle of non-discrimination in Article 3 and as well as in Article 2 (2), states must respect other human rights obligations. For example, states party to the ICESCR, which are also party to CEDAW are under more substantial obligations concerning socio-economic fields for women.[98] When applying Article 3, the United Nations Guiding Principles on Extreme Poverty and Human Rights must be attached,[99] which recommend the Committee's approach. This suggests a good summary of equality between men and women in the context of the enjoyment of economic, social and cultural rights in practice.[100]

95 Farrior, Equality and Non-Discrimination under International Law, p. 111

96 UN Commission on Human Rights, Note verbale dated 5 December 1986 from the Permanent Mission of the Netherlands to the United Nations Office at Geneva addressed to the Centre for Human Rights ("Limburg Principles"), 8 January 1987, E/CN.4/1987/17, Principle. 45, accessed at: https://www.escr net.org/resources/limburg-principles-implementation-international-covenant-economic-social-and-cultura

97 The Global Initiative for Economic, Social and Cultural Rights and ESCR-Net, The ICESCR at 50: The Significance from a Women's Rights Perspective, 2016, p. 6

98 Sepúlveda, The Nature of the Obligations Under the International Covenant on Economic, Social and Cultural Rights, p. 417

99 Human Rights Council, The Guiding Principles on Extreme Poverty and Human Rights, Resolution 21/11, The Office of the United Nations High Commissioner for Human Rights (OHCHR), 2012.
The Guiding Principles on Extreme Poverty and Human Rights are the first global policy guidelines focused specifically on the human rights of people living in poverty. They are intended for use by governments to ensure that public policies, including poverty eradication efforts, reach the poorest members of society, respect and uphold their rights, and take into account the significant social, cultural, economic and structural obstacles to human rights enjoyment faced by persons living in poverty.

100 The Guiding Principles on Extreme Poverty and Human Rights, adopted The Human Rights Council through its resolution 21/11, 2012. Principle 23-31 that requires states

In summary, gender equality rights in Article 3 and Article 2 (2) indicates that gender discrimination is the most important issue in the ICESCR view. Article 3 establishes the fact that "human rights of women and the girl, child are an inalienable, integral and individual human rights."[101] It might be argued that it applies to equal rights for both sexes when ESC rights are at issue and cannot apply to gender equality. In this regard, the CESCR expressed that it be "a necessary flexibility device," concerning gender discrimination, while ICESCR applies to the general realization of ESC rights, it cannot apply to women's right to equality.[102]

On the other hand, the structure of Article 3 provides a general concept of gender discrimination and does not contain detailed requirements for achieving equal rights between sexes. Article 3 has envisaged the international principle of gender equality that generally prohibits gender terms of discrimination. Therefore, Article 3 does not seem to reach its full potential to establish actual equality since the implementation of Article 3 relies on other human rights instruments, as mentioned above, especially Article 2 (2). Nevertheless, in conjunction with other instruments, Article 3 encompasses two significant results: first, it provides express gender equality with regards to ESC rights; and secondly, it holds states accountable to respect women's ESC rights within international monitoring mechanisms.

B.4 Convention on the Elimination of All Forms of Discrimination against Women (CEDAW)

The promotion and protection of women's human rights to ensure equality and non-discrimination has been created especially by the Convention on the Elimination of All Forms of Discrimination against Women (CEADW). It is an important international human rights treaty regarding women's issues. The main objective of the Convention is "the elimination of all forms of discrimination against women", which provides equality rights by eliminating any discrimination against women. Moreover, the enjoyment of equal rights should be exercised in the "political, economic, social, cultural and civil" context. CEDAW emphasizes the recognition of women's rights as formal *(de jure)* and in practice *(de facto)*. This section will address a brief history of CEDAW's adoption and its structure as well.

---

are obliged to eliminate both de jure and de facto discrimination against women and put in place measures to achieve equality between men and women.

101 Ssenyonjo, Economic, Social and Cultural Rights in International Law, p. 136

102 The ICESCR at 50: The Significance from a Women's Rights Perspective, p. 7

B.4.1 Short History of CEDAW

With the growth of women's movements for recognizing their fundamental rights both within the UN system and among women's activists, the Commission on Human Rights established in 1946 a sub-commission under the mandate of the Commission on the Status of Women (CSW). It called immediate attention to the issue of women's rights and the principle of equal rights in the context of gender. Between 1949 and 1959, the Commission prepared some conventions concerning women's rights issues, which then were adopted by the General Assembly. These Conventions provided some discussion on women's issues like the Political Rights of Women, the Nationality of Married Women, the Consent to Marriage, and the Minimum Age for Marriage and the Registration of Marriages. However, the international community decided that should recognize women's rights under the human rights treaty. Thus, the General Assembly on 5 December 1963 adopted resolution 1921 (XVIII), with particular regard to the protection and promotion of women's human rights. It requested the Economic and Social Council invite the CSW to draw up a draft declaration as an instrument international standard with the objective of equal rights of men and women. Drafting began in 1965 by a Committee selected through CSW with the Declaration on the Elimination of Discrimination against Women, and was ultimately adopted by the GA on 7 November 1967. But the declaration was only a statement of political and moral objectives, and it was not envisioned as a human rights treaty.[103]

The following years after the adoption of the declaration and the consideration of a voluntary report by the Economic and Social Commission, in 1972, CSW called upon to articulate a binding treaty that would support the declaration. The Secretary-General then requested the UN Member States to submit their opinions on such a proposal. Within the working group's report in 1974 at the twenty-fifth session, the Commission decided to provide a legal and comprehensive instrument to eliminate discrimination against women in specific fields. After that, at the World Conference of the International Women's Year held in Mexico City in 1975, it decided to prepare the Convention on the Elimination

103 Rai, Suman, Law Relating to Protection of Women from Domestic Violence: An Exhaustive Commentary on Protection of Women from Domestic Violence Act, 2005 with Emphasis on Various Studies by UNO, WHO, UNICEF, Amnesty International and Other National and International Organisations on the Topic Along with Australia, Japan, Malaysia, Mauritius, Singapore, South Africa, Sri Lanka, U.K. and Zimbabwe Laws on Domestic Violence (Orient Publishing Company, 2013), p. 769-771

of All Forms of Discrimination against Women within the working groups CSW and the Third Committee of the General Assembly. In the light of this working group, the General Assembly adopted resolution 34/180, the Convention on the Elimination of All Forms of Discrimination against Women in 1979, by a vote of 130 to none, with ten abstentions. Also, the Secretary-General demanded the presentation of the text of the Convention at the Copenhagen Conference on 17 July 1980 (World Conference on the United Nations Decade for Women: Equality, Development, and Peace). The Sixty-four States signed the Convention, and it was entered into force as comprehensive and international standards for women on 3 September 1981, after the twentieth country had ratified it.[104]

As of 2017, there are 189 states parties to the Convention. The states that have not joined the Convention at the time are Somalia, Sudan, the Islamic Republic of Iran, Tonga, and the Holy See. The United States of America and Palau, previously non-ratifying States, have just signed the Convention.

B.4.2 The Purpose and Structure of CEDAW

The Convention set forth the concept of discrimination against women through a policy of eliminating discrimination by all appropriate means. It also includes a comprehensive agenda to achieve substantive equality that obliges states parties to modify or abolish social/cultural and political attitudes.

Additionally, the design and purpose of the CEDAW constructed by General Recommendation No. 25 were:

- to ensure full equality of women before the law and protection against discrimination in public as well as the private sphere (formal equality),
- to improve the *de facto* position of women (substantive equality),
- to address prevailing gender relations and the persistence of gender-based stereotypes (transformative equality).[105]

The structure of the Convention involves an introduction and six parts. Part 1 (Articles 1-6) defines discrimination and states parties' obligations to eliminate any discrimination with all appropriate measures to ensure the equal enjoyment rights between women and men. Part II (Articles 7-9) covers equality in public life and as well participates at the intentional level. Part III (Articles 10-14) provides for women to access the economy and social rights. Part IV (Articles

104 Ibid, p. 771-772

105 CEDAW, General Recommendation No. 25, para. 7

15-16) affirms full equality in the private/family life. Part V (Articles 17-22) creates a Committee to monitor the provisions of the Convention. Part VI (Articles 23-30) establishes final provisions, which involves administration of the Convention and other details.

B.4.3 The Concept of Equality and Discrimination

CEDAW contains a comprehensive definition of discrimination and, therefore, goes beyond the concept of discrimination so that it is a pattern for the formulation of other General Comments to enhance the concept of discrimination. Article 1 defines discrimination as "any distinction, exclusion or restriction made based on sex which has the effect or purpose of impairing or nullifying the recognition, enjoyment or exercise by women, irrespective of their marital status, on the basis of equality of men and women, of human rights and fundamental freedoms in the political, economic, social, cultural, civil or any other field". There are some significant points concerning Article 1 that must mention.

Discrimination as any distinction, exclusion or restriction: Article 1 defines discrimination as 'any distinction, exclusion or restriction'. 'Distinction' implies differential treatment based on sex/gender that includes distinctions between women and men. 'Exclusion' refers to patterns of legal, social, and cultural actions in practice that opens up the possibility to deny women opportunities where, in contrast, these are available for men. 'Restriction' imposes the limitations on the enjoyment of equal rights to a greater extent than may apply to women's enjoyment of those rights.[106]

On the basis of sex: Also, the Convention recognizes that non-discrimination made 'on the basis of sex'. The Convention uses the term of 'sex', where the meaning of 'sex' refers to biological differences between men and women when it comprises gender identities that may disadvantage women. Also, another issue of 'sex' protects to discrimination against women on the grounds of their sexuality status, for example, sex orientation/gender identity, or when referring to the notion of sex in domestic legislation: either in the form of sex discrimination or the reflection of harmful stereotyped roles for women and men. 'Gender' refers more to socially constructed identities, attributes, and roles for women

106 Freeman, Marsha A.; Chinkin, Christine M.; Rudolf, Beate, The UN Convention on the Elimination of All Forms of Discrimination Against Women: A Commentary (OUP Oxford, 2012), p. 59

and men, and society's social and cultural meaning for these biological differences.[107] Therefore, 'gender' is not a synonym for 'sex' or 'women', but includes a broader concept which addresses socially constructed identities. 'Gender' was not yet recognized as a concept of international human rights law.[108] However, the CEDAW Committee, and in many contemporary rights instruments, use 'sex discrimination against women and men'. For example, the majority of individual communications to HRC and CEDAW are based on sex discrimination, not gender discrimination — toward the recognition of the importance of addressing women's specific experiences of discrimination.[109]

Which has the effect or purpose of — direct and indirect discrimination: Article 1 also encompasses both direct and indirect discrimination. 'Direct discrimination' occurs when explicitly mentioned differential treatment based on sex appeal in the laws, practices, or social beliefs. 'Indirect discrimination' constitutes the application of a natural criterion and *de facto* having another impact on women than on men as well.[110] Additionally, indirect discrimination incorporates the "structural and historical patterns of discrimination and unequal power relationships between women and men".[111] In this regard, states are responsible for eliminating any direct and indirect discrimination at their national level.

Irrespective of their material status: This phrase protects women regardless of their material status, for example, discrimination against married women on the grounds of their marital consequences compared to women who are not married. This phrase includes all women regardless of married/unmarried status. Additionally, in conjunction with 'any other field' makes the Convention dynamic in that it allows an interpretation of new forms and fields of discrimination.[112]

Coverage: CEDAW guarantees the exercise of equal/fundamental rights in all fields of life, notwithstanding the political, economic, social, cultural, and civil,

---

107 CEDAW, General Recommendation No. 28: on the Core Obligations of States Parties under Article 2 of the CEDAW, 2010, para. 5

108 Jänterä-Jareborg, Maarit; Tigroudja, Hélène, Brill, Women's Human Rights and the Elimination of Discrimination, Leiden, 2016, p. 47-48

109 Cusack, Simone; Pusey, Lisa, CEDAW and the Rights to Non-Discrimination and Equality," Melbourne Journal of International Law 14 (2013): 54–92, p. 59

110 eräJänt-Jareborg, Tigroudja, Women's Human Rights and the Elimination of Discrimiantion, p. 49

111 CEDAW, General Recommendation No. 28, para. 16

112 Zwingel, Susanne, Translating international women's rights: the CEDAW Convention in context, Gender and Politics (London: Palgrave Macmillan, 2016), p. 52

or any other. States parties oblige to eliminate discrimination against women in 'any other fields' to ensure women's full development and advancement. The phrase 'any other fields' anticipates the emergence of new forms of discrimination that has not been identified at the time of its drafting.[113] Therefore, CEDAW recognizes a broader range of discrimination against women, expanding the fields explicitly covered by the Convention.

Formal, substantive, and transformative equality: The CEDAW Committee endorsed comprehensive equality, including formal, substantive, and transformative equality.

- The Convention compels states parties to adopt a formal legal obligation of equal treatment of women with men. For example, Article 7 (a) requires states parties to adopt measures to guarantee women equal rights with men to vote, or Article 9 guarantees women equal rights to acquire, change or retain their nationality. In this regard, the Committee expressed that "these obligations should be implemented in an integrated fashion and extend beyond a purely formal legal obligation of equal treatment of women with men".[114] Therefore, formal equality is essential, but it is not sufficient for the full implementation of CEDAW.
- Substantive equality: It is necessary to achieve women's *de facto* equality. Hence, CEDAW requires states parties to take all appropriate measures to ensure substantive *(de facto)* equality between women and men. For example, Articles 3 and 24 require measures to be taken to ensure women's full development and advancement and the full realization of the rights. As a result, it is not enough for states parties to guarantee equal treatment; instead, they must also take biological, socially, and culturally constructed differences between women and men into account, which may require non-identical treatment to address those differences.[115]
- Transformative equality: The principle of transformative equality addresses the structural obstacles that discrimination against women originates from them. In this regard, the Committee requires states parties to "adopt measures towards a real transformation of opportunities, institutions, and systems so that they are no longer grounded in historically determined male paradigms of power and life patterns".

113 CEDAW, General Recommendation No. 28, para. 8
114 CEDAW, General Recommendation No. 25, para. 6
115 CEDAW, General Recommendation No. 25, para. 8

Moreover, the Committee calls on states parties to modify their norms, prejudices, and stereotypes that violate women's rights.[116] This transformative equality aims to change structures rather than making women more equal to men in such structures.[117]

To sum up, Article 1 of the CEDAW contains a more comprehensive definition of gender discrimination when comparing to ICCPR and ICESCR. The CEDAW sets out various forms of discrimination that women have experienced, while ICCPR and ICESCR also prohibit gender discrimination and protect "both men and women from treatment based on arbitrary, unfair and/or unjustifiable distinctions".[118] In fact, the scope of 'discrimination against women' is the "widely-used" pragmatic definition of discrimination,[119] but this broad character of gender discrimination can be divided into two perspectives.

On the one hand, it provides a dynamic and responsive instrument to articulate the content of equality and non-discrimination for the Committee. Thus, the ongoing development of equality and non-discrimination under the Committee's jurisprudence may lead to shaping the discourse on women's human rights at the national, regional, and international levels.[120] On the other hand, in practice, there are inconsistencies between the Committee's interpretative approach and its application of the rights to non-discrimination and equality;[121] therefore, it might be said that a gap exists between the purpose and application of Article1.

B.5 Conclusion

This section briefly examines the definition of equality and non-discrimination principles concerning gender. The UDHR, ICCPR, and ICESR provide a general definition of gender discrimination, and CEDAW containing more details of 'discrimination against women'. The emphasis on gender discrimination in relevant

---

116 CEDAW, General Recommendation No. 28, para. 2
In this regard, the Committee creates the conditions "to develop their personal abilities, pursue their professional careers and make choices without the limitations set by stereotypes, rigid gender roles and prejudices."

117 Zwingel, Translating international women's rights: the CEDAW Convention in context, p. 59

118 CEDAW, General Recommendation No. 25, para. 5

119 Vandenhole, Non-Discrimination and Equality in the View of the UN Human Rights Treaty Bodies, p. 71

120 Cusack, Pusey, CEDAW and the Rights to Non-Discrimination and Equality, p. 28-39

121 Ibid, p. 56

conventions indicates that gender-sensitivity is an essential issue in the view of international human rights treaties, as stated above. Even though international human rights have used their capacity to develop the concept of equality and non-discrimination based on gender, it does not mean that this system "as a whole is now fully satisfactory" because the application of equality depends on the extent to which the content and the interpretation of relevant provisions by states parties are reconciled.[122]

Although most states are parties to ICCPR, ICESCR, and CEDAW, in practice, there is still "a serious rift between standard-setting and implementation", and inequality for women in the enjoyment of equal rights is an ongoing situation. However, states very rarely assert that they are allowed to breach women's equal rights. States generally affirm the legal obligations to respect, protect, and fulfill equal rights for women, but within their jurisdiction.[123] Thus, they try to justify their limitation of rights; in doing so, they practice illegal discrimination while claiming a form of legality. In this regard, the HRC has considered a wide range of gender issues in the public and private sectors. The HRC has acknowledged that legislation does not offer the same level of protection of the family to both sexes and identifies the most critical grounds for discrimination, such as traditions, customs, persistent attitudes and prejudices, which form obstacles for women to enjoy the same rights as men.[124]

Therefore, a comprehensive approach to gender discrimination is sought to transforming prevailing social, cultural, financial, and political structures.[125] In this context, the International Court of Justice (ICJ) has stated that if a state "defends its conduct by appealing to expectation within the rule itself, then whether or not the State's conduct is, in fact, justifiable on that basis, the significance of that attitude is to confirm rather than weaken the rule".[126] However, it would recommend that the Committee of relevant conventions be strengthened to take the appropriate mechanisms to access equality for women in the enjoyment of equal rights.

---

122 Weiwei, Equality and Non-Discrimination Under International Human Rights Law, p. 25

123 Ssenyonjo, Economic, Social and Cultural Rights in International Law. p. 156

124 Vandenhole, Non-Discrimination and Equality in the View of the UN Human Rights Treaty Bodies, p. 115-116

125 Riedel, Giacca, Golay, Economic, Social, and Cultural Rights in International Law, p. 159

126 ICJ, Case concerning Military and Paramilitary Activities in and against Nicaragua, JUDGMENT OF 27 JUNE 1986, supra note 14, p. 98

Chapter 2 Potential Violations of Gender Equality Based on Religion

A. Gender Discrimination to Participation in Public Decision-Making Processes

A.1 The Right to Participation in Political and Public Life

Political participation is defined as citizens' activities affecting politics and includes any voluntary and nonprofessional actions concerning government structures and politics. It is a necessary condition in democratic societies because it emphasizes the role of ordinary citizens in political affairs, so much that "where few take part in decisions there is little democracy; the more participation there is in decisions, the more democracy there is".[127] Therefore, the extent of political participation is a criterion for assessing the quality of democracy. Due to rapid social and political developments, the scope of political participation covers many new modes such as "voting, demonstrating, contacting public officials, boycotting, attending party rallies, guerrilla gardening, posting blogs, volunteering, joining flash mobs, signing petitions, buying fair-trade products, and even suicide protests."[128]

Participation in political and public life is also known as the right of every citizen to take part in the conduct of public affairs. The conduct of public affairs relates to any process, directly or indirectly, in the legislative, executive/administrative, and judiciary branches of government. It also includes the formulation and implementation of policy at the international, national, regional, and local levels.[129]

Most importantly, the right to political participation must exercise without any discrimination. This right must not be restricted based on race, color, sex, language, religion, political or other opinions, national or social origin, property, birth, or another status.[130] Moreover, it should not be subject to 'unreasonable

---

127 Jan W. van Deth, What is Political Participation?, Oxford Research Encyclopedia of Politics, 2016, accessed at: http://oxfordre.com/politics/view/10.1093/acrefore/9780190228637.001.0001/acrefore-9780190228637-e-68

128 Ibid

129 CCPR, General Comment No. 25, The right to participate in public affairs, 1996, CCPR/C/21/Rev.1/Add.7, para. 5

130 Article 25 of the ICCPR

restrictions'; if any restriction exists, it should justify by domestic law where this is necessary, for example, setting a minimum age limit for the right to vote.[131] The following part will provide an overview of gender equality in decision–making processes.

A.2 Women's Equal Participation in Public Decision-Making Processes

Participation at different levels of decision-making processes across genders indicates the degree to which ordinary citizens connect with the democratic process. It is also a tool for assessing the size of gender gaps at the levels of political participation.[132] Additionally, both sexes' equality to engage in the political process provides a unique opportunity to integrate diverse perspectives, in which both sexes can represent their interests. Equal access for men and women to public life contributes to economic empowerment, equitable governance, and public trust "from the community level to top policy-making circles".[133]

In fact, without women's involvement at all levels of decision-making, cannot achieve the goals of equality, development, and peace. Women's participation/ activities in political and public life are defined as their ability to take part in politics through a range of activities such as discussion and debate, lobbying, and activism in formal and informal ways at all levels of decision making.[134] In this regard, women's political participation must go 'beyond numbers' in elected office. It means women must contribute to be effective in the decision-making processes. Women's enable to influence policy processes in three conditions must be fulfilled.[135]

The first condition pertains to the role of ***critical actors*** in decision-making; those who "act individually or collectively to bring about women-friendly policy

---

131 CCPR, General Comment No. 25, para. 10

132 Miki Caul Kittilson, Gender and Political Behavior, Oxford Research Encyclopedia of Politics, 2016, accessed at: https://doi.org/10.1093/acrefore/9780190228637.013.71.

133 OECD Global Forum on Public Governance, Women's Leadership in Public Life: Fostering Diversity for Inclusive Growth, OECD Conference Centre, Paris, 2014, p. 1

134 Womens UN Report Network, EGM/EPDM/ REPORT, Equal Participation of Women and Men in Decision-Making Processes, with Particular Emphasis on Political Participation and Leadership, United Nations, Division for the Advancement of Women (DAW), 2005, p. 21 para.14 and 24, accessed at: http://www.un.org/womenwatch/daw/egm/eql-men/FinalReport.pdf.

135 Ibid, para. 59-60

change", as far as they can transform their priorities into policy initiatives.[136] For example, increasing female representation in parliaments leads to promoting policies for women. Hence, the number of women involved in decision-making is a crucial factor determining whether they will be politically marginalized or whether they become key players in decision-making positions in the public offices that they assume.[137]

The second condition is ***critical structures***: each country's political system's structure and environment influence women's effective participation in policy-making bodies. In this context, governments are held accountable for increasing or limiting women's presence in public participation.[138] Therefore, the degree of government accountability improves the position of women in decision-making branches.

The third condition is called ***critical junctures*** and refers to opportunities for women to influence the policy-making processes, such as international negotiations in peace processes, peacekeeping activities, transitions to democracy, and the drafting of new constitutions. These periods of change and transformation provide different social/political groups with the opportunities to represent their interests, which means that women, too, can press for gender-sensitive reforms.[139] For instance, women's participation in peace processes can facilitate the inclusion of gender issues into a new peace agreement. Additionally, this contributes to the maintenance and promotion of international peace and security at national, regional, and international levels.[140]

To sum up, women's participation in decision-making is "a valid political project and indicator of gender equality in itself and a necessary condition for women to have influence".[141] On the one hand, women have a crucial role in formulating domestic laws and could integrate gender matters into national

---

136 Childs, Sarah; Lena Krook, Mona, Analyzing Women's Substantive Representation: From Critical Mass to Critical Actors, Journal compilation Government and Opposition Ltd Published by Blackwell Publishing, 2009, p. 127

137 Womens UN Report Network, Equal Participation of Women and Men in Decision-Making Processes, with Particular Emphasis on Political Participation and Leadership, para. 61

138 Ibid, para. 25 and 68

139 Ibid, para. 74

140 United Nations Security Council, Resolution 1325 on women and peace and security, 2000, para. 1

141 O'Neil, Tam; Domingo, Pilar, The power to decide, Women, decision-making and gender equality, Overseas Development Institute, 2015, p. 6

legislation. On the other hand, the importance of women's equal participation in decision-making indicates "transparent and accountable government and administration and sustainable development in all areas of life".[142]

A.3 The Status of Women's Participation in decision-making Processes under International law

Women's rights to participate in decision-making recognizes in international human rights treaties. Article 21 of the UDHR provides equal access to political rights without discrimination on any ground[143]— Article 25 of the ICCPR stipulates equal enjoyment of political rights without discrimination based on one's sex or any other ground.[144] CEDAW provides the most comprehensive provision in this context. Article 7 requires states parties "to take all appropriate measures to eliminate discrimination against women in the political and public life of the country".

Additionally, there are some recommendations and declarations where they set out the framework of international standards of equality for participating in public life. The most notable include:

- General Recommendation No. 23 (adopted by CEDAW Committee),
- Convention on the Political Rights of Women (General Assembly Resolution 640 (VII)),
- General Comment No. 25 (adopted by the Human Rights Committee)

---

142 Fourth World Conference on Women, Action for Equality, Development and Peace, Beijing 1995, para. 181

143 Article 21 of the UDHR: (1) Everyone has the right to take part in the government of his country, directly or through freely chosen representatives.
(2) Everyone has the right of equal access to public service in his country.
(3) The will of the people shall be the basis of the authority of government; this will shall be expressed in periodic and genuine elections which shall be by universal and equal suffrage and shall be held by secret vote or by equivalent free voting procedures.

144 Article 25 of the ICCPR: Every citizen shall have the right and the opportunity, without any of the distinctions mentioned in article 2 and without unreasonable restrictions: (a) To take part in the conduct of public affairs, directly or through freely chosen representatives; (b) To vote and to be elected at genuine periodic elections which shall be by universal and equal suffrage and shall be held by secret ballot, guaranteeing the free expression of the will of the electors; (c) To have access, on general terms of equality, to public service in his country.

- Resolution 1325(adopted by United Nations Security Council, 2000—the role of women in the peace process),
- OECD Recommendation on Gender Equality in Education, Employment and Entrepreneurship (2013),
- the OECD Global Forum on Women's Leadership in Public Life (2014) which address promoting gender equality for enabling gender diversity in public institutions for better and more gender-responsive policies and services,
- Beijing Declaration and Platform for Action (1995) provides a comprehensive framework toward the realization of the rights of women in public life.

A.4 Legal Barriers to Women in Public Decision-Making Processes for Religious Reasons

Women's access to decision-making processes varies across Islamic countries, generally due to different social norms, economic factors, and the nature of politics. Beyond the specificities of national contexts, Islam typically recognizes as an official religion in its legal system. Religious scholars traditionally interpret Islamic law, which is typified by the male domination system and often assumes unequal rights for women compared to men in the decision-making processes. In this regard, the essential point is the degree of their interpretation of Islamic law that impacts women's access to the decision-making process. In other words, the interpretation of 'Sharia' shapes the presence of women at different levels in public life; however, it creates obstacles or limitations for women to access the decision-making processes. It generates legal-gender discrimination in domestic laws where women face severe obstacles in public participation. Nevertheless, it also creates non-legal gender discrimination that provides a gate for women to re-interpret Sharia's review to develop their political rights.

In this section, different levels of women's participation in the decision-making processes will address Sharia's grounds in various Islamic countries. The most extensive range of gender discrimination in decision-making includes political parties, executive branches, the national parliament, and the judiciary system.

A.4.1 Political Parties

Political parties perform an essential role in government operation at all levels in which they seek to determine public policy through their candidates who are nominated and elected. They are the channel between civil society and the duly-elected representatives to the government; hence, political parties "fulfill many other vital roles in a democratic society".[145] While political parties mobilize voters, women's groups apply pressure to attach a gender equality agenda to the political programs. Consequently, the role of women in political parties has influenced the shaping of the parties' policies with their perspective.[146]

More importantly, political parties determine the degree to which women and men emerge as elected representatives or political decision-makers.[147] Women's participation in political parties depends on the protection of women in their policy agenda. Internal party regulations are essential in establishing the framework for women's political participation. In other words, political parties' laws can facilitate or hinder women's political progress. For example, some political parties seek to promote the position of women in party leadership. In contrast, other political parties tend to protect females nominated in the local election, where generally women have a better chance of emerging as candidates in such levels.[148] Thus, several factors are significant in the level of women's political participation, such as "the structures, policies, practices, and values of political parties".[149] It follows then that states must take measures to empower women's participation in political parties "to remove all barriers that directly or indirectly discriminate against the participation of women, to develop their capacity to analyses issues from a gender perspective, and to adopt policies to promote the ability of women to participate fully at all levels of decision-making within those political parties".[150]

145 The ACE Encyclopaedia: Parties and Candidates, published by ACE Electoral Knowledge Network, 2013, p. 8

146 Womens UN Report Network, Equal Participation of Women and Men in Decision-Making Processes, with Particular Emphasis on Political Participation and Leadership, p. 69

147 The OSCE Office for Democratic Institutions and Human Rights (ODIHR),Handbook on promoting women's participation in political parties, 2014, p. 16

148 United Nations, Women and Election, Guide to promoting the participation of women in elections, United Nations Office of the Special Adviser on Gender Issues and Advancement of Women (OSAGI), 2005, p. 35-36

149 United Nations Development Programme; National Democratic Institute for International Affairs, Empowering Women for Stronger Political Parties: A Good Practices Guide to Promote Women's Political Participation, 201, part III

150 Resolution 66/130, Women and political participation, adopted by the General Assembly, 2011, para. 6(c)

In various Islamic countries, political parties' policies have led to different levels of women's political participation, in which a brief of these different levels is as follows.

At the first level, some political parties have supported women at the highest levels of political structure, such as Prime Minister *Tansu Çiller* of Turkey(1993-1996, first female prime minister to date), *Benazir Bhutto* (1988- 1990, 1993 - 1996 Premier minister of Pakistan) and *Megawati Sukarnoputri* (2001-2004, President of Indonesia).

In **Bangladesh**, women have experienced a high level of political participation, e.g., Prime Minister *Sheikh Hasina* (1991-2001, 2014 until now, 2018) and *Khaleda Zia*(1991-1996, 2001- 2006), who were also in the leadership of their respective political parties. In this regard, two significant factors had influenced these women's seating in the high level of political participation. First, even though Bangladesh's state religion is Sunni Islam,[151] it is intertwined with indigenous religions in what is now Bangladesh. As a result, Bengali culture has had a significant effect on Sharia law interpretation regarding women's political participation. Consequently, they do not have a strong understanding of Islamic laws and provides a more open arena for women to promote their political rights.[152] The second factor is the role of the Islamic party in Bangladesh. The *Jammat-E-Islami (BJI)* as an Islamic political party has shifted "from an Islamic conception of democracy to support secular democracy" and has also supported equality for women.[153] Therefore, they could not exclude women in political participation for religious reasons, and, accordingly, women have achieved this level of political participation.

At the second level, some Islamic countries, such as Tunisia, Algeria, Djibouti, Libya, Mauritania, and Morocco, have adopted laws or executive decrees to encourage political parties to include a certain proportion of women on their lists of candidates.[154]

---

151 Article 2 of the Bangladesh Constitution 1988: "The state religion of the Republic is Islam, but other religions may be practiced in peace and harmony in the Republic"

152 Rolland, Abby M, Muslim Women Political Leaders and Electoral Participation in Muslim-Majority Countries, Gettysburg College's institutional, 2015, p. 4-6

153 Kurzman, Charles; Naqvi, Ijlal, ISLAMIC POLITICAL PARTIES AND PARLIAMENTARY ELECTIONS, United States Institute of Peace, 2009, p. 19

154 Economic and Social Commission for Western Asia (ESCWA), A Review of the Status of Women and Gender Equality in the Arab Region, 20 Years after the Adoption of the Beijing Declaration and Platform for Action, 2016, p. 16

In **Tunisia,** before the 2011 elections, which were the first elections after the revolution in January 2011, they had unequal gender composition that applied directly to men without exception. Activists and feminists struggled to attach gender equality to the electoral law, emphasizing adequate women's representation in the assembly. This mobilization led to adopting the Decree of May 10, 2011 (Article 16), which concerned the election of the National Constituent Assembly. It established "parity in candidacy between men and women alternating male and female names in the electoral lists and canceling the lists that do not respect this rule".[155] This Decree granted legal gender equality through political parties in their electoral lists. Hence, political parties should nominate males and females in their electoral lists.[156]

It is also important to point out that the *Nahda* party (founded in 1981) won the election in 2014. It is the most prominent of all Tunisia's Islamic parties and brought the most women to the Chamber (59 women were nominated, 42 women were successfully elected), and it has placed one non-veiled woman ahead of the list.[157] The leadership of *Nahda* (*Rachid Ghannouchi*) acknowledged that "the new government should be realistic and align with Tunisian society's real-life".[158] Although the *Nahda* party is an Islamic party, the Tunisian women joined the *Nahda* party to pursue their political rights by the law and society.[159] Indeed, the *Nahda* considered the quota as positive discrimination against women to guarantee political participation for women and force them to participate. In general, women in the *Nahda* party have a unique experience in political rights/ involvement in that they have succeeded in obtaining a 50 percent quota in the parliamentary elections. This considered being one of the highest percentages in the world.[160]

---

155 Toperich, Sasha; Mullins, Andy, A New Paradigm: Perspectives on the Changing Mediterranean, Center for Transatlantic Relations, 2014, p. 227

156 Ibid, p. 228
There were 5502 women candidates which 128 lists are headed by women, 85 are lists of parties and 43 independent candidates

157 Ibid, p. 229

158 Bary, Ida, Women's Political Participation in Muslim Brotherhood between the Hammer of Ambiguity and the Anvil of Inclusion moderation: (The Case of Egypt and Tunisia), Norwegian University of Life Sciences Faculty of Social Sciences Department of International, Environmental and Development Studies (NORAGRIC), 2015, p. 15

159 Ibid, p. 27

160 Ibid, p. 41

At the third level of participation, there are no female legal activities within the political parties. In **Saudi Arabia**'s constitution, political parties are officially banned.[161] Saudi women are excluded from legal activity in political parties; this may ultimately hinder women's rights advancement in other areas. In **Qatar,** political parties are also banned,[162] which is an obstacle to the expansion of women's political participation.

The crucial point regarding women's political participation in Islamic countries is the degree of prevalence of Islamic political parties. They determine how women can gain political participation. That is to say, they may limit or advocate strict controls over women's participation in politics. Therefore, to a better understanding of how these women access political participation, one must understand the role that Islamic parties have played.[163]

A surprising fact is that Islamic political parties are more likely to have been a significant force in a shift toward more liberal positions and an emphasis on the issues of democracy and gender equality as well.[164] For example, **Hizbullah** is a *Shi'ite*Islamist political party in Lebanon, which understands Lebanon's political and social dynamics. Therefore, they switched from religious ideology to political ideology and added gender equality in their political programs. In 2004, the party decided to encourage women's participation in political life and for the first time in its history, has appointed the head of its Women's Organization as a member of its 18-member Political Council.[165]

In contrast, the **Muslim Brotherhood** in Egypt switched from secular democracy to Islamic democracy.[166] The Muslim Brotherhood (founded in 1928) is the Islamic ideology party in Egypt, which had traditionally restricted women from political participation. The Egyptian Muslim Brotherhood has allowed women to participate in politics; thus, in 2000, women were nominated for the Muslim Brotherhood's list of candidates for the parliamentary elections. Subsequently, in 2005, 21 women from the Muslim Brotherhood were nominated as their candidates, but only one woman become a member of the parliament for the first time.

161 Cavendish, Marshall, World and Its Peoples (Marshall Cavendish, 2006), p. 78

162 Qatar, 29. Januar 2017, accessed at: https://freedomhouse.org/report/freedom-world/2017/qatar.

163 Muslim Women Political Leaders and Electoral Participation in Muslim-Majority Countries, p. 8

164 Kurzman, Naqvi, p. 19

165 Elie Alagha, Joseph, The Shifts in Hizbullah's Ideology: Religious Ideology, Political Ideology, and Political Program, Amsterdam University Press, 2006, p. 58

166 Kurzman, Naqvi, p. 19

In contrast, women do not have any right to participate in the Brotherhood's hierarchal structure; therefore, there is an obstacle within the conservative and *Salafist* view to preventing women from full political participation.[167]

Interestingly, can argue the flexibility of Islamic parties to embrace women's political participation against the position that "religiously motivated parties are more detrimental to women's political representation than are their secular counterparts". When in fact, women's access to political participation has increased under the watch of conservative and religious, not under liberal reformist or secular parties.[168] It could potentially instigate more reforms for women in political decision-making under Islamic political parties.

A.4.2 Executive Branches

The executive branches "set the policy agenda of a nation, determine the content of many policies, and oversee and guide policy implementation and administration".[169] Therefore, the presence of women in the executive branch introduces a gender-sensitive approach to government halls. Women's administrative posts' participation tends to bring about policies to advance women, especially when women access high positions in government. For instance, female ministerial positions seek to modify the gender issues that women have suffered and lead to reviewing in public women's empowerment in a high level of decision-making processes. In this regard, the political structure is an essential factor for the inclusion or exclusion of women in government.

This section examines the role of women in governmental branches in Pakistan and Iran. Pakistan would be a compelling case to address because *Benazir Bhutto* was the first woman to rise to the head of government in a Muslim majority. Moreover, within women's political history, the military-dominated center mobilized the religious scholars to exclude women from power centers, but the election of a woman indicated a dynamic between religion and gender issues at a high level of government.

The case study of Iran also is interesting; on the one hand, the traditional *Shiʿite* interpretation of Islam has impacted women's political rights in like

167 Ibid, p. 21

168 Tajali, Mona, Islamic Women's Groups and the Quest for Political Representation in Turkey and Iran, The Middle East Journal, 2015, p. 564

169 Womens UN Report Network, Equal Participation of Women and Men in Decision-Making Processes, with Particular Emphasis on Political Participation and Leadership, p. 21

manner as in Pakistan. However, it cannot create legal gender discrimination against access to higher positions of government; therefore, it has opened up areas for women's activities and reformists to push the decision-maker to allow women access to higher government levels. Notwithstanding, for the first time, a female minister has been elected under the conservative administration, but this election was not under a reformist faction. It indicates that the conservative line has accepted the participation of women in higher positions of government.

Pakistan. In the early nineteenth century, Indian Muslims lost their power to the British, and they began their struggle to find an autonomous political center. They demanded a new province for a separate Muslim political identity where Islamic principles would apply. The Islamic identity of Indian Muslims impacted the partition of British India and, as a result, Pakistan gained independence from Britain with the Muslim-majority of Indian Muslims in 1947. Hence, Islamic identity has been intertwined in Pakistan's political history, so much that successive regimes have used Islam as an instrument to gain legitimacy for their rules.[170]

Pakistan's 'Islamic identity' has affected women's legal, political participation; thus, women have had many ups and downs in diverse regimes. On the one hand, some regimes needed the support of the *ulama*[171] to restrict women's political activity for religious reasons; on the other hand, *Benazir Bhutto* was elected as the first woman to head the government in 1988. The following summarizes how women's political participation developed.

Initially, in 1930 when Pakistan was still part of India, The Government of India apportioned women in the Council of State and the Federal Assembly, despite a small percentage of women. This tradition of women's participation in the political process carried over into the following decades.[172] Since independence from Britain, women have voted and also held office in the new country (1947). Even though women faced threats by conservative Muslim religious groups to

---

170 Pakistan - Oxford Islamic Studies Online, accessed: http://www.oxfordislamicstudies.com/print/opr/t236/e0616

171 *Ulama* means: a body of Muslim scholars who are recognized as having specialist knowledge of Islamic sacred law and theology.

172 Friedhoff, Anna, Bras and Ballots: Comparing Women's Political Participation in Pakistan and Saudi Arabia, OREGON REVIEW OF INTERNATIONAL LAW, 2013, p. 274 compare also: Awan, Muhammad Ali, Political Participation of Women in Pakistan, Historical and Political Dynamics Shaping the Structure of Politics for Women, FGI, Frankfurter Forschungszentrum Globaler Islam, 2016, p. 1

exclude them from political participation, women were achieved two seats of total seats in the first and second legislative assembly (1947-1958).[173]

Later, when the first military coup *d'état* assumed power under General *Ayub Khan* (1958-1968),[174] he attempted to install a modernist version of Islam through public policies; he also removed 'Islamic' from the name of the country, the Republic of Pakistan in the new constitution in 1962.[175] In particular, he challenged conservative *ulama*'s views about the status of women, family, and inheritance law.[176] He adopted the Muslim Family Laws Ordinance (1961) that gave women rights in marriage and family law, despite protests from religious groups.[177] It must mention that *Ayub Khan* applied two different policies concerning women's participation in the political sphere. On the one hand, he reserved for women (according to article 20 of the Constitution 1962) six seats in the National Assembly and five seats in the provincial legislature.

On the other hand, he restricted women when it came to power issues in the first presidential elections (1965); and, a coalition of politico-religious parties challenged him. *Fatima Jinnah*, who the sister of Pakistan's founder of the country, was a presidential candidate in opposition to *Ayub Khan*. As a result, *Ayub Khan* mobilized the *ulama* to issue a *fatwa*[178] against the candidature of any woman who aspired to be the head of an Islamic state.[179] The *fatwa* expressed that Islam does not permit a woman to be head of state. By doing so, *Ayub Khan* referred to this religious premise to eliminate a woman from the power center;

173 Awan, Muhammad Ali, Political Participation of Women in Pakistan, p. 1
Compare also: Friedhoff, Anna, p. 275

174 It must be mentioned that during the period of 1947 to 1956 the head of state was the governor general; there was no office of the president.
See also: Awan, Muhammad Ali, p. 1

175 It must be mentioned that Pakistan's first constitution promulgated in 1956.

176 Pakistan - Oxford Islamic Studies Online, accessed: http://www.oxfordislamicstudies.com/print/opr/t236/e0616

177 Shaheed, Farida, Gender, Religion and the Quest for Justice in Pakistan, United Nations Research Institute for Social Development (UNRISD) and HeinrichBöll-Stiftung, 2009, p. 7

178 *Fatwa* defined as: "Authoritative legal opinion given by a mufti (legal scholar) in response to a question posed by an individual or a court of law. " accessed at: Fatwa - Oxford Islamic Studies Online", accessed at: http://www.oxfordislamicstudies.com/article/opr/t125/e646.

179 Ansari, Sarfraz Husain, Forced Modernization and Public Policy: A Case Study of Ayub Khan Era (1958-69), Journal of Political Studies, Vol 18, Issue – 1, 2011, p. 53 and 57

however, the constitution does not provide any gender discrimination in the head of the state's designation.[180]

In the 1970s, *Zulfiqar 'Ali Bhutto* came to power (1971-1977). He used Islamic identity to incorporate a deeply divided nation under the name of 'Islamic socialism'. The emphasis on Islam led to adopting a new constitution in 1973, which contains more Islamic provisions as well as returning 'Islamic' to the name of the state, The Islamic Republic of Pakistan.[181] This constitution recognized gender equality (Article 26) as well as the full participation of women in all spheres of public life (Article 33). He launched the adoption of the "Declaration on the Rights of Women of Pakistan", in 1976. Article 1 of this Declaration stated that "Discrimination against women is contrary to the injunctions of Islam, violates Constitutional guarantees and constitutes an offense against human dignity".[182] However, women achieved ten percent of the seats in the National Assembly and five percent in the provincial assemblies.[183]

Next, *General Muhammad Zia ul-Haq* (1977–1988) came to power with religious leaders' support. The *Zia* initiated a process of Islamisation by imposing discrimination against women that moved women to the political margins again.[184] He applied a series of informal regulations and unwritten policies to his agenda to curtail women's liberty, visibility, and political rights.[185] Despite

---

180 Constitution of Pakistan 1962 provided: The president must be Muslim and not less than 35 years old.
Dawood, Muhammad; Afridi, Manzoor Khan, Comparison between 1956 and 1962 Constitution of Pakistan, Ma'arif Research Journal, 2016, p. 132

181 Pakistan - Oxford Islamic Studies Online

182 Shaheed, Farida, p. 8

183 Pakistan Council for Science & Technology, History of women empowerment in Pakistan, accessed at: "http://www.pcst.org.pk/wst/wst_hwep.php."

184 Nicholas, Sarah, Islam and Women's Rights in Modern Pakistan, SPRING 2016, accessed at: "https://history.libraries.wsu.edu/spring2016/2016/01/19/womens-rights/"

185 Human Rights Watch, CRIME OR CUSTOM?, Violence Against Women in Pakistan, 1999, accessed to: "https://www.hrw.org/reports/1999/pakistan/Pakhtml-03.htm#P336_49235."
For example he prohibited women from participating and from being spectators of sports and promoted purdah or, he launched to adopt a series of laws that gave legal sanction to women's subordinate status which relegates women to inferior legal status and, in some circumstances, renders the testimony of a woman equal to only half the weight of a man's. See also: CRIME OR CUSTOM? Human Rights Watch.

this backsliding, he appointed 20 women in the National Assembly.[186] However, during the 1980s, women have experienced "an uneasy balance between women's rights and religion in Pakistani politics." In the late 1980s, a series of discrimination against women provoked a social movement by the Women's Action Forum (WAF), which became one of the leading voices of opposition to *Zia*.[187]

In 1988, when the sudden death of *General Zia* precipitated elections, Pakistan elected a woman, *Benazir Bhutto,* as Prime Minister: the first woman to serve as head of government in a Muslim majority country (1988 – 1990 and 1993-1996). During her election campaigns in 1988, *Benazir Bhutto* called to remove any legal discrimination against women. *Bhutto* believed that "the need to maintain a balance between various political forces and conservative religious community" was essential for promoting women's rights.[188] After the election of 1988, there was a disagreement on whether Sharia allowed a woman to serve as prime minister. A religious pronouncement made it clear that a prime minister is not the head of the state (the president who must be a man) but is rather the head of a political party; therefore, it is not contrary to Sharia law.[189]

Even though *Bhutto* challenged laws in the name of Islam instituted by *Zia* that resulted in legal discrimination against Pakistani women, she could not make any changes.[190] Since Pakistan's main Islamist parties had only two parliamentary seats in the National Assembly (1993-1997), they had the military establishment's backing, which pressured the weak civilian regimes to impose Sharia law.[191] Therefore, *Bhutto* did not repeal a single one of *Zia*'s Islamisation laws that she promised to remove. With regard to non-legal discrimination, *Bhutto* measured to improve women's participation in public life, such as expanding the five percent quota for women in all federal services, setting up women's police stations, promoting several women as high court judges (the first female judge in high court occurred in 1994) and women's development banks.[192]

On the whole, women's representation in the National Assembly made much less progress. While were filled the ten percent assigned quota for women in (22 women) and five percent of the seats in the provincial assemblies in 1988,

---

186 Pakistan Council for Science & Technology

187 Human Rights Watch, CRIME OR CUSTOM

188 Ibid

189 Friedhoff, Anna, Bras and Ballots, p. 278

190 Shaheed, Farida, Gender, Religion and the Quest for Justice in Pakistan, p. 22

191 Pakistan - Oxford Islamic Studies Online.

192 Pakistan Council for Science & Technology

in 1990-1997, women's representation dropped dramatically. Since the provision for reserved seats had lapsed, there were no seats mandated for women. Hence, women's representation was nine-tenths percent in 1990 and one-point-eight percent in 1993. For the 1997 national assembly, however, the percentage of women in elected assemblies increased to two-point-eight percent.[193]

Although *Bhutto* had two incomplete terms in office, her tenure had a transformative impact on improving women's position to be head of government. *Bhutto* launched programs to promote women's rights or highlighted their obstacles. These 'soft' measures had a minor impact on the societal attitudes that became entrenched under *Zia*.[194] Consequently, several women served as federal and state ministers, such as *Hina Rabbani Khar* who became the first Minister of Foreign Affairs of Pakistan in 2011; *Sherry Rehman*, the ministers of Information and Broadcasting, in 2008; and *Saira Afzal Tara*, appointed Minister of National Health Services in 2017.

As a Muslim woman, *Benazir Bhutto* not only impacted Pakistan women's political history, but also paved the way for other female politicians to follow her path to access higher governmental branches, such as *Chandrika Kumaratanga* in Sri Lanka, and *Sheikh Hasina* and *Khaleda Zia* in Bangladesh.

Additionally, significant progress was made in increasing the quota for women at all levels of the decision-making processes. For the first time, in 2000 was raised the quota for women's political participation to 33 percent at the local government level. The Political Parties Act 2002 specified that women's quota increased to 17 percent in all country law-making bodies. It was an important legislative development for women as political decision-makers.[195] Since then, the quota for women's political participation has carried into the following decades. In the 2008 election, women reserved 17 percent of the total number of seats, and in the 2013 election, almost 20.5 percent of the total number of seats. However, in the 2008 and 2013 elections, there are some fluctuating trends, but there are positive signs of an increase in women's political participation.[196]

To sum up, Islam has not created legal gender discrimination in political participation in like manner. As far as this is concerned, the constitution guarantees

193 Awan, Muhammad Ali, Political Participation of Women in Pakistan, p. 1-2

194 Shaheed, Farida, Gender, Religion and the Quest for Justice in Pakistan, p. 25

195 United Nations Development Programme Pakistan: Political and Legislative Participation of Women in Pakistan, Issues and Perspectives. Research Report, Islamabad, 2005, p. 1

196 Awan, Muhammad Ali, Political Participation of Women in Pakistan, p. 2

women's rights in political participation and public life, but women cannot enjoy this legal mandate. Moreover, women confront other obstacles such as social-cultural attitudes, patriarchal structures, and economic factors. However, Pakistani women in political participation may be relatively progressive; therefore, their experience with religious, political participation and gender issues would be an effective pattern for other women in Muslim majority countries.

Iran. Under the *Pahlavi* regime (*Reza Shah and Mohammad Reza Shah*, 1925-1979), Iranian women on the whole developed rights. The changing position of women was due to anti-religious attitudes and the perception that women's emancipation was a secular issue. Furthermore, they encouraged women to participate in social affairs unlike the prevailing norms of religious and traditional society. During *Reza Shah*'s regime (the First Pahlavi regime) social activities of women improved, such as the opening up education and employment for women, and the forceful unveiling of women; nonetheless, women's political participation did not improve significantly.[197] In *Mohammad Reza Shah*'s period (the Second *Pahlavi* regime), women's rights improved, especially in family law: The Family Protection Act (1967), which modestly enhanced women's rights within marriage.[198] The *Pahlavi* regimes were undemocratic regimes within the structure of the patriarchs of the nation of Iran; hence, the process of political development confronted limitations in which was included women's political participation.[199] However, women's political rights changed in like manner by the recognition of female suffrage in 1963, as well as the first female (*Farokhroo*

---

197 Moinifar, Heshmat Sadat, PARTICIPATION OF WOMEN IN IRAN'S POLITY, GEMC journal, 2013, p. 26

198 For example, the new Act imposed some restrictions on the right of the husband to divorce his wife which was hitherto enjoyed freely by him. It created that all family disputes arising out of matrimonial relations shall be referred for arbitration before the parties are allowed to separate. The arbitration is intended to make all possible endeavors to bring about a reconciliation between the spouses, and in case of failure of these efforts, the parties shall be allowed to separate. (Section 1133 of the Civil Code) Moreover, regarding custody of children section 12 reads: "in all cases of dispute when a certificate of non-reconciliation is issued, the court shall determine and order the method of the custody of the children".
That was not an automatic right of the father regarding the custody of children
Naqavi, Ali Reza, The Family Protection ACT of Iran, Islamic Research Institute, International Islamic University, Islamabad, 1967, p. 242-244

199 Karimi, Behzad, WOMEN'S POLITICAL PARTICIPATION IN THE CONTEMPORARY IRAN: A STUDY OF WESTERN IRAN, IMPACT (International Journal of Research in Applied, Natural and Social Sciences), 2014, p. 70

Parsa, 1968) serving as Minister of Education of Iran. In fact, the *Shah*'s modernization programs about women's rights provoked the anger of the religious conservatives, thus providing one of the main reasons for the outbreak of the Islamic revolution in Iran.[200]

During the Islamic revolution, *Ayatollah Khomeini,* the Islamic revolution's religious leader,[201] needed significant support from women's political participation. While granting female suffrage in1963, the *Ayatollah* later issued a declaration that female suffrage was un-Islamic. In contrast, he encouraged women to vote as an Islamic duty. Undoubtedly, his shift was not because women had the right to vote, but rather to legitimize an Islamic republic.[202]

The establishment of an Islamic regime led to prioritizing Sharia law interpretations by the most conservative clerics. As a result, they imposed limitations on women concerning family and gender issues in Islam's name in the new Iranian constitution (1979), and other domestic laws. These limitations also impacted women's political life and were cited as justification to curtail women's access to key political decision-making positions.[203] Thus, under the Iranian Constitution, women faced obstacles accessing some decision-making positions, such as the presidency and other ministerial positions.

Iran Presidency: In principle, Article 115 of the Iranian constitution concerning the position of the president does not explicitly prohibit women from being elected as the president.[204] This Article stipulates the president should be from amongst "a Muslim and political *rejal*"; it uses the notion of '*rejal*' or 'maleness'. *Rijal* comes from Arabic, which can be understood either as 'men' or as a gender-neutral term of 'personalities'. Therefore, it is open to interpretation concerning *rejal.* Technically, the notion of *rijal* means men, but it can also argue

200 Ibid. 71

201 Ayatollah Khomeini was before the Islamic Revolution as religious opposition, but further he was the founder of Iran as an Islamic republic and the leader of its 1979 Iranian Revolution.

202 Tajali, Mona, Notions of Female Authority in Modern Shi'i Thought, Religions Open Access Journal of Theology, 2011, p. 453

203 Ibid, p. 452

204 Article 115 of Iranian Constitution: "The President of the Republic must be elected from among the religious and political elite who meet the following qualifications: Iranian origin, Iranian nationality, administrative leadership, clear past record, honesty and piety, believing in the fundamentals of the Islamic Republic of Iran and the official religion of the country."

that women can advance to the extent that they become like 'men'. As a result, it can be interpreted as respectable personalities, regardless of gender.[205]

In the 7th presidential election in 1997, for the first time, nine women nominated themselves for the presidency; therefore, requiring clarification from the Council of Guardians of this the ambiguous term of '*rijal*'. The members of the Council have the power to approve or disqualify the candidates as well as the authority to interpret the constitution.[206] The Council has disqualified all of the female candidates, without any legal reason for their disqualification. Since then, in the presidential election in 2005, 89 women registered to run for president, and all-female candidates were disqualified. The Council argued that the world '*rejal*' is only limited to men as well as it is against religious law. However, it was not an official interpretation of the term of '*rijal*'.[207] Thus, it provided an opportunity for women's groups and activists to protest against the disqualification of female presidential candidates [208] and pressured the Council to clarify their interpretation of the term '*rijal*'.

Consequently, for the first time, the spokesman for the Guardian Council (*Abbas Ali Kadkhodaei*) in 2009, expressed that the Council had never reached its position based on an individual's gender; therefore, women can be considered politicians and religious '*rejal*'. Nonetheless, the argument does not remain in the framework of official interpretation. It can be argued that this shift from a conservative decision has been the result of the various reformists, especially those who belong to the links parties and the discourses launched by women's activism. Moreover, the Council's silence on the issue of gender encouraged more women presidential candidates to register in future elections. For example, in the presidential election of 2013, 100 women, and in 2017, 137 women registered;

---

205 Can Iran Have a Female President?, accessed at: https://www.trtworld.com/mea/can-iran-have-a-female-president--6402.
Compare also: Tajali, Mona, Notions of Female Authority in Modern Shi'i Thought, p. 455

206 The Guardian Council is an upper chamber of the parliament that has 12 members, including jurists and clerics, none of whom are women.
Iranian Parliament Seeks Ruling on Women's Presidential Eligibility, 16 Mar 2004, accessed at: http://www.payvand.com/news/04/mar/1120.html.

207 Kadivar, Jamileh, An Unofficial Boy's Club, Majalla Magazine (blog), 24. Mai 2013, accessed at: http://eng.majalla.com/2013/05/article55241743/an-unofficial-boys-club.

208 Iran: Women Call For Rights Ahead Of Presidential Poll, RadioFreeEurope/RadioLiberty, 2005, accessed at: "https://www.rferl.org/a/1059254.html."

however, they were disqualified for religious and political grounds, but without mentioning gender as a reason for the disqualification.[209]

To sum up, there is no legal gender discrimination against the accessibility of Iranian women to high positions in the government. The Iranian constitutional law has the potential for women to access the position of president. Still, the patriarchal system and the conservative tendency in the high level of decision-making create limitations for women. However, cannot disregarded movements' role cannot be disregarded; it provides a dynamic for the re-interpretation or review of Islam to access the female president position.

Iran Ministerial positions: Even though women could not ascend to the presidency, some positive steps have been taken to improve women's political participation in government branches, resulting in a conservative president administration electing women to serve as ministers.

Mohammad Khatami (1997–2005), was Iran's first reformist president. He launched a gender issue campaign and integrated them into his election agenda. As a result, he received a great deal to support female voters (69.7 percent), especially among younger and well-educated women. Many women with other reformists were hopeful that he would nominate women to his cabinet. Nevertheless, *Khatami* declared that appointing a woman as a minister was risking to anger conservative clerics, who "might issue *fatwas* instructing citizens not to pay taxes to his un-Islamic government."[210] Therefore, a female minister was not practical.

On the other hand, he tried to mollify the reformists by appointing women to different positions. During his presidency, particularly, he appointed two female cabinet members; one at the rank of vice-president and the head of Environmental Protection Department and the other as a presidential advisor and the head of the Center for Women's Participation, which is part of the President's office. Despite the demands of women for nominations to ministerial positions, women did not include in his cabinet.[211]

The neo-conservative president *Mahmoud Ahmadinejad* (2005-2013) came to power with generous support from the conservative clergy line. In his first administration, there was no drastic change either in favor of or against women's status.[212] In fact, he had not committed to improving women's rights; rather,

---

209 Ibid, p. 457

210 Shahrokni, Nazanin, All the President's Women, 2009, MER253, accessed: "https://www.merip.org/mer/mer253/all-presidents-women"

211 Ibid

212 Moinifar, Heshmat Sadat, p. 31

he emphasized women's traditional domestic duties. His election to a second term in 2009 was widely disputed, thus incredibly challenging his legitimacy. He needed to appeal to the Iranian public on the whole, as well as make a fresh plea to women voters among the reformists.[213] Therefore, he made the bold move of nominating three women to be ministers in the new cabinet, despite his conservative views on women's issues. *Ahmadinejad's* willingness was not without controversy.

On the one hand, the nomination of female candidates met with opposition by the number of conservative clerics because they argued that there are 'religious uncertainties' to choosing women as ministers; nevertheless, the appointment of a female minister in the conservative-dominated parliament was eventual.[214] Notwithstanding, he did not back down on having his choice of female minister even when the clerics publicly opposed his decisions. He declared that it is a rightful demand by women, and there was no need even to consult the clergy. Consequently, the Supreme Leader (*Ayatollah Khamenei*) tacitly approved, and the uproar in the conservative-dominated parliament quieted down.[215] As a result, one woman nominee, *Marzieh Vahid-Dastejerdi*, became Iran's minister of health, who belonged in the conservative camp.

Regardless of *Ahmadinejad*'s motives, the nomination and approval of a female minister had two significant Iranian female authority results. First, it opened once again a discussion on whether women should have access to political decision-making positions. Therefore, it challenged the traditional interpretations of *Shi'ite* that banned women's access to decision-making positions. It was "a shift in *Shi'ite* clerical discourse from the conventional stance".[216]

Second, the approval from the highest religious authority in Iran, the Supreme Leader *Ayatollah Khamenei*, was the most significant gain for women's activities. Thus, the upper ranks of different groups followed *Ayatollah Khamenei's* approval on the subject of women ministers. Eventually, women appointed as

---

213 Tajali, Mona, Protesting gender discrimination from within: women's political representation on behalf of Islamic parties, British Journal of Middle Eastern Studies, 2017, p. 189

214 Tajali, Mona, Notions of Female Authority in Modern Shi'i Thought, Religions, p. 459 compare also: Tajali, Mona, Islamic Women's Groups and the Quest for Political Representation in Turkey and Iran, p. 575

215 Shahrokni, Nazanin, All the President's Women

216 Tajali, Mona, Notions of Female Authority in Modern Shi'i Thought, Religions, Open Access Journal of Theology, p. 464

ministers with the Supreme Leader's approval can undoubtedly enhance women's access to higher positions.[217]

In particular, other Islamic countries' women participate at a high cabinet level. For example, in Algeria in 2012, three female ministers of 31cabinet members were women, and with the re-election in 2014 of President *Bouteflika*, seven women were appointed as ministers in his cabinet. This was remarkable progress to high government level participation in Arab countries. Furthermore, in Malaysia under *Najib Razak* (2009-2015), 14 female cabinet ministers and 25 female deputy ministers were appointed. Moreover, Egypt, Morocco, and the Palestinian Authority also appointed several female ministers. [218] In this regard, it must add that women as ministers in most Islamic countries are often responsible for 'soft' portfolios that focus on social policy issues, In other words, their access to crucial economic decision-making positions remains marginalized. In Arab countries, neither has a woman ever held the position of head of government or head of state.[219]

A.4.3 National Parliaments

Inasmuch as many countries have removed the legal obstacles for women to enter parliament, the important point is the degree of women's parliamentary participation. The number of female representatives in a parliament is influential in determining debate's nature on political priorities. Thus, by increasing women's representation, which results in greater participation, parliaments would seek to prioritize gender equality laws on the legislative agenda.[220] Therefore, legislatures play a critical role in addressing gender-related concerns in the legislative agenda through laws and policies, aiming to promote gender equality.[221]

---

217 Ibid, p. 459

218 It must be added that women's participation improved in other executive positions in Arab countries. For example, women serve as ambassadors, in Egypt, Iraq, Jordan, Kuwait, Morocco, Lebanon, Oman, the Palestinian Authority, Syria, Tunisia and Yemen, and some have elected female mayors in Egypt, Jordan, Morocco and the Palestinian Authority.
see also more: OECD/CAWTAR, Women in Public Life: Gender, Law and Policy in the Middle East and North Africa, OECD Publishing, Paris, 2014, p. 136-137

219 Ibid, p. 138

220 United Nations Development Programme; National Democratic Institute for International Affairs, Empowering Women for Stronger Political Parties: A Good Practices Guide to Promote Women's Political Participation, p. 35

221 OECD/CAWTAR, Women in Public Life, Gender, Law and Policy in the Middle East and North Africa, p. 78

In Islamic countries, there are different levels for women in parliament. These differences are due to Sharia as a source of law or the establishment of lower levels (quotas) for women in parliament, but both result in institutionalizing barriers for women to their political participation.[222] The Inter-Parliamentary Union in 2000 reported 'zero female parliamentarians' for several countries, including Djibouti, Jordan, Kuwait, and the United Arab Emirates; on the other hand, the highest levels of women in parliament found in Tunisia. Since 2000 significant legal and public policy reforms have occurred, resulting in women's parliamentary participation, especially in Arab countries.[223] Hence, some countries such as Kuwait, Morocco, Tunisia have been obliged to remove discrimination in their legal system through reviewing constitutional provisions or the implementation of electoral codes that support a gender equality principle in the election process.[224] In the following examples, the different levels of women in some Islamic countries' legislatures will be considered.

Algeria. The introduction of a legislative gender quota in 2012 increased the percentage of women's parliamentary representation. However, as a pioneer in the Arab countries, Algeria renewed the makeup of its legislature in 2017. The Algerian National Front party in the 2017 election presented the country's first all-female parliamentary candidates in an electoral list, while no other similar elections were held in the Arab countries.[225]

Kuwait. The new electoral reform bill granted women the right to run for office in 2005. Since then, the first election for the 12th National Assembly held in 2008, 27 out of the 274 candidates were women but none were elected. This is because Islamists had contested the election as they were opposed to women's participation in politics and promised to impose Sharia law in public affairs. After the dissolution of the assembly in 2009, 210 presented female candidates, and, consequently, for the first time, four women were elected.[226] In the 2016 election, only eight women ran, but two were elected then that time.[227]

---

222 Haas '06, Sherri, Female Parliamentary Representation in Islamic Countries, Res Public - Journal of Undergraduate Research: Vol. 11, 2006, p. 77.

223 OECD/CAWTAR, Women in Public Life, Gender, Law and Policy in the Middle East and North Africa, p. 80

224 Ibid, p. 135

225 Inter-Parliamentary Union (IPU), Women in parliament in 2017, The year in review, United Kingdom, 2018, p. 4-5

226 Jyoti Das, Hirak, National Assembly Elections in Kuwait, 2016, Contemporary Review of the Middle East, 2017, p. 199.

227 Inter-Parliamentary Union (IPU), Women in parliament in 2016, The year in review, 2017, p. 6

Saudi Arabia. In 2005, King *Abdullah bin Abdul Aziz* made an important decision that allowed women to enter or be nominated for candidacies in the *Majlis Ash-Shura* (Council National Parliament of Saudi Arabia). Saudi women's political participation was faced with strong opposition from the powerful religious establishment. However, the reform movement in 2005 leads to the renewal of religious thought as a prerequisite for social and cultural change. Therefore, it opened up the opportunity for the re-institutionalization and reformulation of laws and regulations in the scope of social, political, and economic structures.[228] Thus, women ran for Parliament for the first time in 2015; 30 females were appointed to the 150-member *Shura* Council, which has the mandate of preparing draft laws.[229] It must note that this political women's decision demonstrated a division between the religious establishment on the one hand and the political decision-making. This division "can unleash the potential for broader change in Saudi women's rights".[230]

The legislative body in **Iran** includes two parts, the Islamic Consultative Assembly (National Parliament) and the Guardian Council.[231] Women can enter parliament without structural barriers. In the latest election, 2016, 17 women of reformists were elected to the chamber; these were small electoral gains for Iranian women that "were accompanied by seismic shifts in attitudes away from hard-line conservatives".

On the other hand, the Guardian Council compromises six Islamic jurisprudents or *Fiqh*[232]and six legal scholars.[233] According to the Sharia-based

---

228 Al-Heis, Abdulaziz, Women Participation in Saudi Arabia's Political Arena, Al Jazeera Centre for Studies, 2011, p. 2 and 6

229 OECD/CAWTAR, Women in Public Life, Law and Policy in the Middle East and North Africa, p. 128

230 Al-Heis, Women Participation in Saudi Arabia's Political Arena, p. 3

231 Accordingly to the Article 74 of the Iranian Constitution, the Guardian Council is responsible for protect the commands of Islam: "the Islamic Consultative Assembly cannot legislate laws that contradict the canons and principles of the official religion of the country or the constitution. The Guardian Council is responsible for the evaluation of this matter….."

232 *Faiqh* means: "Conceptually, the human attempt to understand divine law (shariah). Whereas shariah is immutable and infallible, fiqh is fallible and changeable. *Fiqh* is distinguished from usul al-fiqh, the methods of legal interpretation and analysis. *Fiqh* is the product of application of usul al-fiqh, the total product of human efforts at understanding the divine will."
Fiqh - Oxford Islamic Studies Online accessed at: http://www.oxfordislamicstudies.com/article/opr/t125/e659.

233 Article 91 of the Iranian Constitution: "An assembly named the Guardian Council is established in order to protect the commands of Islam, and the constitution from

constitution, women are not allowed as Islamic jurists or *Fiqh*; [234] therefore, there is legal gender discrimination based on religious reasons. Moreover, in practice, the designation of legal scholars are always men, while the provisions have not explicitly affirmed men's position in this context. As a result, Sharia's reference creates discrimination against women in law that has negatively affected the percentage of women's participation, either as lower-level participation or legal barriers to the legislative body.

A.4.4 Judiciary Bodies

Judiciary institutions play essential roles as change agents for gender equality. They can be powerful agents for social change to bring about justice for women and support for gender reforms when they work without gender prejudice.[235] In this regard, the social and political dynamics influence how much Judiciary institutions can contribute to women's equality. Significant factors determine the scope of the judiciary for action, such as the legitimacy of court authority, the judiciary's relationship to other state structures, the independence of the courts themselves, and the existence of explicitly gender equality laws.[236] In fact, judiciary bodies cannot always be an effective means to follow the gender equality agenda; preferably, it may by itself be "the driver of gender-progressive change, or it can be a tool of the state in bringing about change."[237] For example, the state by establishing special courts, e.g., family courts, courts for rape, or specific

---

discord with the proceedings of the Islamic Consultative Assembly". The Guardian Council has the following composition:

1. Six just Islamic jurisprudents who are conscious of the issues and needs of the time. These are selected by the leader.
2. Six legal scholars (hoquqdan), specialized in different fields of law, from among Muslim jurists who are presented by the head of the judiciary to the Islamic Consultative Assembly and are selected by the vote of the Assembly.

234 Mirshahvalad, Minoo, Can Iranian Women Compensate for Their Absence From the World of Fiqh?, Jura Gentium, XIV, 2017, 2, p. 87

235 Chiongson, Rea Abada; Desai, Deval; Marchiori, Teresa; Woolcock, Michael, The Role of Law and Justice in Achieving Gender Equality, World Bank. 2012, World Development Report 2012, "Gender Equality and Development", 2011, p. 21

236 World Bank. 2012, World Development Report 2012: Gender Equality and Development, The International Bank for Reconstruction and Development / The World Bank, 2011, p. 347

237 Ibid, p. 347

regimes in family matters reserved to religious or customary courts can influence the role of the judiciary in promoting gender equality.[238]

Judiciary institutions enforce justice in society; therefore, they must provide equal opportunity for women and men to engage in the judicial system. Gender diversity enables the judiciary to better respond to diverse social and individual contexts and experiences.[239] The scope of women's participation in the judiciary includes judges, police, prosecutors, heads of agencies, and village chiefs at the national and local levels. In this area, female judges play vital roles in ensuring justice for women. The most crucial function of a female judge is the commitment to recognize gender equality; thus, they can impact judicial reasoning/ decision making, primarily when cases concern women's rights.[240]

However, in many countries, women may not have the same rights as men in the judiciary. In Islamic countries, there are also obstacles for women to equal participation. These legal obstacles or limitations for women in the judiciary in Muslim countries often are justified on religious grounds. In particular, religious arguments claim that women have "perceived deficiencies in religion and intellect"; in effect, they are opposed to women's appointment in the judiciary, especially as judges.[241] Despite this opposition, women can participate in the judiciary system but at different levels. This difference is due to the very breadth of Islamic jurisprudence as it "takes into consideration the circumstances in which people are living."[242] Hence, Islamic countries' different views on being a female judge based on religious reasoning can divide into three parts. First, no women are judges in the judiciary; second, more female judges are in the lower courts than in the higher courts; third, female judges in the higher courts and Islamic courts. A summary of these is as follows.

First, there are still no women in the judiciary. Saudi Arabia and Iran ban women in the judiciary. In **Saudi Arabia,** in general, Islamic Sharia is the primary authority for Saudi Courts, and the judicial system consists of Sharia courts and a Supreme Judicial Council. A judge must be qualified to hold the position

---

238 The Role of Law and Justice in Achieving Gender Equality, p. 22

239 Geneva Forum Series no. 1, Women and the Judiciary, International Commission of Jurists, 2014, p. 20

240 Ibid, p. 21

241 Sonneveld, Nadia; Lindbekk, Monika, Women Judges in the Muslim World: A Comparative Study of Discourse and Practice, BRILL, 2017, p. 11

242 Commission on Human Rights, Report of the Special Rapporteur on the independence of judges and lawyers, Report on the mission to the Kingdom of Saudi Arabia, E/CN.4/2003/65/Add.3, 2003, para. 29

of the judge under Sharia laws. Moreover, the Judiciary law requires each judicial candidate to have a degree from one of the Sharia colleges in the Kingdom of Saudi Arabia and capable of relative degrees of '*ijtihad*'.[243] Therefore, according to Sharia law, women are not capable of '*ijtihad*', as a result, they are prohibited from becoming judges, so there are no women in the Saudi Arabian judiciary.[244] On the other hand, Saudi women have been able to enter law schools since 2006; for the first time, in 2013, women were admitted as lawyers,[245] taking not only cases concerning women's issues, but also covering a range of matters such as commercials, personal and labor affairs.[246] It was significant progress for Saudi women in the legal area, but they are still not allowed to become judges.

With regard to **Iran,** before the Islamic revolution, women were allowed to serve as judges. Still, after the revolution (1979) due to Islam's conservative interpretation, women judges are un-Islamic. The new constitution did not explicitly formulate a legal prohibition against female judges, and the conditions of the judge determine by law and Islamic jurisprudence.[247] After that, in 1982, the Judges' Appointment Conditions Act adopted the provision that "judges were selected from the eligible men".[248] Hence, the new law excluded women from

243 Brief Overview of the Saudi Arabian Legal System - GlobaLex, accessed: http://www.nyulawglobal.org/globalex/Saudi_Arabia.html#_Toc200894588.
"ijtihad" means Islamic legal term meaning "independent reasoning," as opposed to taqlid (imitation). It is considered a required religious duty for those qualified to perform it. It should be practiced by means of analogical or syllogistic reasoning (qiyas). Its results may not contradict the Quran, and it may not be used in cases where consensus (ijma) has been reached, according to many scholars.
See also, *Ijtihad* - Oxford Islamic Studies Online", accessed at: http://www.oxfordislamicstudies.com/article/opr/t125/e990.

244 Commission on Human Rights, E/CN.4/2003/65/Add.3, 2003, para.29
It was also believed that women were unlike men physically, emotionally and in thought… furthermore more women are attaining the high level of intellectual maturity required, society was not ready to accept the change.

245 Women and the Judiciary, p. 45

246 Female Lawyers in Saudi Courts: 'We Are Equal to Male Counterparts', Arab News, 29. December 2016, accessed at: http://www.arabnews.com/node/1030991/saudi-arabia.

247 Article 163 of the Iranian Constitution: The attributes and qualifications of a judge are defined through the law in accordance with the criteria of jurisprudence.

248 Kar, Mehrangiz, Who are the Judges in the Islamic Republic of Iran, LEGATUM INSTITUTE, 2011, p. 2
The Act was passed by the Parliament and judges were selected from the eligible men as described below:

judgeships. However, since 1995, women have been permitted to serve as advisors in the family courts and the Office of the Guardianship of Underage. Furthermore, women cannot make decisions, and their role restricted to an advisory capacity.[249]

Second, some Islamic countries permit women to become judges, particularly in matters concerning women. Still, more female judges are in the lower courts than in the higher courts in countries such as Bahrain 2006, UAE 2008, Kuwait 2010, and Mauretania 2013.

As much as the legal system of the **United Arab Emirates** is based on Sharia and civil law, the first women to become judges occurred in 2008. Women can appoint as judges and prosecutors in the local judiciary. In **Abu Dhabi**, since 2015, there are currently nine female judges and 18 female prosecutors, and in **Dubai,** there are three female judges and 17 female prosecutors. However, women's representation in the judiciary remains limited; that is, women are prohibited from becoming federal judges and federal prosecutors under Federal Law No. 3 of 1983.[250] In **Qatar,** the first female became a judge in 2010, but one female judge in the family circuit, one woman in the civil circuit, and one female

---

1. Those who have faith and are just and possess a practical commitment to the Islamic principles and loyalty to Iran's Islamic Republic system.
2. Legitimacy of birth.
3. Iranian citizenship and completion of the mandatory military service unless legally exempt.
4. Soundness of mind and ability to work and be clear of drug addiction.
5. Having achieved *ijtihad* with approval of the Judicial High Council or having a Judgment Permission from the Judicial High Council for those who are holding a bachelor degree in law or theology or a bachelor from the College of Judicial and Administrative Studies affiliated with Justice Administration or a degree from the College of High Judicial Studies of Qum or those seminary students who finished their classes and also passed two years of *fiqh* kharij and are certified by the *Fiqhi* Teachers' Association, if the Judicial High Council does not have enough qualified clergyman of Islamic jurisprudence available.

(Judges' Appointment Conditions Act approved on May 14, 1982, published in the Code Collection of 1982, Official Gazzette.)

249 Abdelkader, Engy, To Judge or Not to Judge: A Comparative Analysis of Islamic Jurisprudential Approaches to Female Judges in the Muslim World (Indonesia, Egypt and Iran), Fordham International Law Journal, Volume 37, Issue 2, 2014, p. 365

250 Human Rights Council, Report of the Special Rapporteur on the independence of judges and lawyers, Gabriela Knaul, Mission to the United Arab Emirates, A/HRC/29/26/Add.2, 2015, para. 66-67

assistant judge out of 14. There are no female judges to the higher court in the Qatar judiciary system.[251]

Third, some Islamic countries appointed women to serve as judges in higher courts and the religious courts for the first time, such as Egypt in 2015, Gaza in 2010, Malaysia in 2010, and Pakistan in 2013.

Egypt. In 1949, the first time a woman (*Aisha Ratib*) had requested to have become a judge, but her request was turned down. The Administrative Court stated that while there is no Islamic law or Egyptian law prohibiting women from appointment to the judiciary, it is instead that Egyptian society is not ready to accept the right for women to be appointed judges. A few decades later, in 1978 and 1989, two women responded to vacancies on the State Council, and their applications were rejected. This was the first time that provided religious argumentation to justify the barring of women from occupying a position as judge.[252] Following this, the formal religious authorities (*Egypt's Grand Mufti and Imam*) issued some *fatwas*. The important *fatwa* from the *Sheikh* of *Al Azhar* stated that "there is no express provision from the Quran or from the Sunna that prohibits women from assuming judicial posts".[253] These *fatwas* were able to reform Egyptian women's legal position in the judiciary; as a result, the first Egyptian female judge was appointed in 2003. Moreover, in 2003, former President *Mubarak* appointed a woman as the first Egyptian female (*Tahany al-Gebali*) to the Supreme Constitutional Court. In 2010, the first woman (*Dalia al-Namaky*) was appointed to serve as a Chief Judge in the Family Courts, and in 2009, the first female judge became to serve in a criminal court. In Cairo, in 2012, a total of 42 female judges had been appointed across criminal, civil, family, and commercial courts. In 2015, 26 additional women were appointed from the Administrative Prosecution, and at least seventy-two women are serving in the State Litigation Authority.[254] Notably, the new Egyptian constitution of January 2014 for the first time in history explicitly states that the Egyptian state shall guarantee women's appointments to judicial bodies without discrimination (Article 11). Egyptian

---

251 Human Rights Council, Report of the Special Rapporteur on the independence of judges and lawyers, Gabriela Knaul, Mission to Qatar, A/HRC/29/26/Add.1, 2015, para. 77

252 Sonneveld, Lindbekk, Women Judges in the Muslim World, p. 77-78

253 The International Commission of Jurists (ICJ), Egypt's Judiciary: A Tool of Repression: Lack of Effective Guarantees of Independence and Accountability, 2016, p. 88

254 Messieh, Nancy; Gaber, Suzanne, A Win for Women in Egypt's Courts, Atlantic Council, accessed at: http://www.atlanticcouncil.org/blogs/menasource/a-win-for-women-in-egypt-s-courts.

women achieved significant progress in the higher courts; however, the overall percentage of women judges in Egypt is one of the lowest in the world.[255]

Malaysia is a multiracial and multi-religious society, but two-thirds of the population is Muslim. The Federation of Malaysia is currently made up of 13 states and three federal territories. The Judiciary has been influenced by the common law of England and Islamic law and comprises civil courts, Sharia courts, and Native courts.[256] There is no prohibition on female judges' appointment in the civil courts and Native courts, which guarantee participation under the Malaysian Federal Constitution of 1957. Therefore, female judges were appointed to the civil courts as early as the 1960s.

On the other hand, women's appointment as judges in Sharia courts has been a controversial issue. Sharia courts fall under states' jurisdiction and deal with personal status law, which is related to Islamic family law only for Muslims. The issue of female judgeship in the Sharia court has provoked much disagreement between classical Islamic law and contemporary Muslim scholars. Islamic classical law expressly prohibits women from being judges. They believed that "justice would not be served due to women's lack of exposure to mundane matters".[257] This argument brought inequality for female judgeship positions in Sharia courts, which was adopted by the Malaysian *Shari'a* system. In contrast, contemporary religious writings asserted the need for reinterpretation of Islamic law to qualify female judges. This move by contemporary scholars affected the appointment of women as judges in the Malaysian Shari'a courts. The National Fatwa Committee issued a *fatwa* in 2006 that the post is equal to the position of a judgeship. Since then, in 2010, two female Shari'a court judges were officially appointed in Sharia courts.[258] As of August 2017, out of 160 judges in Sharia courts 27 are women.[259] Therefore, this progress in the appointment of female

255 Egypt's Judiciary: A Tool of Repression: Lack of Effective Guarantees of Independence and Accountability, p. 89

256 Shuaib, F. S., Kamal, M. H., Bustami, T. A., Othman, N. and Sulaiman, M. S, Towards an Apex Sharia Court in Malaysia, Shuaib, F. S.*, Kamal, M. H., Bustami, T. A., Othman, N. and Sulaiman, M. S, SOCIAL SCIENCES & HUMANITIES, 2017, p. 309

257 Ibid, p. 155

258 Ibid, p. 162

259 Gooch, Liz, The female face of Islamic law in Malaysia, accessed at: https://www.aljazeera.com/indepth/features/2017/08/female-face-islamic-law-malaysia-170802110726630.html.

judgeships in the Malaysian Sharia courts should be viewed as "an attempt to open up the Sharia judicial system to women".[260]

Furthermore, there are two High Courts in Malaysia which have general supervisory and revisionary jurisdiction over all the subordinate courts.[261] Females have been allowed to serve as judges to the High Court since 1983. The provisions of the Administration of Islamic Law (Enactment 2003) mentioned the same criteria for candidates to be appointed as judges of the High Court and the Subordinate Courts.[262] Thus far, the presence of female judges in the High Courts has increased, and there is almost equality with male judges. For example, in 2012, there were 30 female judges and 35 male judges in the High court. In general, the presence of female judges in the subordinate courts is relatively high, so that no legal prohibition based on gender to become judges.[263] Also, for the first time, the judiciary appointed female judges in Shaira High court in 2016.[264]

It must be added that some Islamic countries have female judges in sharia courts, such as **Indonesia** (2010), **Pakistan** (2013), and **Palestinian** (2009, in the West Bank).

A.4.5 Conclusion

To sum up, in recent years, most Islamic countries tend to facilitate women's participation in public decision-making processes. The political structures have understood that they need women for their legitimacy, as this represents half of the population; hence, the area for women to participate in decision-making processes has opened. In the first step, they recognize the right to vote for women as the fundamental right to participate in public decision-making processes; even Saudi Arabia, known as a conservative Islamic country, has recognized women's right to vote (2015). In several Islamic countries, Muslim women have gone further to develop their capacity in participatory decision-making processes. Considering the above, women could serve in high levels of governmental branches,

260 Ibid p. 175

261 Shuaib, F. S., Kamal, M. H., Bustami, T. A., Othman, N. and Sulaiman, M. S, p. 310

262 Wan Muhammad, Ramizah, WOMAN AND SHARI'AH COURT: A STUDY OF MALAYSIA AND INDONESIA, International Journal of Cross-Cultural Studies, 2015, p. 46

263 Sonneveld, Lindbekk, Women Judges in the Muslim World, p. 163

264 Shariah High Court appoints first women judges in Malaysia, 27. Juni 2016, http://www.themalaymailonline.com/malaysia/article/the-first-two-women-shariah-high-court-judges-in-malaysia.

judicial systems, and increased membership in national-local parliaments as a whole.

Most importantly, the extent of women's participation in public decision- making processes depends on whether a political structure has initiated an Islamisation or reformation process. As previously mentioned in this part, women have been marginalized from participation in public decision-making processes when political structures have initiated the process of Islamisation, which happened as a result of the Islamic revolution in Iran (1979), or in Pakistan (1977–1988). In this way, political structures supported by the conservative clergy line, who also has the backing of political-legal structures, curtail women's to access decision-making positions based on a hard interpretation of Islam, especially when women have wanted to access key political positions. As a result, women are disengaged from public decision-making positions. In contrast, in reformation environments, political structures have embraced women in public decision-making processes, as a message toward more liberal views, that they can receive support from plenty of female voters and link parties. For example, Egypt, Morocco, Algeria, and Tunisia (2010) started to reform a series of gender inequality rights, which resulted from the Arab Spring toward the reformation process in such countries. Thus far, the participation of women in public life may be relatively progressive.

However, the question must be answered whether the presence of women in public life could seek to reform gender discrimination in family law, where women have been subject to discrimination. In other words, whether the presence or marginalization of women in public decision-making positions impacts on different legislative agendas of women's life.

B. Gender Discrimination Based on Family Laws

B.1 The Right to Equality in Family Laws

The family is the basic unit of society that includes a social and legal construct, a religious construct, and an economic construct. Legal systems often define the family as a unit founded on marriage between a man and a woman. However, different forms of families result from diverse cultural, religious, customs, and social systems, for example, the recognition of same-sex couples, for both women and men. It must note that not all forms of marriage deserve recognition, especially those that violate the dignity of women and have serious emotional and financial consequences for women and their dependents. These include forced marriage, temporary marriage, and polygamy.[265]

The family has a vital role in the growth and well-being of children and their social development. Therefore, all legal definitions of the family should recognize the right to equality, *de jure* and *de facto*, of women and girls within the family. In fact, family law guarantees the legal equality rights for women in the family relations, when marriage entered into, during the marriage, and at its dissolution. Family law's legal sources may derive from constitutions, domestic laws, and judicial decisions, religious and customary codes. Thus, there are three central systems of family law: secular law systems, religious law systems, and plural systems.[266]

1) **Secular family law systems**: In most countries, family laws are formulated by secular codes under civil or common law systems, and have no basis in religious or customary norms. Within secular law systems, the discriminatory laws have been eliminated, and in parallel, these systems promote gender equality in the family. Many states have reformed their family laws by separating religion from the state and have moved from being a patriarchal structure, thereby guaranteeing women's equality within marriage and family relations. For example, in many European countries, family law was referred to as primarily Christian. At the end of the nineteenth century, was removed the religious jurisdiction, and were placed all matters relating to the family under the secular jurisdiction of the state.[267]
2) **Religious family law systems**: Several countries have based their domestic family laws on religious laws. A large number of Islamic countries recognize Islam as their religion, and they apply religious or customary law to family law. Thus, women do not have equal rights as men under Sharia law on marriage and marital or personal status.[268]
3) **Plural legal systems:** in general, several countries use multiple legal systems due to their cultural diversity. Within plural legal systems, countries are generally civil and codified, and parallel the state courts addressing matters

265 CEDAW, General Recommendation No. 21: Equality in marriage and family relations, 1994, para. 13-14

266 Human Rights Council, Report of the Working Group on the issue of discrimination against women in law and in practice, A/HRC/29/40, United Nations, 2015, para. 31 and 37

267 Ibid, para. 42-45

268 Ibid, para. 48

> relating to the public sphere. They include "various combinations of codified civil law, religious law systems, indigenous or customary legal codes, community arbitration or other dispute settlement procedures". Moreover, these systems are often patriarchal interpretations of culture, religious, customary, or indigenous laws that tend to discriminate against women generally.[269]

Regardless of family law sources, states are obliged to respect, protect, and realize women's right to equality in the family, as stated in international human rights law. International human rights laws recognize gender equality in family law. The most notable include:

- The Universal Declaration of Human Rights (Article 16),
- The International Covenant on Civil and Political Rights (Article 23), the Convention on the Elimination of All Forms of Discrimination against Women (Article 16),
- The Convention on Consent to Marriage, Minimum Age for Marriage and Registration of Marriages, 1962. (articles 1 to 3),
- General Recommendation No. 21(adopted by the Committee on the CEDAW, 1994): Equality in marriage and family relations,
- General Recommendation No. 29 (adopted by the Committee on the CEDAW, 2013): Economic consequences of marriage, family relations, and their dissolution.
- Resolution 26/11: Protection of the family (adopted by Human Rights Council, 2014).

B.2 The Essential of Gender Discrimination in Family Laws

In Islamic countries, family law is often justified on religious grounds, and women do not have the same rights as men in family matters. Women have generally been subject to discrimination when the law is applied. In fact, in these jurisdictions, most discrimination against women occurs in divorce, inheritance, guardianship, and custody of children.

B.2.1 Divorce

Under international human rights standards, states should recognize a woman's ability to divorce her husband without any discrimination. Moreover, women must be able to access fault-based divorce regimes because husbands may abuse

269 Ibid, para. 52-54

these regimes to eliminate any financial obligation towards their wives. Therefore, the differences in assessing fault for both spouses must be removed from divorce provisions so that equal access to the financial consequences of divorce be ensured.[270]

In many Islamic countries, women generally do not have the same right to divorce as men. Within traditional Islamic jurisprudence, divorce (*Talaq*) is a unilateral and unconditional right for men without a stated reason, and men do not need to notify the court. However, women can ask for a dissolution of marriage but under many or limited conditions.[271]

Divorce provisions are different across Islamic countries. In general, they can divide into two groups. First, several Muslim countries have made significant legislative divorce reforms in which they recognize the equal right to divorce and equality in reasons for divorce for both women and men. The second group of Islamic countries recognizes the right to divorce for men, while women can only obtain a divorce on specified grounds.

The first group of Muslim countries that seek to reform divorce law in their domestic laws follows:

Egypt was the first Muslim country to improve divorce provisions in its legal system in 1929. Furthermore, the personal status code of 2000 empowers women with the right to divorce (*khul'*)[272] even without the consent of her husband. This reform allows Egyptian women to divorce with the judge's consent but without the husband's consent. The opponents' argument against this law is that this reform conflicts with religion; thus, it diverges from the Islamic jurisprudence, and

270 CEDAW, General Recommendation No. 21: Equality in marriage and family relations, 1994, para. 39.40

271 The Woodrow Wilson International Center for Scholars, "Best Practices" Progressive Family Laws in Muslim Countries, 2005, p. 19

272 *Khula* means: "the situation in which the wife initiates divorce proceedings is known as Khul'a."

The most grounds for khula divorce incudes:

1) Where the wife suffers physical, financial or emotional harm from the husband. Any violence in the marriage is condemned by Islam, and the Council takes allegations of such violence very seriously.
2) Where the husband suffers certain physical defects, such as impotency.
3) Adultery or infidelity.
4) Where there is difference of religion.

accessed at: „KHULA", Islamic Sharia (blog), 9. Mai 2014, http://www.islamic-sharia.org/khula/.

it has an illegal character. However, *Muhammad Tantâwî* from the Cairo Islamic University of *al-Azhar* justified the reform by arguing that it does not conflict with the Sharia law.

Moreover, President *Mubarak* and his wife were at the origin of this reform. In fact, this law imposes divorce by the judge's consent and not by the Islamic jurisprudence.[273] Furthermore, according to this declaration, women are not obligated to justify the reasons for divorce; rather, women need only formally declare the decision to leave the husband.[274]

In **Tunisia**, unilateral divorce has been removed, and divorce recognizes by mutual consent. Divorce is possible only through the courts and after the judge has made reconciliation efforts, which states in the Tunisian Code of Personal Status (1956). Hence, both spouses can apply for dissolution under equal grounds, "at the will of the husband or the request of the wife" without proof of fault.[275]

Pakistan aimed to improve women's rights in family law under the Muslim Family Law enacted in 1961. Hence, women are allowed to obtain a dissolution marriage on the grounds of incompatibility, which does not distinguish between husband and wife.[276]

The second group of Islamic countries recognizes the right to divorce as unilateral for men; however, their domestic laws allow women to dissolve marriage under many or limited reasons.

Bangladesh. According to the Hanafi School of Jurisprudence, the law of divorce in Bangladesh is based on Islamic Sharia. The right to divorce was given to men, as stated in the Muslim Family Law of Bangladesh, 1961.[277]

---

273 Fortier, Corinne, The Right to Divorce for Women (khul') in Islam: Comparative Practices in Mauritania and Egypt, OALib Journal, 2010, p. 164-165

274 Ibid, p. 168

275 The Woodrow Wilson International Center for Scholars, "Best Practices" Progressive Family Laws in Muslim Countries, p. 21.
and also see: Mayer, Ann Elizabeth, Reform of Personal Status Laws in North Africa: A Problem of Islamic or Mediterranean laws?, WLUML Occasional Paper No. 8, 1996, p. 5

276 The Woodrow Wilson International Center for Scholars, "Best Practices" Progressive Family Laws in Muslim Countries, p. 20

277 Article 7(1) of the Muslim Family Law of Bangladesh, 1961: Any man who wishes to divorce his wife shall, as soon as may be after the pronouncement of divorce (talaq) in any form whatsoever, give the Chairman notice in writing of his having done so, and shall supply a copy thereof to the wife.

However, there is a judicial divorce by which Muslim women can apply for the dissolution of marriage for any one or more reasons that are regulated by the Dissolution of Muslim Marriages Act, 1939.[278] This form of divorce differs from the right to divorce. The right to divorce is granted to Muslim men without any given reasons, but women do not have this right; instead, they can apply under the legal conditions for the dissolution of marriage.[279] Therefore, there is gender discrimination in the granting and exercising of divorce rights.

Iran. The husband can divorce his wife without citing any reasons;[280] however, divorce is permissible only through the courts. On the other hand, women can request a divorce without their husband's consent, which is called 'judicial divorce'. This type of divorce provides for women to request and be granted a divorce by getting a divorce attorney, under certain conditions.[281] Moreover, there is a divorce based on the agreement of couples known as the *khul* divorce. Hence, women can obtain a divorce and, in return, may have

---

278 Article 2 of the Dissolution of Muslim Marriages Act 1939: A woman married under Muslim law shall be entitled to obtain a decree for the dissolution of her marriage on any one or more of the following grounds, namely:

1) The whereabouts of a husband are unknown for four years,
2) The husband has failed to provide maintenance to the wife for two years,
3) The husband has taken an additional wife, in contravention of the Muslim Family Law Ordinance 1961, meaning that he has not taken the permission of court for the second marriage,
4) The husband is imprisoned for at least seven years,
5) Where the husband has failed to meet marital obligations for three years for no reasons,
6) Where the husband is impotent at the time of marriage and continues to be so,
7) If the husband is insane for two years,
8) If the husband is suffering from leprosy or virulent venereal diseases.

279 Compare also: International Law: Muslim Divorce in Bangladesh, International Law (blog), Prof. Gabriel Sawma, 10. Juli 2013, accessed at http://gabrielsawma.blogspot.com/2013/07/muslim-divorce-in-bangladesh.html.

280 Article 1133 of the Iranian Civil Code: "A man can divorce his wife whenever he wishes to do so."

281 These reasons include: the absence of husband (Article 1029), refusal of man to pay alimony (Article 1129), *Asr* and *Haraj* (Article 1130), and the attorney in divorce (Article 1119)
Asr and *Haraj* means "a situation which cause the continuity of the life for the wife to be along difficulties and the bearing of that situation to be hard."

ceded some property to the husband. This property would be more or less than the contracted quantity.[282]

In **Saudi Arabia**, a husband has the exclusive right to unilateral divorce without stating any reason, and women have no right to unilateral divorce. However, this right may be delegated to the wife through a stipulation in the marriage contract, but it is not acceptable socially and is presumed to be un-Islamic.[283]

On the other hand, women have two legal ways to request a divorce. First, *Fasakh* (Judicial Divorce) is when women may only obtain a divorce through the courts based on a limited number of grounds, including spousal mistreatment. In this regard, due to the absence of the family law code, the determination of abuse is often "inconsistent and arbitrary, and it is not uncommon for judges to act in a biased manner."[284] This is because judges do not have codified guidelines on what constitutes mistreatment as grounds for divorce.[285] The second legal way is *Khul'* (Redemptive Divorce) in which women can apply a *khul'* divorce through a mutually-agreed upon the sum of money is given to the husband in exchange for a final divorce.[286] Additionally, before the final divorce, women must also first undergo mandatory mediation, usually run by two or more male religious officials, but men do not have the same requirement.[287]

Therefore, women do not have an equal right to divorce as men. On the one hand, in divorce proceedings, women face many obstacles established by judges and mediators. Men can obtain divorce papers from courts within days of requesting them, but in a divorce initiated by women, judges take delays to

---

282 Article 1146 of the Iranian Civil Code: "a Khul'a divorce occurs when the wife obtains a divorce owing to dislike of her husband, against property which she cedes to the husband. The property in question may consist of the original marriage portion, or the monetary equivalent thereof, whether more or less than the marriage portion." Mohammadzadeh Rahni, Mohammad Reza; Kavousi, Peyman; Fatemeh, Kavousi, Divorce in Iran and Cases in Which the Woman Has the Right to Divorce, Journal of Applied Environmental and Biological Sciences, 2014, p. 33-35

283 Musawah for equality in the family, THEMATIC REPORT ON MUSLIM FAMILY LAW AND MUSLIM WOMEN'S RIGHTS IN SAUDI ARABIA, 69th CEDAW Session, Geneva, Switzerland, 2018, p. 22

284 Ibid, p. 22

285 Compare also: Human Rights Watch, Boxed In: Women and Saudi Arabia's Male Guardianship System, 2016, p. 52

286 Musawah, THEMATIC REPORT ON MUSLIM FAMILY LAW AND MUSLIM WOMEN'S RIGHTS IN SAUDI ARABIA, p. 22

287 Compare also: Human Rights Watch, Boxed In: Women and Saudi Arabia's Male Guardianship System, p. 51-52

get documents. On the other hand, following a divorce, women have limited access to economic status division. Hence, the lack of a written family law code provides an unequal legal right to divorce for women; as a result, women face significantly more restrictions than men.[288]

B.2.2 Custody of Children

Custody refers to the post-divorce or post-separation living arrangements of minor children. Although one parent typically has responsibility for the child's supervision, joint custody law may lead to an equal balance of responsibility upon divorce or separation. Hence, in the event of a divorce, parents undertake a legal obligation to support a child regardless of the child's living arrangements.[289] A child defines as "every human being below the age of 18 years".[290]

Specific international instruments address children's rights where custody is at issue. They emphasize 'the child's best interests' that must guarantee "by appropriate legislative and administrative measures".[291] Most importantly is the Convention on the Rights of the Child (CRC) that provides the most comprehensive document on the rights of children. Moreover, the Hague Conference also had adopted a standard of 'best interests of the child' to determine custody arrangements between parents who separate or divorce.[292] Therefore, according to international laws, custody determines the 'best interest of the child'; it should guarantee equal access to the custody of children for both the mother and the father.

In most states, especially in Western countries, custody is based on the "best interest of the child", although this standard requires a detailed case-by-case

288 Ibid, p. 52

289 Stark, Barbara, International Family Law: An Introduction, Ashgate Publishing, Ltd., 2013, p. 182

290 Article 2 of the U.N. Convention on the Rights of the Child (1989)

291 Article 3 of the U.N. Convention on the Rights of the Child (1989)
Article 2 of the U.N. Declaration of the Rights of the Child (1959): "The child shall enjoy special protection, and shall be given opportunities and facilities, by law and by other means, to enable him to develop physically, mentally, morally, spiritually and socially in a healthy and normal manner and in conditions of freedom and dignity. In the enactment of laws for this purpose, the best interests of the child shall be the paramount consideration."

292 Convention on Jurisdiction, Applicable Law, Recognition, Enforcement and Co-operation in Respect of Parental Responsibility and Measures for the Protection of Children, (1996)

analysis in family court. But in Islamic countries, in general, custody is determined by the age of the child. Under Islamic jurisprudence, a divorced mother is typically entitled to custody of boys until seven years and girls until nine years, and after that, custody automatically shifts to the father.[293] Additionally, the custody rights cite a 'natural right' of fathers to have guardianship over their children, even in the event of the father's death, paternal grandfathers or other male relatives of the father have a preference regarding the custody of the children, regardless of the best interests of the child.[294] Hence, there is discrimination based on gender concerning custody rights in Islamic countries. However, the provisions are different in custody from one country to the next.

In **Malaysia,** the civil court operates over the non-Muslim laws, and the Sharia court serves over the Muslim ones. Therefore, the provisions of child custody are governed by two separate laws, one for non-Muslims and one for Muslims.[295] For non-Muslims, the Law Reform (Marriage and Divorce, Act of 1976 (Act 164)), "the interest of the child" or minor child is considered in child custody cases. After the final divorce process, the court suggests mediation between the parents. During the mediation period, the parents must decide child custody and maintenance. But there is no 'automatic transfer' of guardianship from the mother to the father; instead, they must return to court. The age of the minority in Malaysia is seven years for girls and nine years for boys; when a child has reached adult age, the court would ask the child if she/he would prefer to stay with the mother or the father.[296] So, custody of children for non-Muslims is based 'on the interest of the child' by judicial decision.

On the other hand, under the Islamic Family Law (Federal Territories, ACT 1984), women do not have equal custody rights as their husbands. Thus, a child below the age of puberty will go to the mother while a child above the age of puberty has a right to choose between the parents.[297] Additionally, Article 83 endorsed several circumstances in which the mother loses her right to custody

293 Stark, International Family Law, p. 182-183

294 The Woodrow Wilson International Center for Scholars, "Best Practices" Progressive Family Laws in Muslim Countries, p. 24

295 Mohamed Adil, Mohamed Azam, Custody and Religion of Minors in Malaysia, Islam and Civilisational Renewal (ICR) 8, Nr. 2 (16. August 2017): 272–74, p. 273

296 Ashraf Nemat, Orzala, Comparative Analysis of Family Law in the Context of Islam, The Heinrich Böll Foundation, 2006, p. 49

297 Islamic Family Law and Justice for Muslim Women, Asia Society, accessed at: https://asiasociety.org/islamic-family-law-and-justice-muslim-women.

of a child since this right does not recognize by Muslim men.[298] As a result, custody rights in the non-Muslim Act provide equal guardianship rights for both father and mother, but under Islamic family law for Muslims, the father is to be the primary guardian of the children and women do not have equal guardianship rights as men.[299]

Morocco. In the new Family Law (2004) were introduced a series of reforms regarding gender equality in the family law and custody issues. Custody is based on "the best interests of the child", and in the event of the divorce, custodianship goes firstly to the mother. If the mother is unable to fulfill the duty of custodianship, it confers upon the father, then the maternal grandmother.[300] However, the judge has the authority to decide who should be awarded custody and gives a child who has attained the age of fifteen the right to choose whether it will be the mother or father.[301] Furthermore, the mother will not lose custody if the child is under the age of seven, or the child's separation from the mother would cause significant harm, even if she were to remarry.[302]

Jordanian family law codifies gender-based discrimination concerning child custody issues when the marriage partners are Muslim, and disputes are resolved

298 The right of custody (*hadanah*)of a woman is lost: (a) by her marriage with a person not related to the child within the prohibited degrees if her custody in such case will affect the welfare of the child but her right to custody will revert if the marriage is dissolved; (b) by her gross and open immorality; (c) by her changing her residence so as to prevent the father from exercising the necessary supervision over the child, except that a divorced wife may take her own child to her birth-place; (d) by her abjuration of Islam; (e) by her neglect of or cruelty to the child.

299 Islamic Family Law and Justice for Muslim Women

300 Article 171 of the Moroccan Family Code: "Child custody shall be awarded first to the mother, then to the father, then to the maternal grandmother of the child...."

301 Article 166 of the Moroccan Family Code: "...[a] child who completes fifteen years of age has the right to choose either the father or mother as custodian."

302 Reunite International Child Abduction Centre, Morocco, Approved by Jean Gabriel Tomaly, 2005, p. 2-3

Article 175 of the Moroccan Family Code: The marriage of the custodial mother shall not result in the loss of her custody of the child in the following cases: 1. If the child has not attained the age of seven years; or if such a separation may inflict harm on him or her; 2. If the child suffers from an illness or a handicap which renders his or her custody difficult for any person other than the mother; 3. If her husband is in a degree of kinship relations precluding marriage, or is the child's legal representative; 4. If she is the child's legal representative.

in the Sharia court.[303] Under Jordanian law, the father is legally responsible for the children. In the event of death or nonattendance of the father or the paternal grandfather, the legal responsibility for the children gives to the mother.[304] A woman has the right to custody of sons until the age of nine and girls until the age of eleven. Additionally, a mother can lose her right to custody of a child under the following conditions: if she is incapable of safeguarding the child or of bringing the child up under the appropriate religious standards; or by remarrying; or by residing in a home with people that might be strangers to the child. Hence, Jordanian law is not based on the best interest of the children, as the father has automatic legal guardianship of the children, and women do not have the same rights as men concerning the custody of children.[305]

Family law in **Kuwait** is based on Islam, but there are different interpretations of Islam concerning custody issues, according to *Sunni* Law and *Shiá* Law. In *Sunni* law, fathers designate as the legal guardians of their children under the Personal Status of Kuwait (1984). In the event of the divorce, a woman may be granted custody of the children upon divorce for her sons until they reach the age of 15 years and her daughters until they are married.[306] If the court finds the mother not fit to have custody, will choose a maternal grandmother living in Kuwait or a paternal grandmother. However, the mother can lose her primary right to custody of a child, if she remarries.[307] In *Shiá* Law, the mother has custody of her daughter until the daughter is nine and of her son until he is two, and she cannot have remarried.[308]

In **Pakistan**, the Guardians and Ward's Act (1890) concerns guardianship and custodial issues and based on the "best interests of children". Moreover, this law applies to the whole of Pakistan "without differentiating between people of different faith traditions". In other words, it refers to "minors of all creeds and races"

---

303 International Family Law Firm, JORDAN AND CHILD ABDUCTION, accessed at: http://www.international-divorce.com/ca-jordan.htm.

304 Yacoub Al Rabadi, Rania Farah, Legal Reform in Women's Rights: A Comparative Study Between Jordan and Bahrain Concerning Citizenship and Political Participation, Cuvillier, 2012, p. 80-81

305 International Family Law Firm

306 Kuwait Marriage Law - Kuwaiti Family Law and Divorce, accessed at: https://www.visit-kuwait.com/living/marriage-law.aspx.

307 International Parental Child Abduction Kuwait, accessed at: http://www.passportsusa.com/family/abduction/country/country_503.html.

308 The United Nations Children's Fund (UNICEF), KUWAIT, MENA Gender Equality Profile Status of Girls andWomen in the Middle East and North Africa, 2010, p. 2

and provides that "in the selection of guardians and other matters; regard shall be had to the personal law of the minor".[309] In this regard, the Supreme Court of Pakistan states that the primary consideration in custody cases "must be the child's welfare, but also that the child's welfare is not coterminous with the child's religious tradition".[310] As a result, the custody does not apply automatically to the fathers, and the court has the power to determine who the best guardian for children by reference to the factual circumstances of the particular case. [311]

In **Iran**, the father has automatic legal guardianship over the children. In the event of a divorce, the mother's custody of both girls and boys ends at seven years. If the mother remarries during the custody period, the custody will devolve to the father.[312] It is the traditional *Shi'ite* interpretation of Islam that creates legal gender discrimination in Iranian family law.

B.2.3 Inheritance

In many countries, women and girls face discriminatory laws related to inheritance, affecting their enjoyment of the right to adequate housing. As a result, women may receive either a smaller share of the husband's or father's property at his death or have limited and controlled rights and receive income only from any heritage of their deceased husbands or fathers. Therefore, women should also have equal inheritance rights to their husbands, sons, and brothers when the dissolution is caused by death.[313] In this regard, the Economic and Social Council (Resolution 884D (XXXIV)) recommended that states should ensure "men and women in the same degree of relationship to a deceased are entitled to equal shares in the estate and equal rank in the order of succession".[314]

Women's equal rights to inheritance recognize in various international human rights instruments. The most important specific provisions protecting gender equality to inheritance rights include:

- International Covenant on Civil and Political Rights (ICCPR): Arts. 3, 17, and 26,

---

309 Anver, M. Emon; Khaliq, Urfan, Private International Law, Islamic Law, and Cross-Border Child Abduction, A Historico-Legal Analysis, Institute Letters, 2016, p. 63

310 Ibid, p. 64

311 Ibid, p. 66

312 Fazaeli, Roja, Islamic Feminisms: Rights and Interpretations Across Generations in Iran (Taylor & Francis, 2016), p. 106

313 CCPR, General Comment No. 28, para. 26

314 CEDAW, General Recommendation No. 21, para. 34

- International Covenant on Economic, Social and Cultural Rights (ICESCR): Arts. 11 (1) and 2 (2),
- Convention on the Elimination of All Forms of Discrimination against Women (CEDAW): Arts. 14 (h) (2), 15, 16 (1) (c) and (h),
- The Human Rights Committee, General Comment No. 28 (Equality of rights between men and women, 2000),
- Committee on the Elimination of Discrimination against Women, General recommendation on article 16 of the Convention on the Elimination of All Forms of Discrimination against Women (Economic consequences of marriage, family relations and their dissolution, 2103),
- UN Commission on Human Rights Resolution 2005/25 Women's equal ownership of, access to and control over land and the equal rights to own property and to adequate housing,
- UN Commission on the Status of Women Resolution 42/1, Human rights and land rights discrimination.

In general, these international instruments obligate states parties to ensure that women do not experience discrimination in respect of having access to, acquiring, and securing housing, land, and other property. Also, denying women's equal rights to own, access, and control housing and land violates women's fundamental human rights.[315]

However, in many countries, women have fewer inheritance rights than men, as well as women are disadvantaged under Sharia provisions on inheritance. Under Islamic jurisprudence, if women (daughters) more than two, then for them two-thirds of the inheritance, and if there is only one, then it is half. Moreover, the wife's share is one-quarter in the absence of a child or agnatic grandchild and one-eighth in the presence of a child or agnatic grandchild. Two or more wives share equally in this prescribed share.[316] In particular, within Sharia, women are entitled to half/ or two-thirds of the inheritance than men. However, some Islamic countries have taken various positive developments to reform equality right in terms of inherence law, while some Islamic countries have not yet made such steps.

---

315 Center on Housing Rights and Evictions (COHRE), In Search of Equality: A Survey of Law and Practice related to Women's Inheritance Rights in the Middle East and North Africa (MENA) Region, Geneva, Switzerland, 2006, p. 3

316 Hussain, Dr. Abid, THE ISLAMIC LAWS OF INHERITANCE, accessed at: https://www.islam101.com/sociology/inheritance.htm

Tunisia. Although the Personal Status Code (1956) contained some progressive provisions for Tunisian women in family law, it failed to provide for equal inheritance rights. Tunisian inheritance law is based on Islamic jurisprudence, which grants women half of what it gives men an inheritance. The Tunisian Association of Democratic Women and the Tunisian Association of University Women for Research in Development attempted to bring issues of women's inheritance into the focus of public debate.[317] A controversial reform of the inheritance law prescribed by Tunisian President *Beji Caid Essebsi* (2018), called equal rights for men and women in inheritance law. After that, on National Women's Day (March 2018), many women took to the streets and demand to establish equal inheritance rights for both sexes and an end to inheritance laws based on Islamic law.[318] On the other hand, some Muslim clerics described "gender equality in inheritance as a flagrant violation of Islamic precepts".[319]

The President announced the formation of the Committee on Individual Freedoms and Rights, and a woman (*Bushra Belhaj Hamida*) heads the nine-member committee. She announced in a statement the drafting of the bill that comprised essential reforms of equality rights in inheritance between male and female children into the country's legal code.[320] This draft does not remain in the legal formwork; however, Tunisia is the first Arab country to take measures in reforming equality in inheritance between genders.[321]

Algeria. Inheritance law is based on the Sharia which women receive half of their brother's share or relevant male relative. However, women's inheritance issue was a discussion in Algeria. However, women's rights activists launched a camping to enforce gender equality in inheritance law in 2011. But it is faced

---

317 Center on Housing Rights and Evictions (COHRE), p. 101 and 103

318 Tunisians Divided Over Women's Inheritance Rights, The North Africa Post (blog) accessed at: http://northafricapost.com/19367-tunisians-divided-womens-inheritance-rights.html.

319 Tunisian Women Stand up for Gender Equality in Inheritance, The North Africa Post (blog), 12. März 2018, http://northafricapost.com/22654-tunisian-women-stand-gender-equality-inheritance.html.

320 The New Arab, "Tunisia Takes Groundbreaking Steps towards Gender Equality", alaraby, accessed at: https://www.alaraby.co.uk/english/news/2018/1/20/tunisia-takes-groundbreaking-steps-towards-gender-equality.

321 Tunisia becomes the first Arab nation to approve gender equality in inheritance law, Dhaka Tribune, 25. November 2018, accessed at: https://www.dhakatribune.com/world/africa/2018/11/25/controversial-gender-equality-in-inheri tance-law-approved-by-tunisian-cabinet.

by the rejection of clerics; they argued that men are responsible for the material wellbeing of women under Islamic law, and thus they need more share of the inheritance.[322] As a result, *Sheikh Ali Ferkous*, a *Salafist* theologian, issued a *Fatwa* that "the settlement in the Sharia-required inheritance between males and females with which justice would be realized is for males to receive double of what females receive in the division of inheritance".[323] Hence, inheritance law remains the unequal share between men and women in Allergies inherence law.

Kuwait. Inheritance is unequal to share between women and men that a woman's share of the inheritance is half of her brother's share. However, the rules differ between *Sunni* and *Shi'a* inheritance law. For example, under *Shi'a* law, the wife inherits all of her husband's property when there is no direct male heir. *Sunni* law limits the wife to one-eighth of the estate.[324]

Lebanon. Inheritance laws differ between Non-Muslims and Muslim communities. Non-Muslims refer to the 1959 Civil Law of Inheritance, which grants equality share of inheritance between men and women. Although, inheritance law for Muslims is established under Sharia law that generally man inherits twice as much as a woman.[325]

Pakistan. The Muslim Family Laws Ordinance (1961) codified discrimination against women in the inheritance of property. These provisions have been legitimized "by the formal legal system and religious scholars based on arguments like the compensatory property regime provided by Islam for women". However, the National Commission of Inquiry 1997 has recognized that "women's inheritance rights are half those of men and that even these rights are ignored".[326]

---

322 Freedom House, Women's Rights in the Middle East and North Africa 2010, p. 15, accessed at: https://freedomhouse.org/report/women039s-rights-middle-east-and-north-africa/womens-rights-middle-east-and-north-africa-2010.

323 Algerians debate female inheritance rights, accessed at: http://www.algeria.com/forums/algeria-en-alg%E9rie/28514-algerians-debate-female-inheritance-rights.html.

324 Family Law in Kuwait, U.S. Embassy in Kuwait (blog), accessed at: https://kw.usembassy.gov/u-s-citizen-services/local-resources-of-u-s-citizens/family-law-kuwait/.

325 Freedom House, Women's Rights in the Middle East and North Africa 2010, p. 17

326 Ahmad, Nausheen, Land Rights for Pakistani (Muslim) Women: Law and Policy, Policy Brief Series, Nr- 23, 2010, p. 2

C. Conclusion

In this chapter, the substantial violation of gender discrimination for religious reasons considered. It has focused on public decision-making processes and family law, targeting the root of fundamental women's human rights.

To sum up, the degree to which women access equal rights varies across Islamic countries is mainly due to different social-culture norms, traditional, economic factors, and nature of politics. Regardless of such factors, Islamic law's interpretation is the most critical factor that directly affects women's access to equal rights in their public and private law. Thus, religious scholars have the competence to interpret Islamic law, which is considered a male domination system and often assumes unequal rights for women compared to men. As a result, they impose a range of discriminatory practices on women on the grounds of religion. This form of gender discrimination for religious reasons has two consequences for women. First, it claims a form of legality; in this form, discrimination against women institutionalized in domestic laws; thus, women meet severe legal challenges under Islam's name. Second, when they do not define in the legal system, it is possible to put them into effect via social, cultural, and patriarch structures. In other words, there are no legal obstacles; rather, there are social-cultural obstacles for religious reasons.

Nevertheless, discrimination against women under Sharia's name is a 'practical instrument' because religious clerics refer to religious reasons in the form of the *fatwa*, without any legal justification for their actions. In doing so, they do not need to go through legal channels or take into consideration public discussion. In other words, it is a 'unilateral statement' by religious clerics on women, when especially discussing women's access to key political decision-making positions and property law, which are male-dominant structures. Furthermore, a religious declaration or *fatwa* can mobilize civilian regimes to maintain discrimination against women.

However, on the one hand, women have made significant progress, especially in their public lives, on their presence in decision-making processes in general, which have led to reform in gender-equal rights in some matter of family law. In other words, where women's representation has increased, particularly in legislative branches, in general, family law has reformed. For example, in several Islamic countries in North- Africa (Egypt, Morocco, Algeria, Tunisia), and East-Asia (Pakistan, Malaysia, and Bangladesh), the parallel to the increasing women's presence in public decision-making processes, particularly in parliamentary participation and the judiciary system, has resulted in reform in some matters of family law. But in the Middle East, as considered, the extent of women in public decision-making processes is weak; thus, the reform of gender equality rights in family law often lags behind. It could be concluded that the degree of participation of women in decision-making processes leads to dynamic or static other legislative agendas of women's rights.

On the other hand, it seems that Islamic governments do not lean towards more family law reform because they may face stiff opposition from the dominant religious attitudes, which tend to preserve a patriarchal structure in the family. In this regard, the major obstacle is in property rights through inheritance, in which Islamic governments do not take serious measures to give women this financial advantage. As a result, significant legal and public policy reforms for women have occurred more during participation in decision-making processes, than in family law.

Chapter 3 International Monitoring Mechanisms of the Implementation of Women's Human Rights

A. Introduction to Human Rights Monitoring Mechanisms

International human rights treaties set out legal obligations on states parties to protect and promote fundamental human rights. In this regard, ratification or accession by states on paper cannot guarantee that will be enjoyed the protection of human rights in practice. Therefore, the nine core international human rights treaties constitute a crucial mechanism for monitoring the implementation of each treaty.[327] The violation of human rights obligations by states parties will be

327 The application of the human rights treaties is monitored by the following committees:

- The Committee on the Elimination of Racial Discrimination (CERD). The first treaty body to be established has reviewed the application of the International Convention on the Elimination of All Forms of Racial Discrimination since 1969. It has 18 members.)
- The Committee on Economic, Social and Cultural Rights (CESCL) was created in 1985 to carry out the functions of the Economic and Social Council under the International Covenant on Economic, Social and Cultural Rights. It has 18 members.
- The Human Rights Committee (HRC) was created in 1976 to review the application of the International Covenant on Civil and Political Rights. It has 18 members.
- The Committee on the Elimination of Discrimination against Women (CEDAW) has reviewed the application of the Convention on the Elimination of All Forms of Discrimination against Women by its State parties since 1981. It has 23 members.
- The Committee against Torture (CAT), created in 1987, reviews the application of the Convention against Torture and Other Cruel, Inhuman or Degrading Treatment or Punishment. It has 10 members.
- The Subcommittee on Prevention of Torture ("SPT") held its first session in February 2007. Its mandate is twofold: to visit all places of detention in State parties; and to provide assistance and advice to both States parties and their independent national bodies for the prevention of torture and other cruel, inhuman or degrading treatment or punishment, the national preventive mechanisms. It has 25 members.
- The Committee on the Rights of the Child (CRC) has since 1991, reviewed the application of the Convention on the Rights of the Child, as well as its Optional Protocols relating to the involvement of children in armed conflict and to the sale

identified through these mechanisms. There are various procedures for monitoring under an international Committee known as the 'treaty-monitoring body'. These procedures include submitting reports periodically, engaging in dialogue with the treaty body established, advising, and making recommendations. Some states have accepted to be bound by petitions procedures within an Optional Protocol.[328]

These monitoring procedures of treaty bodies have developed in practice and strengthened over time. In other words, they have made a significant contribution to the development of human rights. For example, the reporting process has indicated to which degree states parties have met their obligation under human rights treaties, which aim at "strengthening the capacity of states to fulfill their reporting obligation".[329] Moreover, individual complaints concluded as the progressive development of international instrument monitoring, which has resulted in individual relief for victims; though it is in accord with the approaches of the Committee, it is not legally binding.[330]

However, the role of the Committees has highlighted, on the one hand, their jurisprudence in the interpretation and application of human rights referred to frequently by national courts.[331] On the other hand, human rights development is grounded more in the interests of states parties facing human rights monitoring. The monitoring system needs support by state parties in their work by

---

of children, child prostitution and child pornography, by their State parties. It has 18 members.

- The Committee on Migrant Workers (CMW) held its first session in March 2004 and reviews the application of the International Convention on the Protection of the Rights of All Migrant Workers and Members of their Families. It has 14 members.
- The Committee on the Rights of Persons with Disabilities (CRPD), established in November 2008, held its first session in February 2009. It has 18 members.

See also: OHCHR | Core International Instruments, accessed at: https://www.ohchr.org/EN/ProfessionalInterest/Pages/CoreInstruments.aspx

328 The United Nations Human Rights Treaty System (An Introduction to the Core Human Rights Treaties and the Treaty Bodies Fact), Office of the United Nations High Commissioner for Human Rights Fact Sheet No. 30/Rev. 1 (2012), accessed at: http://www.ohchr.org/Documents/Publications/FactSheet30Rev1.pdf. p. 19- 21.

329 Alfredsson, Gudmundur; Grimheden, Jonas; G. Ramcharan, Bertrand, International Human Rights Monitoring Mechanisms: Essays in Honour of Jakob Th. Möller (Martinus Nijhoff Publishers, 2009), p. 23

330 Ibid, p. 24

331 Ibid, p. 10

ensuring that they have "competent members, adequate resources of information and data, opportunities for discussing and reflecting on the issue, and adoption of efficient methods of operation".[332] Therefore, part of this increased contribution to the monitoring system is based "on genuine interest from States in consolidating and improving the system while others seem to be driven by a wish to control and reverse some of the achievement". [333]

B. The Committee on the CEDAW

CEDAW establishes 'the Committee' in Articles 17 to 30, which is a crucial mechanism for monitoring the state's measure in the fulfillment of the Convention's obligations.

Since 1981, the Committee comprises twenty-three independent experts by which their autonomy is essential. That means that they "may not be subject to direction or influence of any kind or to pressure from a State party". In fact, they are accountable only to the Committee, not to their Country. Following this, Chairpersons have adopted the statement about the independence of experts that acknowledges: "members of treaty bodies [will] refrain from participating in any aspect of the consideration of the reports of the States parties of which they were nationals, or communications or inquiries concerning those States parties, in order to maintain the highest standards of impartiality, both in substance and in appearance'. Moreover, all members will be individuals of 'high moral standing and competence in the field'. They should have significant expertise in gender and related women issues such as social or political science, law, education, human rights, and equal treatment. Indeed, in practice, diverse knowledge and expertise are important for the Committee's function, particularly in the examination of reports. The members nominated by their Governments and elected by the states parties for a term of four years with due regard to equitable geographical representation, as well as the different forms of civilization and the principal legal systems.[334]

---

332 Ross, Susan Deller, Women's Human Rights: The International and Comparative Law Casebook (University of Pennsylvania Press, 2013), p. 14

333 Alfredsson, Grimheden, G.Ramcharan, International Human Rights Monitoring Mechanisms, 2009, p. 12

334 Article 17 of the CEDAW and compare also: Freeman, Rudolf, Chinkin, The UN Convention on the Elimination of All Forms of Discrimination Against Women: A Commentary, p. 467-482

The Committee elects a chairperson, three Vice-Chairpersons, and the Rapporteur 'with due equitable geographical representation', who are chosen for two years terms and may be re-elected "provided that the principle of rotation is upheld". Furthermore, each year the Chairperson participates on behalf of the Committee on the Commission on the Status of Women, the Commission on the Human Rights, and the Third Committee of the General Assembly.[335] CEDAW members have also participated in the regular meeting with the chairpersons of the treaty bodies and the subsequent inter-Committee institutes' meetings, which have been "an important venue for sharing information and working toward improvement".[336]

B.1 Functioning of the Committee to Monitoring

This section provides a general overview of the functioning of the Committee on monitoring Convention obligations. In this regard, the monitoring system by the Committee envisaged by various means; through a reporting procedure (Article 18), and making General Recommendations (Article 21). These mechanisms have supported many important issues of gender equality, and the Committee has "contributed through progressive thinking to the clarification and understanding of the substantive content of CEDAW".[337] Moreover, the Optional Protocol of the CEDAW empowers the Committee to examine individual communications and inquiry procedures.

B.1.1 Consideration of States' Periodic Reports

Under Article 18, states parties upon ratifying or acceding to the CEDAW are obliged to submit a report to the United Nations' Secretary-General for examination by the Committee. The report includes the legislative, judicial, administrative, or other measures taken within one year after the entry into force and after that every four years if requested.[338]

In general, states parties' reports are the main procedure for monitoring the obligations of CEDAW; as a result, the process for the submission of reports by

335 Compare also: Inter-parliamentary Union and United Nations, The Convention on the Elimination of All Forms of Discrimination Against Women and Its Optional Protocol: Handbook for Parliamentarians (United Nations Publications, 2003), p. 23

336 Hellum, Anne; Aasen, Henriette Sinding, Women's Human Rights: CEDAW in International, Regional and National Law (Cambridge University Press, 2013). p. 31

337 CEDAW, General recommendation No. 25, para. 3

338 According to Article 18 of CEDAW

states parties should be followed in the preparation of the initial report and also all subsequent periodic reports.[339] The initial report is a first opportunity for states parties to present to the Committee degree to which its domestic laws comply with the Convention's provisions, which it has ratified. The initial report at the time of submission should explain factors and difficulties affecting the extent of compliance obligations of the convention. It includes the establishment of domestic law for the implantation of the Convention. It should also outline any restrictions or limitations imposed by law in practice or tradition to the fulfillment of each provision of the Convention.[340] The initial report examined the presence of a representative of the reporting state, who is to respond to answers or supporting material and may make a supplementary presentation. Besides,

---

339 See also, United Nations, The Convention on the Elimination of All Forms of Discrimination Against Women and Its Optional Protocol, Inter-Parliamentary Union (IPU), 2003, p. 61
The committee has adopted reporting guidelines which apply to the initial and subsequent periodic reports submitted after 31 December 2002.
These guidelines provide that:

- In preparing reports, the terms of articles, together with the Committee's general recommendations, should be taken into;
- Detailed information should be provided on any reservations or declarations that the State party may have lodged;
- Any factors or difficulties affecting the fulfilment of the obligations under the Convention should be explained, and information on the steps being taken to overcome these provided;
- Sufficient data and statistics disaggregated by sex should be included in order to enable the Committee to assess progress in the Convention's implantation.

340 The report should explain: (1)Whether the Convention is directly applicable in domestic law on ratification, or has been incorporated into the national Constitution or domestic law so as to be directly applicable; (2) Whether the provisions of the Convention are guaranteed in a Constitution or other laws and to what extent; or if not, whether its provisions can be invoked before and given effect to by courts, tribunals and administrative authorities;(3) How article 2 of the Convention is applied, setting out the principal legal measures which the State party has taken to give effect to Convention rights; and the range of remedies available to persons whose rights may have been violated."
See also, UN. Committee on the Elimination of Discrimination against Women, Compilation of Guidelines on the Form and Content of Reports to Be Submitted by States Parties to the International Human Rights Treaties, International Human Rights Instruments, HRI/GEN/2/Rev.1/Add.2, 5 May 2003, p. 3-4

individual members have the right to ask for clarification or elaboration of related issues to the report.[341]

The subsequent periodic reports of states parties should focus on the period between examining their previous report and the presentation of the current reports. Therefore, they should include the concluding comments of the previous report, as well as elaborate significant progress that has occurred over the last four years. Besides, the subsequent periodic reports should give information about identifying obstacles in the state party's legal and political approach to the achievement of the Convention.[342] These reports will have been considered by a pre-session working group which comprises no more than five Committee members. The working group shall formulate a list of questions on substantive issues arising from reports submitted by other states parties several months in advance, and then submit them to the state representative,[343] who should be prepared with the list of issues which are related to its report through "their knowledge and competence and their position of authority or accountability".[344] Moreover, the state representative must respond to such questions or any others that members may request, with updated information; and may be required to do this within the time allocated for addressing the report. Also, reports are processed as UN documents and published in the six languages of the Organization.[345]

The Committee at each of its sessions (usually a three-week session) examines the periodic national reports in a public meeting in the presence of a representative from the reporting state and regularly invites eight states parties to

---

341 CEDAW Reporting, accessed at: http://www.un.org/womenwatch/daw/cedaw/reporting.htm.
See also, CEDAW, General Recommendation No. 1: Reporting by States Parties, 1986, which addressed to submit initial report under Article 18: "... reports should be submitted at least every four years after the first report was due and should include obstacles encountered in implementing the Convention fully and the measures adopted to overcome such obstacles."

342 UN. Committee on the Elimination of Discrimination against Women, Compilation of Guidelines on the Form and Content of Reports to be submitted by States Parties to the International Human Rights Treaties, HRI/GEN/2/Rev.1/Add.2, p. 4-5

343 CEDAW Reporting, accessed at: http://www.un.org/womenwatch/daw/cedaw/reporting.htm.

344 CEDAW, Fifteenth meeting, CEDAW/SP/2008/1, 30 July 2008, para. K.3

345 UN. Committee on the Elimination of Discrimination against Women, Compilation of Guidelines on the Form and Content of Reports to be submitted by States Parties to the International Human Rights Treaties, International Human Rights Instruments, HRI/GEN/2/Rev.1/Add.2, p. 6, para. H.2.1

present their reports. That done to open a 'constructive dialogue' with the states parties concerned as well as to make clear or to exchange views on the policies of discriminatory law in that state.[346] Following the consideration of the reports, the Committee makes "Concluding Observations" on the periodic report as a completion of the consideration, which, on the whole, has strengthened the reporting procedure.[347] Thus, Concluding Observations are a primary source of information about the Committee's views, and they are an opportunity for the Committee "to speak with one voice in identifying its priorities, obstacles to progress in Convention implantation, and practice that it considers contrary to convention norms".[348]

B.1.2 Suggestions and General Recommendations

The UN human rights treaty bodies have adopted their interpretation of substantive provisions based on the consideration of states parties' reports in the form of 'general comments' or 'general recommendations'. In general, they intend to clarify the state reporting concerning specific articles and suggest approaches to implementing treaty obligations.[349]

Article 21 provides making "suggestions and general recommendations" as a result of the examination of reports and information received from states parties to which it could attach comments, if any, from states parties to the reports of the Committee, too.[350] Suggestions are usually included in the Committee's

346 Committee on the Elimination of Discrimination against Women, accessed at: http://www.un.org/womenwatch/daw/cedaw/committee.htm.

347 The Committee decided, for the first time, to prepare concluding comments on each report considered but, owing to its tight schedule, it was not able to prepare comments on all the reports. For the status of the submission of reports by States parties.

348 Freeman, Rudolf, Chinkin, The UN Convention on the Elimination of All Forms of Discrimination Against Women: A Commentary, p. 22

349 The United Nations Human Rights Treaty System (An introduction to the core human rights treaties and the treaty bodies Fact), p. 36

350 Article 21 of CEDAW:

1. The Committee shall, through the Economic and Social Council, report annually to the General Assembly of the United Nations on its activities and may make suggestions and general recommendations based on the examination of reports and information received from the States Parties. Such suggestions and general recommendations shall be included in the report of the Committee together with comments, if any, from States Parties.

annual report and directed at UN entities, while general recommendations are addressed to any issue affecting women and on specific provisions of the Convention. Most of them outline matters that the Committee wishes to see addressed in the report of states parties; thus, they are the guidance to all states parties in understanding the obligations of the Convention.[351] Thus, as of early 2018, the Committee had adopted thirty–four General Recommendations.[352]

---

2. The Secretary-General of the United Nations shall transmit the reports of the Committee to the Commission on the Status of Women for its information.

351 Ross, Women's Human Rights: The International and Comparative Law Casebook, p. 335-336

352 All General Recommendation as of 2018:

- General Recommendation No. 1–fifth session, 1986 reporting guideline
- General Recommendation No. 2–sixth session, 1987 reporting guidelines
- General Recommendation No. 3–sixth session, 1987 education and public information programmes
- General Recommendation No. 4–sixth session, 1987 reservation
- General Recommendation No. 5–seventh session, 1988 temporary special measures
- General Recommendation No. 6– seventh session, 1988 effective national machinery and publicity
- General Recommendation No. 7– seventh session, 1988 resources
- General Recommendation No. 8– seventh session, 1988 article 8
- General Recommendation No. 9– eighth session, 1989 statistical data
- General Recommendation No. 10–eighth session, 1989 tenth anniversary of the adoption of CEDAW
- General Recommendation No. 11 –eighth session, 1989 technical advisory services for reporting
- General Recommendation No. 12 –eighth session, 1989 violence against women
- General Recommendation No. 13 –eighth session, 1989 equal remuneration for work of equal value
- General Recommendation No. 14 –ninth session, 1990 female circumcision
- General Recommendation No. 15 – ninth session, 1990 women and AIDS
- General Recommendation No. 16 – tenth session, 1991 unpaid women workers in rural and urban family enterprises
- General Recommendation No. 17 – tenth session, 1991 measurement and quantification of the unremunerated domestic activities of women and their recognition in the GN
- General Recommendation No. 18 – tenth session, 1991 disabled women
- General Recommendation No. 20 – eleventh session, 1992 reservations
- General Recommendation No. 21–thirteenth session, 1994 equality in marriage and family relations

The early General Recommendations were short and resolution-style documents that addressed substantive matters, reservations to the Convention, and other resources. In 1991, at the 10th session, the Committee decided to expand in more detail on specific provisions of the Convention and the relationship between the Convention articles and specific issues related.[353]

- General Recommendation No. 22–fourteenth session, 1995 article 20 of the Convention
- General Recommendation No. 23–sixteenth session, 1997 women in political and public life
- General Recommendation No. 25 – thirtieth session, 2004 article 4 paragraph 1 - Temporary special measures
- General Recommendation No. 26–forty-second session, 2008, Women Migrant Workers
- General Recommendation No. 27–forty-seventh session, 2010 - Older women and protection of their human rights
- General Recommendation No. 28–forty-seventh session, 2010 - The Core Obligations of States Parties under Article 2 of the Convention on the Elimination of All Forms of Discrimination against Women
- General Recommendation No. 29–fifty-fourth session, 2013 - Article 16 - Economic consequences of marriage, family relations and their dissolution
- General Recommendation No. 30 (fifty-sixth session, 2013) on women in conflict prevention, conflict and post-conflict situations
- General Recommendation No. 31–fifty-ninth session, 2014 - of the Committee on the Elimination of Discrimination against Women and No. 18 of the Committee on the Rights of the Child on harmful practices
- General Recommendation No. 32–fifty-ninth session, 2014 - on the gender-related dimensions of refugee status, asylum, nationality and statelessness of women
- General Recommendation No. 33–sixty-first session, 2015 - on women's access to justice
- General Recommendation No. 34–sixty-third session, 2016 - on the rights of rural women

353 The Committee decided: "that analyses of selected articles of the Convention, as well as of special issues related to the formulation of general recommendations and suggestion… [I]t further decided, in conformity with existing general recommendations, that if States parties whose reports were overdue by the conclusion of the tenth session so wished, they could submit a combined report to the Committee. In cases where the report due was an initial one, it was decided that the combined report should be comprehensive, covering all aspects of the Convention as well as the general recommendations of the Committee, and that it should describe the current situation of women and seek to show the changes that had occurred since the Convention had entered into force in the country concerned, as well as the obstacles encountered in

Since that time, the Committee has adopted a three-stage process for the formulation of general recommendations. The first stage provides an open dialogue on the General Recommendation between the Committee, non-governmental organizations, and others. The second stage is the preparation of the draft of the General Recommendation by the Committee members, and the final step is the adoption of the General Recommendation by the Committee.[354] Following that decision, the Committee prepares more detailed and comprehensive recommendations[355] that offer states parties a resource for legal and policy guidance on applying Convention obligations that the Committee describes as 'cross-cutting' themes. For example, the most important General Recommendation No. 19 addresses the conceptualization of violence against women as a form of discrimination against women. This Recommendation provides that states parties have obligations of "due diligence" to take reasonable measures to ensure that women are not subject to discrimination in the context of the violence against them. Moreover, General Recommendation No. 25 concerns the development of the concept of non-discrimination and substantive equality through temporary special measures.[356]

---

its implementation. Such reports should be numbered by the secretariat in a way that facilitated the identification of reports that were being combined."
CEDAW, Report of the Committee on the Elimination of Discrimination Against Women, 10th Session, A/46/38, 1991, para. 369-370

354 Hellum; Aasen, Women's Human Rights. p. 39

355 For example, the Committee adopted General Recommendation No. 19 in 1992, requires that States parties' reports provide statistical data on the incidence of violence against women, information on the provision of service for victims, and legislative and other measures taken to protect from abuse in the family and sexual violence. Moreover other comprehensive general recommendations have addressed equality in marriage and family relations (No. 21), women's participation in public life (No. 21), and access to health care (No. 24). as well as several general recommendation relevance to the other articles of the Convention— General Recommendation No. 28 in that on Article 2 which explains the Committee's understanding of concepts as gender, equality, and intersectionality.

356 Hellum; Aasen, Women's Human Rights. p. 41
In addition to general recommendations, the Committee has adopted a number of other statements in which it clarifies "its position on major international developments and issues that bear upon the implementation of the Convention." Statements may address thematic issues or the situation of women in a specific States, for instance, Statements on the situation of women in the Middle East (2006), or Statements on the situation of women in Iraq (2005).

Additionally, the process of drafting general recommendations has indicated a procedure for the development and elaboration of the Committee's view that has been incorporated with increasingly transparent and open to contributions from a wide range of interested states parties.[357]

B.2 Optional Protocol to the CEDAW (OP-CEDAW)

The Optional Protocol to the CEDAW came into force in December 2000. It consists of two procedures: communication and an inquiry procedure. Through these procedures, women enable the justice system at the international level in the CEDAW, whose rights have been violated. This section briefly considers the background of the Optional Protocol and the main elements of the two procedures.

An Optional Protocol: The majority of human rights treaties are followed by an 'Optional Protocol', which are separate treaties in their rights. An Optional Protocol addresses issues not covered or insufficiently developed in the treaty. In general, most optional protocols to human rights treaties include a complaints procedure by which "individuals and groups of individuals can file formal complaints in cases where States have violated rights set forth in a human rights treaty".[358] Hence, the monitoring bodies elaborate through complaints and inquiry procedures on the meaning of the provisions and contribute to the development of international jurisprudence on the subject of

---

357 Ibid. p. 40

358 OP CEDAW > What is OP CEDAW? > OP CEDAW Overview : IWRAW Asia Pacific, accessed at: https://www.iwraw-ap.org/op-cedaw/what-is-op-cedaw/op-cedaw-overview/.

International complaints procedure exist in universal human rights treaties including:

- The first Optional Protocol to the International Covenant on Civil and Political Rights;
- The International Convention on the Elimination of all Forms Racial Discrimination ;
- The Convention against Torture and other Cruel, Inhuman or Degrading treatment or Punishment;
- The International Convention on the Protection of all Migrant Workers and Members of Families;
- The Optional Protocol to the Convention on the Elimination of all Forms Discrimination against Women.

In addition, some regional human rights instruments have optional complaints procedures.

the treaty within and issue "views, Opinions or Decisions of a quasi-judicial nature".[359] Usually, they are open to signature, ratification, or accession by states parties, who are already party to the main treaty. However, states are not obliged to become a party to it.

Background of the Optional Protocol-CEDAW: The introduction of a complaints procedure was suggested at the World Conference on Human Rights in Vienna (1993), which called for examining a new procedure to strengthen the implantation of women's human rights through the formulation of an 'Optional Protocol to the CEDAW'. In this regard, the Commission on the Status of Women (CSW) established the open-ended working group to prepare the text to the OP-CEDAW from 1996-1999 with the participating states, non-governmental organizations and members of the CEDAW Committee. After that, the General Assembly adopted Optional Protocol articles to the CEDAW on 6 October 1999 at the fifty-fourth session by Resolution A/RES/54/4 a 21- and came into force in December 2000. States that are already CEDAW Convention states parties must independently ratify or accede to the agreement. As of 2015, there were 104 OP-CEDAW states parties.[360]

It is interesting to note that the distinctive feature of the OP-CEDAW is that non-reservation can be entered into the Protocol. At the time of the negotiations on the OP-CEDAW, states parties would be tempted to limit the Protocol's scope, especially in economic, social and cultural fields in which many states consider "to be non-justiciable".[361] Therefore, the OP-CEDAW explicitly affirms the prohibition of reservation (Article 17) to its terms; thereby, a woman or a group of women may submit a communication on the violation of any of the rights created in the CEDAW, when a state is ratifying or accessing the OP-CEDAW. It makes clear that OP-CEDAW has two strategies; on the one hand, it impossible for states parties to restrict the issue of the communications procedure to the substantive provisions of the CEDAW, a 'pick-and-chose' policy.[362] On the other hand, states parties to the OP-CEDAW may not accept the inquiry procedure at the time of ratification or accession, which is the so-called 'opting out' clause

359 Alfredsson, Grimheden, G.Ramcharan, International Human Rights Monitoring Mechanisms, 2009, p. 35

360 OP CEDAW > What is OP CEDAW? > OP CEDAW Overview : IWRAW Asia Pacific.

361 Alfredsson, Grim, heden, G. Ramcharan, International Human Rights Monitoring Mechanisms, 2009, p. 93

362 Ibid, p. 93

(Article 10).[363] However, from the moment the CEDAW Committee receives a communication or initiates an inquiry, it works within "a set of rigid Rules of Procedure".[364]

B.2.1 Communications Procedure

Articles 2 to 7 of the OP-CEDAW set out the communications procedure through which specific conditions that an individual complaint may be lodged and considered by the Committee. The communications procedure permits submitting claims to the Committee, an individual or group of individuals within a state's jurisdiction. A complaint can only refer a state party to the Convention and its Protocol; alleged violations must be related to "any of the rights set forth in the Convention" (Article 2).

Furthermore, the communication must show how an issue is personally affected by the law, policy, and practice, which must be linked to "State action or inaction or conduct of State officials in their public functions".[365] In this regard, to assist the Committee in considering they have established a Working Group or Rapporteur on Individual Communications under the OP-CEDAW.[366]

Communication can be divided into two stages of consideration: the first is based on the 'admissibility test', and the second consideration is on 'its merits'.[367]

---

363 Ibid, p. 94
Article 10(1): Each State Party may, at the time of signature or ratification of the present Protocol or accession thereto, declare that it does not recognize the competence of the Committee provided for in articles 8 and 9.
For example: Bangladesh has ratified the CEDAW Convention on 6 November 1984 with reservations and the Optional Protocol on 6 September 2000, accepting the individual communications procedure under the Op-CEDAW, but opting out of the inquiry procedure.
Declaration of Bangladesh to Op-CEDAW: "The Government of the People's Republic of Bangladesh declares in accordance with Article 10 (1) thereof, that it would not undertake the obligations arising out of Articles 8 and 9 of the said Optional Protocol."

364 OP CEDAW > What is OP CEDAW? > OP CEDAW Overview : IWRAW Asia Pacific.

365 Union und Nations, The Convention on the Elimination of All Forms of Discrimination Against Women and Its Optional Protocol, p, 86

366 Rules of Procedure - Annex I To the CEDAW Report A/56/38, accessed http://www.un.org/womenwatch/daw/cedaw/cedawreport-a5638-RulesOfProcedure.htm. Rules.62

367 Union und Nations, The Convention on the Elimination of All Forms of Discrimination Against Women and Its Optional Protocol, p. 88

At this point, the Committee makes its decision on the admissibility of a communication. There are several admissibility tests; for instance, "the exhaustion of domestic remedies" Article (4(1)) must be met.

Moreover, the communications must concern violations that have occurred before the entry of the OP-CEDAW (Article 4 (2-e)) into force. If the communication contains sufficient information relating to admissibility, the Committee will deliberate on its merits.[368] In other words, if any of these factors are not met, the communication will be declared inadmissible and may not be considered on its merits. In this regard, the Committee reports to the relevant State party its explanations or statements "to avoid irreparable damage to the victim or victims of the alleged violation" of the case (Article 5). In the case-law, for example, concerning a German woman, the Committee acknowledged the 'non-admissibility' of her communication.

Case law on the inadmissibility of the communication: Concerning a German woman; the communication concerned the adverse financial consequences of an unwanted divorce in 2002.[369] The author alleged that she was subjected to gender-based discrimination under the law's statutory regulations on the legal consequences of divorce. After the consideration of the State party's observations on admissibility and other processes, the Committee decided that

---

368 Rules of Procedure, A/56/38, Rules 56-71

369 B.J. was a 56-year-old German citizen, married since 1969. She agreed upon marriage to assume the role of 'homemaker', allowing her husband to further his career. She maintained this role for 30 years, bringing up three children, despite wishing to continue her education in the early 1980s. She was a nurse by profession. In May 1999 her husband applied for a divorce, which became final in July 2000. B.J. claimed before the Committee that the statutory regulations in Germany regarding the law on the legal consequences of divorce allowed for gender-based discrimination, in respect of equalization of accrued gains, equalization of pensions and maintenance-in particular, against older women who are divorced after long marriages and are left in situations of 'discrimination, disadvantage and humiliation" The author had sought judicial resolution of her claim at the domestic level and, whilst this was mostly unsuccessful, in April 2004, the Court of Göttingen did award B.J. monthly maintenance payments backdated to the last payment by her ex-husband. B.J. had also written, without success, to the Federal Ministry of Justice and the Ministry of Justice and Women's Issues, claiming a disregard for marriage and family, and gender-based discrimination by the courts.

See also: Sokhi-Bulley, Bal, The Optional Protocol to CEDAW: First Steps United Nations and Regional Human Rights Systems: Recent Developments, Human Rights Law Review 6 (2006): 143–59. p. 145-146

the communication was inadmissible for failure to exhaust domestic remedies, and the disputed facts occurred before the entry into force of the Optional Protocol for the State party and did not continue after that date.[370]

It is clear that to be admissible, a communication should concern CEDAW rights or based on discrimination against women, but since the Convention has not formulated a vital issue such as the violence against women, which is subject of General Recommendation No. 19, the Committee has taken up cases in this regard. It has made substantive contributions to women's human rights. *Karen Tayag Vertido v. The Philippines*, the author's allegations were based 'on gender-based myths and misconceptions about rape and rape victims'. The Committee acknowledged that the Convention's text does not expressly provide for a right to a remedy, but it considers that such a right implied in the Convention; however, it violates the provisions of the Convention. To this case, the Committee has made the recommendation that matters: "...... [I]nvolving crimes of rape and other sexual offenses [be] impartial and fair, and not affected by prejudices or stereotypical gender notions. To achieve this, a wide range of measures are needed, targeted at the legal system, to improve the judicial handling of rape cases, as well as training and education to change discriminatory attitudes towards women".[371] Other case law in this regard can point to *Alyne da Silva Pimentel Teixeira (deceased) v. Brazil*, in which a young woman ended up dead because of a failure to secure her safety during pregnancy and childbirth. The author argued that, according to the Convention, States parties to achieve equal rights "not only ... guarantee in law measures to struggle discrimination (*de jure*), but also to ensure in exercise through practical implementation of such measures and the realization of rights without delay *(de facto)*".[372] The Committee found the violence had been sufficiently substantiated for consideration under the concept "the violation of her right to life and health"; and recommended "women's right to safe and affordable obstetric care to reduce maternal deaths, establish a maternal mortality monitoring committee and provide necessary training to the medical profession on women's reproductive health rights".[373] After this recommendation, Brazil established "an inter-ministerial group to oversee the implementation of

---

370 Compare also Ibid, p. 150
and CEDAW, Communication No. 1/2003, Ms. B.-J. v. Germany. Decision adopted on 14 July 2004, thirty-first session. Excerpt from A/59/38.

371 CEDAW, Communication No. 18/2008, CEDAW/ C/46/D/18/2008, p. 17

372 CEDAW, Communication No. 17/2008, CEDAW/C/49/D/17/2008, p. 4

373 CEDAW, Communication No. 17/2008, CEDAW/C/49/D/17/2008, p. 21-22

the Committee's recommendation"; however, there remain concerns about its effectiveness.[374]

In general, case law concerning individual communications is growing under OP-CEDAW; as a result, the Committee is empowered to decide individual communications 'on crucial socio-economic rights'. In fact, the Committee performs a 'dual-purpose'. On the one hand, these decisions resolve the individual claims and facilitating improvement at the domestic level within law, policy, and administration. On the other hand, the Committee makes contributions to developing CEDAW, particularly the substantive decisions. This may enforce an accountability role in developing CEDAW and strengthening women's rights. But in many countries, the decisions may not have the jurisdiction to consider these claims because they are not legally binding. The implementation depends on the state's willingness to pursue the guidance of the Committee. Therefore, the state may decide the Committee's reasons are objectionable and reject its recommendations. It is because there is a difference between the state and the Committee in their respective understanding of women's human rights standards, which so far "can significantly undermine the potential of the OP-CEDAW".[375]

B.2.2 Inquiry Procedure

The inquiry procedure set out in Article 8-9 of the OP-CEDAW and modeled on Article 20 procedure under the UN Convention against Torture and Other Cruel, Inhuman or Degrading Treatment or Punishment. Under this procedure, the Committee is enabled "to initiate inquiry into reliable indications of grave or systematic violation by a State party of rights set forth in the Convention". However, Article 10 allows states parties on ratification or accession to 'opt-out' of the inquiry mechanism.[376] In other words, it may not recognize the competence of the CEDAW Committee to conduct an inquiry procedure into a grave or systematic violation of rights under the jurisdiction of the states party.[377] A 'grave' violation refers to severe abuse of women's human rights, which provides any discrimination against women linked to violations of their right to life, physical and mental integrity, and security. A

---

374 Campbell, Meghan, Women's Rights and the Convention on the Elimination of all Forms of Discrimination Against Women: Unlocking the Potential of the Optional Protocol", Nordic Journal of Human Rights 34, Nr. 4 (1. Oktober 2016): 247–71. p. 270

375 Ibid, p. 251 and 268-270

376 This mechanism applies to all states at the time of ratification by making a declaration under article 10; four states have opted out Bangladesh, Belize, Colombia and Cuba.

377 Rules of Procedure, rules 76-82.

'systematic' violation refers to the massive scale or prevalence of the violation or the existence of the direct intention of a State Party of a uniform character.[378]

The Committee's investigation may be instigated based on information reviewed from any source, including women's organizations, non-governmental organizations, or other groups that assist the Committee on alleged systematic or grave violations of women's human rights. The information submitted to initiate an inquiry must be forwarded by the secretariat to the Committee and maintained in a permanent register. The Committee examines the information and ascertains that it is "reliable information indicating grave or systematic violations"-Article 8. Moreover, the examination may set out a broad range of recommendations, any additional information, including from representatives of the state party, governmental organization, and any relevant UN documentation. Though an inquiry may conduct without the consent of the related state party, for an on-site evaluation of the state party, the Committee needs the state party's cooperation. After completing the inquiry's finding, the Committee transmits it to the state party with its comments and recommendations within six months. Moreover, under Article 18 of the Convention, the state party must provide further details of any measures taken in response to the Committee's requests.[379]

The case of the Philippines will point out regarding the inquiry procedure. The Committee received a joint submission from three non-governmental organizations requesting to conduct an inquiry issued by the former *Mayor of Manila* in 2008. She alleged systematic and grave violations of rights guaranteed under the Convention resulting from the implementation of an executive order which governed the provision of sexual and reproductive health rights, services, and commodities in *Manila*.[380] The Committee investigated the problem

---

378 Alfredsson, Grimheden, G. Ramcharan, International Human Rights Monitoring Mechanisms, 2009, p. 96

379 Rules of Procedure, rules 82-91.

380 Under the Local Government Code of 1991, provides that the local government units are to be responsible for the provision of basic services and facilities, including health services, family planning services and population development services. Local government units exercise power through their respective legislative bodies, such as the Manila City Council, which enacts legislation by ordinance, while a mayor has the power to issue executive orders. According to the information received by the non-governmental organizations, while the executive order did not expressly prohibit the use of modern contraceptives, its continued implementation in practice severely limited women's access to sexual and reproductive health services and effectively resulted in a ban on modern contraceptives in Manila.
CEDAW Committee, UN Doc. CEDAW/C/OP.8/PHL/1, 22 April 2015, para. 2

in-depth and met the designated members of the territory of the State party. After the inquiry, the Committee found that the state party is "responsible for ensuring compliance with the standards of the Convention by all its organs".[381] Therefore, the number of persons affected by the policies set out in the executive orders is significantly high, given that thousands of women of childbearing age continue to have inadequate access to sexual and reproductive health services in *Manila*.[382] In 2015, the Committee recommended that the government challenge the law and policy as soon as possible to ensure the immediate implementation of the Reproductive Health Act. So far, the local government units do not constitute barriers to the implementation of the new legal framework and to establish mechanisms at all levels of government.[383]

Thus, the Committee had at least three inquiries in mid-2017, the Philippines, Canada, and Mexico, which are still in their early days. One of the obstacles to lodging and deciding cases through the inquiry procedure is the 'opt-out' system created in OP-CEDAW. It is a separate procedure, not widened by accession to or ratification of the Protocol. Therefore, states parties can exclude the inquiry procedure.

B.2.3 Challenges of the OP-CEDAW in Practice

As mentioned above, OP-CEDAW is the first specific supervisory mechanism on gender at an international level. In itself, it does not establish new substantive rights; instead, it creates the complaints procedures for addressing the violation of women's rights as enshrined in the CEDAW. Most importantly, in the OP-CEDAW lies the capacity to be used as a means in the development of the Committee's jurisprudence, through holding governments accountable for identifying and removing existing discriminatory laws and practices.[384] However, women continue "to face specific challenges in seeking redress for their grievances under general human rights mechanisms". [385]

States are not obliged to become parties to it, especially many Islamic countries that still have not ratified the OP-CEDAW[386] because of it not permitting

381 Ibid, para. 21

382 Ibid, para. 47

383 Ibid, para. 51(b)

384 Alfredsson, Grimheden, G.Ramcharan, International Human Rights Monitoring Mechanisms, 2009, p. 92

385 OPTIONAL PROTOCOL TO WOMEN'S CONVENTION COMES INTO FORCE, accessed at: http://www.un.org/womenwatch/daw/cedaw/protocol/wom1242.htm.

386 As 2017, only Tunisia (2008) and Bangladesh (2001) are ratified the OP-CEDAW.

any reservation to it, though they have adhered to the CEDAW Convention already. So, they should be encouraged to do so. In doing so, they would need to widely circulate information on access to an international justice system concerning violations of women's human rights.[387] With awareness of the existence of these procedures, the women's activities or non-governmental organizations can play a dynamic role than the government branches.

Furthermore, following the decisions/recommendations by the Committee, states parties may accept and apply the consequences of any decisions or recommendations. That means there would be formal, non-binding enforcement, which would be dependent on the state's willingness to pursue them. This would appear to be a justification for establishing new policy measures in the legislative and budgetary areas. Therefore, in parallel with recommendations or decisions, the Committee can use other monitoring instruments, such as a state's reporting process, to reinforce and oversee as requested already. Hence, there are practical barriers to t implementing the decisions or recommendations by the Committee in states parties.

C. Reservations by Islamic Countries on the CEDAW for Religious Reasons

The first step in this analysis should be a brief overview pointing out the meaning of reservation and the implementation of reservations concerning international human rights treaties.

C.1 The legal Regime of Reservation

The reservation regime codified in the Vienna Convention on the Law of Treaties (VCLT), was adopted on 23 May 1969 and entered into force on 27 January 1980. The Vienna Convention covers the provisions and procedures for the creation, operation, and termination of a treaty, which is a matter for the negotiating states.[388] It also sets out the codification of the right to formulate reservations and enter them into treaties. Article 2 paragraph1 (d) of the Vienna Convention defines a reservation:

387 Alfredsson, Grimheden, G. Ramcharan, International Human Rights Monitoring Mechanisms, 2009, p. 97

388 Vienna Convention on the Law of Treaties (1969), accessed: http://opil.ouplaw.com/view/10.1093/law:epil/9780199231690/law-9780199231690-e1498.

> "Reservation means a unilateral statement, however, phrased or named, made by a State, when signing, ratifying, accepting approving or acceding to a treaty, whereby it purports to exclude or to modify the legal effect of certain provisions of the treaty in their application to that State";

Therefore, a reservation is a 'unilateral statement', which means it has not been agreed to by the negotiating states, although some states may make the same reservations upon ratification or accession.[389] After this, they have wanted to exclude or modify the legal effect of specific provisions in their obligations.

To make a reservation, Article 19 of the Vienna Convention covers the basic rule for formulating it:

A state may, when signing, ratifying, accepting, approving, or acceding to a treaty, formulate a reservation unless:

(a) The reservation is prohibited by the treaty;
(b) The treaty provides that only specified reservations, which do not include the reservation in question, may be made, or
(c) In cases not falling under sub-paragraphs (a) and (b), the reservation is incompatible with the object and purpose of the treaty.

Under subparagraph (a), a state cannot formulate a reservation if the treaty does not permit it. For example, the Rome Statute of the International Criminal Court of 1998[390], Article 21 of the European Convention for the Prevention of Torture and Inhuman or Degrading Treatment or Punishment of 1987,[391] and the UN Convention on the Law of the Sea of 1982,[392] provide that reservation is not permitted.

Another exception to formulating a reservation is subparagraph (b); it means a state party may exclude some specific subjects to the treaty, or relevance to one or more specified articles, or obligations of the treaty.[393]

---

389 Shqarri, Fjorda, Reservations to Treaties, Prohibited Reservations and some Unsolved Issued Related to Them, Mediterranean Journal of Social Sciences, 2015, p. 97

390 Article 120 of the Rome Statute of the International Criminal Court of 1998 provided that: "[n]o reservations may be made to this Statute"

391 That states "no reservation may be made in respect of the provisions of this Convention", European Convention for the Prevention of Torture and Inhuman or Degrading Treatment or Punishment, ETS, 126, entered into force 1 Feb. 1989.

392 Article 309 of the UN Convention on the Law of the Sea of 1982 stated that "[n]o reservations or exceptions may be made to this Convention unless expressly permitted by other articles of this Convention".

393 Aust, Anthony, Modern Treaty Law and Practice, Third Edition, (Cambridge University Press, 2013), p. 109-110

When a reservation is not prohibited under exceptions (a) or (b), a 'compatibility test' will be applied under exception (c). Subparagraph (c) affirms that reservations are not "incompatible with the object and purpose of the treaty," but none define the notion of "object and purpose" of the treaty. The Special Rapporteur *Mr. Enrique Candioti*, a member of the International Law Commission, noted that "... it was difficult to define objectively the grounds for the invalidity of reservations to treaties. A general definition according to which a reservation was incompatible with the object and purpose of a treaty is if it affected an essential element of the treaty".[394] The Commission was currently considering another group of guidelines concerning non-derogable norms and human rights treaties.[395]

In other words, the essential elements can be affected by the *raison d'être,*[396] which constitute the core obligations of the treaty. In fact, the *raison d'être* distinguishes between all obligations and core obligations in the treaty, that be preserved.[397] The object and purpose of the treaty can find by the examination in *good faith* of its text. In particular, to understand being in *good faith* can refer to resources of the treaty such as the title, the preparatory work, the circumstances of its conclusion, and the subsequent practice agreed upon by the states parties.

---

394 The ILC debated on the draft Article 19 in the Vienna Convention:
"The question of the admissibility of reservations could only be determined by reference to the terms of the treaty as a whole. As a rule it was possible to draw a distinction between the essential clauses of a treaty, which normally did not admit of reservations, and the less important clauses, for which reservations were possible".
Yearbook of the International Law Commission, Vol. I. 651st meeting. 25 May 1962. Law of treaties (A/CN.4/144 and Add.l), accessed at: http://legal.un.org/ilc/publications/yearbooks/english/ilc_1962_v1.pdf, para 35.
Also by reference to the commendatory on guideline 3.1.5, ILC Report (2007), A/62/10, can be understood the notion of "essential clauses": "A reservation is incompatible with the object and purpose of the treaty if it affects an essential element of the treaty that is necessary to its general thrust, in such a way that the reservation impairs the raison d'être of the treaty."

395 Meeting with Human Rights Bodies, International Law Commission, Fifty-Ninth Session, ILC(LIX)/RT/CRP.1, July 26, 2007. p. 16, para. 16.

396 *Raison d'être* means in Oxford dictionary: The most important reason or purpose for someone or something's existence

397 Corten, Olivier; Klein, Pierre, The Vienna Conventions on the Law of Treaties: A Commentary (Oxford University Press, 2011). p. 450-451

These are general guidelines to determine the compatibility or incompatibility of reservation.[398]

International human rights treaties have set up minimum standards for protecting human rights, which are universally accepted regardless of the independent domestic structure and national law of any state. Therefore, on the one hand, the 'object and purpose' criteria provide for "the necessary flexibility to take the special nature of human rights treaties into due account". On the other hand, the 'object and purpose' are essential elements for determining the admissibility of reservation.[399]

A reservation to human rights treaties can be viewed as cultural diversity, domestic law, or religious grounds, but some reservations have a more unlimited scope in this context. For example, the reservation by an Islamic country to human rights treaties grounded within the Sharia bounds. The following will show the consequence of acceptance or objection to reservation by other states' participation in human rights treaties.

Denmark has submitted a reservation to Article 20, paragraph 1 of the ICCPR, which affirms to prohibit any propaganda for war. From the Government of Denmark's perspective, freedom of expression is under the vote cast by Denmark against the prohibition against propaganda for war.[400] This reservation is acceptable because other contracting parties did not make any objection to it. On the other hand, some Islamic states have entered general reservations to CEDAW with reference to the Islamic laws or national law. Therefore, such reservations are unlimited and undefined, and other states parties raise objections that they are unacceptable. In this regard, the objecting state will soon be able to modify or withdraw the reservation or change general domestic law provisions.

For a better understating of the general reservation, see General Comment No. 24, wherein it was pointed out by the Human Rights Committee. It elaborated:

---

398 Text of the draft guidelines on reservations to treaties provisionally adopted so far by the Commission, A/62/10. 2007. guideline 3.1.6, accessed at: http://legal.un.org/docs/?path=../ilc/documentation/english/ilc_lix_rt_crp1.pdf&lang=EF.

399 Ziemele, Ineta; Reservations to human rights treaties and the Vienna convention regime: conflict, harmony or reconciliation, The Raoul Wallenberg Institute human rights library / Raoul Wallenberg Institutet för Mänskliga Rättigheter och Humanitär Rätt. - Leiden [u.a.] : Nijhoff, 1997- ; ZDB-ID: 2026501-3 17 (Leiden [u.a.]: Nijhoff, 2004). p. 191

400 United Nations, Treaty Collection, accessed at: https://treaties.un.org/Pages/ViewDetails.aspx?chapter=4&clang=_en&mtdsg_no=IV-4&src=IND#EndDec

"Reservations must be **specific and transparent**, so that the Committee, those under the jurisdiction of the reserving State and other States parties **may be clear as to what obligations of human rights compliance have or have not been undertaken**. Reservations may thus **not be general** but must refer to a particular provision of the Covenant and indicate in precise terms its scope in relation thereto. When considering the compatibility of possible reservations with the object and purpose of the Covenant, States should also take into consideration the overall effect of a group of reservations, as well as **the effect of each reservation on the integrity of the Covenant, which remains an essential consideration**. States should not enter so many reservations that they are, in effect accepting a limited number of human rights obligations and not the Covenant as such. So that reservations do not lead to a perpetual non-attainment of international human rights standards, reservations should not systematically reduce the obligations undertaken only to the presently existing in less demanding standards of domestic law."[401]

Despite the absence of a legal procedure in the Vienna regime for the validity of a reservation, the question still arises whether it is competent to determine if a reservation is compatible or incompatible. Nonetheless, the international human rights treaties provide different instruments for monitoring the respective treaties that are accepted by states parties. Moreover, the human rights treaty bodies have begun to determine the permissibility of reservation to accordingly its conditions of the treaty. For example, General Comment No. 24 (Human Rights Committee, 1994) pointed out that the Committee can determine whether a reservation is "compatible with the object and purpose" of the Covenant.[402] On the other hand, other treaty bodies have not followed this mechanism for determining a reservation, such as the European Court of Human Rights (ECHR) consider the validity of a reservation after the examination of individual communications. Still, the practice has been limited because few bodies had received such communications. As a result, with respect to the diversity of human rights bodies, it was not possible to adopt a general method for determining a reservation's validity within the 'object and purpose' of the treaty.[403]

However, the human rights bodies have established a practice of persuasion through 'reservation dialogue' with states. In this regard, the Committees

401 CCPR, General Comment No. 24: Issues Relating to Reservations Made upon Ratification or Accession to the Covenant or the Optional Protocols thereto, or in Relation to Declarations under Article 41 of the Covenant, CCPR/C/21/Rev.1/Add.6 1994, para. 19

402 Ibid, para.16

403 International Law Commission, The discussion during of Meeting with Human Rights Bodies, International Law Commission, Fifty-ninth session, ILC(LIX)/RT/CRP.1, 26. Juli 2007, para. 9 and 15

encouraged opening up a discussion with states about the scope of reservation and their justification. *Mr. Alexandre Sicilianos* member of the Committee on the Elimination of Racial Discrimination stressed that the importance of dialogue with states depends on studying domestic law during the consideration of the report. He recommended that "it was essential to deal with political considerations as well as with practical problems...."[404] In other words, the issue of 'reservation dialogue', which is "extremely useful for understanding the political considerations underlying reservations and that the pragmatism and discretion exercised by the human rights bodies had already met with success".[405]

C.2 Objections to Reservations

A point which is generally noticed is that when a reservation has passed under Article 19 of the Vienna Convention, other contracting states have a choice between acceptance of and 'objection' to it,[406] an objection to a reservation is not an acceptance. An 'objection' to a reservation defines as:

> "a unilateral statement, however, phrased or named, made by a State or an international organization in response to a reservation formulated by another State or international

404 Ibid. para. 19

405 Ibid. para. 35

406 Article 20 paragraph (4) and (5) of the Vienna Convention state the acceptance/ or objection to reservation.
Article 20(4): In cases not falling under the preceding paragraphs and unless the treaty otherwise provides:
(a) acceptance by another contracting State of a reservation constitutes the reserving State a party to the treaty in relation to that other State if or when the treaty is in force for those States; (b) an objection by another contracting State to a reservation does not preclude the entry into force of the treaty as between the objecting and reserving States unless a contrary intention is definitely expressed by the objecting State; (c) an act expressing a State's consent to be bound by the treaty and containing a reservation is effective as soon as at least one other contracting State has accepted the reservation. And paragraph 5 of Article 20: For the purposes of paragraphs 2 and 4 and unless the treaty otherwise provides, a reservation is considered to have been accepted by a State if it shall have raised no objection to the reservation by the end of a period of twelve months after it was notified of the reservation or by the date on which it expressed its consent to be bound by the treaty, whichever is later.

organization, whereby the former State or organization purports to preclude the reservation from having its intended effects or otherwise opposes the reservation".[407]

In fact, states parties, through a reservation, preserve the integrity of human rights established to pursue their interests, and formulating an objection to such reservations may endanger this integrity.[408]

Most objections concern reservations that are incompatible with the object and propose the treaty and made on the compatibility test grounds. Objecting states should show that a reservation sets a negative precedent, and it is not acceptable. However, they should state the reasons why the objection is being made, and in doing so, call on the reserving states as soon as possible to change their domestic law (s) to withdraw or modify the reservations.[409] Thus, objections play an essential role in the evaluation of the admissibility or inadmissibility of a reservation.[410]

C.3 Reservations to Specific Obligations by Islamic Countries

CEDAW had "the highest number of reservations of all in international human rights treaties".[411] Article 28 of the CEDAW provides for formalizing a reservation at the time of ratification of, or accession to, the Convention, affirming that the reservations are not incompatible with the object and purpose of the present Convention (Article 28, paragraph 2). Some states parties have attached reservations to particular articles based on cultural reasons, religious beliefs, traditions, or national law. States parties justify their reservations for violating substantive gender equal rights on this basis. In general, there is a conflict between

407 United Nations, Guide to Practice on Reservations to Treaties, adopted by the International Law Commission sixty-third session (A/66/10), Yearbook of the International Law Commission, 2011, vol. II, Part Two, p. 11
Official document of the United Nations accessed at: http://legal.un.org/docs/?path=../ilc/texts/instruments/english/draft_articles/1_8_2011.pdf&lang=EF.

408 Ziemele, Reservations to Human Rights Treaties and the Vienna Convention Regime, p. 194

409 Report of the International Law Commission, Sixty-third session, A/66/10/Add.1, 2011, p. 27

410 Ziemele, Reservations to Human Rights Treaties and the Vienna Convention Regime. p. 194

411 CEDAW, Report of the Committee on the Elimination of Discrimination Against Women, 11th Session, A/47/38, 1992, para. 460

the constitution of states and its reservations to the Convention because of the prohibition of discrimination established in their constitution law.[412]

For instance, the Constitution of Algeria (1996) recognizes the right to equal treatment and equal rights before the law on the basis of gender. Article 29 states "all citizens are equal before the law. No discrimination shall prevail because of birth, race, sex, opinion, or any other personal or social condition or circumstance". Moreover, Article 31 acknowledges "the aim of the institutions is to ensure equality of rights and duties of all citizens, men, and women, by removing the obstacles which hinder the progress of human beings and impede the effective participation of all in the political, economic, social and cultural life".

Also, Qatar's Constitution 2003 stresses non-discrimination in relation to the general right on the basis of sex. Article 34 reads, "The Citizens of Qatar shall be equal in public rights and duties. Article 35 states "All persons are equal before the law and there shall be no discrimination whatsoever on grounds of sex, race, language, or religion". As a result, several states recognize the general terms of gender equality and non-discrimination in their national constitution, which does not formulate any detailed content.

Since some members of the CEDAW are from Muslim countries, these states have entered reservations to the CEDAW based on religious reasons. The formulation of such reservations is 'incompatible with the object and purpose', thus, violating the fundamental issues of the CEDAW such as equality in private and public life, policy measures, and legal capacity to eliminate discrimination against women. As a result, the reservations may challenge to preserve the core provisions of the Convention. On the other hand, impermissible reservations can affect the relationship between reserved states and other states parties. So, the objecting state requests to review and modify or withdraw the reservations through a declaration or notification as soon as possible.

It is interesting to note that, as discussed above, OP- CEDAW does not permit the reservation of any articles. Therefore more Islamic countries have not yet ratification this Protocol. As a result, communications by individual women or groups of individual women of such countries cannot be lodged.

This section involves two parts. The first part addresses the Articles' content and the reservations to them by Islamic countries for religious reasons. The second part is the reaction of other states to that reservations.

---

412 CEDAW, Report of the Committee on the Elimination of Discrimination Against Women, 19th session, A/53/38, 1998, para. 3

C.3.1 Articles Affected Based on Religious Reasons

The substantive reservations based on religion refer to articles 2, 9, 15 and 16, which are key provisions of the CEDAW and target women's fundamental human rights. The content of such reservations is in Article 2, related to general measures on the elimination of discrimination against women; Article 9, respect to nationality law; Article 15, freedom to choose one's residence and domicile; and, Article 16, equality in marriage and family relations.

In 1994, the Committee on the CEDAW considered Articles 2 and 16 "to be core provisions of the Convention". The Committee viewed Article 2 to be "central to the objects and purpose of the Convention", and the reservation to the whole or part to Articles 2 and 16 are of particular concern; thus, they will be subject to modification or withdrawal.[413] A state party would indicate the removal or modification of reservations, especially under Articles 2 and 16, seeking to eliminate all obstacles against women's fundamental rights in their private and public life. Thus, a state would be obligated to comply with the essential provisions of the Convention and apply them in its domestic law, if impermissible reservations were removed.[414]

C.3.1.1 Article 2

a) Content of Article 2

Article 2 is a core provision of the Convention[415] that emphasizes eliminating existing discriminatory laws, regulations, and customs. Furthermore, this Article

---

413 CEDAW, Report of the Committee on the Elimination of Discrimination against Women, 13th Session, A/49/38, 1994, para. 41-47
accessed at: http://www.un.org/documents/ga/docs/49/plenary/a49-38.htm.

414 Reservations to CEDAW, accessed at: http://www.un.org/womenwatch/daw/cedaw/reservations.htm.

415 Article 2: States Parties condemn discrimination against women in all its forms, agree to pursue by all appropriate means and without delay a policy of eliminating discrimination against women and, to this end, undertake:

(a) To embody the principle of the equality of men and women in their national constitutions or other appropriate legislation if not yet incorporated therein and to ensure, through law and other appropriate means, the practical realization of this principle;

(b) To adopt appropriate legislative and other measures, including sanctions where appropriate, prohibiting all discrimination against women

imposes accountability on the state party to take the policy and other 'appropriate measures' to prevent discrimination at the national and international levels. In General Recommendation No. 28, the Committee has drawn the three significant obligations for states parties under Article 2:

- Formally condemn discrimination against women in all its form;
- Agree to pursue by all appropriate means and without delay a policy of eliminating discrimination against women;
- Utilize all appropriate measures.[416]

The first part of the chapeau of Article 2 is the obligation "to condemn discrimination against women in all its forms". In this context, states parties "have an immediate and continuous obligation to condemn discrimination". The reference to "discrimination in all its forms" clearly states that states parties are "to be vigilant in condemning all forms of discrimination, including forms that are not explicitly mentioned in the Convention or that may be emerging".[417]

The second part of the chapeau requires states parties to adopt a policy to eliminate "all forms of discrimination" against women and develop a strategy for implementing such a policy. The policy should cover legal and non-legal measures in all branches and levels of government within the Convention's scope. Accordingly, the state must create a policy "without delay", and it cannot justify any delay "on any grounds, including political, social, cultural, religious, economic, resources, or other considerations or constraints within the State".[418] The

---

(c) To establish legal protection of the rights of women on an equal basis with men and to ensure through competent national tribunals and other public institutions the effective protection of women against any act of discrimination;
(d) To refrain from engaging in any act or practice of discrimination against women and to ensure that public authorities and institutions shall act in conformity with this obligation;
(e) To take all appropriate measures to eliminate discrimination against women by any person, organization or enterprise;
(f) To take all appropriate measures, including legislation, to modify or abolish existing laws, regulations, customs and practices which constitute discrimination against women;
(g) To repeal all national penal provisions which constitute discrimination against women.

416 Freeman, Rudolf, Chinkin, The UN Convention on the Elimination of All Forms of Discrimination Against Women, p. 75

417 Ibid, p. 75

418 CEDAW, General Recommendation No. 28, para. 29

obligation to "pursue" is access to "participate actively in the development, implementation, and monitoring of the policy".[419]

A point to be emphasized is the phrase in Article 2, "all appropriate measures" as the third part of Article 2. The state party is allowed to select flexibility and design regarding the most effective measures through legislative means and other types of measures. Also, "appropriate measures" includes temporary measures to fulfill the practical realization of equality.[420] General Recommendation No. 25 establishes the measures under Article 2 and other provisions of the Convention. Therefore, states parties should "report on the legal or other basis for such measures, and their justification for choosing a particular approach. States parties are further invited to give details about any legislation concerning temporary special measures, and in particular, whether such legislation provides for the mandatory or voluntary nature of temporary special measures".[421]

In general, Article 2 stresses the establishment of fundamental provisions of the Convention domestically, and attempts to modify or remove discrimination in all fields of 'customs and practices'. CEDAW-Committee acknowledged that when states parties "ratify the Convention do so because they agree that discrimination against women in all its forms should be condemned and that the strategies set out in Article 2(a) to (g), should be implemented by States parties to eliminate it".[422]

b) Reservation

As noted above, Article 2 is "central to object and purpose of the Convention", in which states parties shall review their obligations under Article 2 to implement CEDAW's provisions. Thus, reservations to Article 2 or subparagraphs of Article 2 may be incompatible with the object and purpose following paragraph 2 of

---

419 CEDAW, General Recommendation No. 28, para. 27

420 Freeman, Rudolf, Chinkin, The UN Convention on the Elimination of All Forms of Discrimination Against Women, p. 77
Brief obligations of States parties created by Article 2:
"to condemn discrimination against women;
to embody the principle of equality of men and women in their national constitutions, or other legislation;
to adopt legislative measures, including sections, to prohibit discrimination against women;

421 CEDAW, General Recommendation No. 25, para. 30

422 CEDAW, Report of the Committee on the Elimination of Discrimination Against Women, 19th session, A/53/38, 1998, para. 16

Article 28. As a result, reservations to Article 2 can be particularly problematic, regardless of the reasons for them, because Article 2 is "the very essence of the obligations of States parties under the Convention".[423]

The reservations to Article 2 have referred to inconsistencies between the obligations of the Convention and the requirements of customary law, religious or traditional practices. Therefore, reserving states intend to preserve existing national law, since most cases are brought without determining what those inconsistencies might be. In General Recommendation No. 28, the Committee reiterated that reserving states to Article 2 or subparagraphs of Article 2 should make clear the practical effect of reservations to the implementation of the Convention and should indicate a view to withdrawing or removing them as soon as possible.[424]

Twenty-two states have entered reservations to all or part of Article 2, and eleven Islamic countries are among them. It will show Islamic countries' reservation to Article 2 linked in general to Sharia; some of such reservations.

Bangladesh made the following reservation concerning Article 2:

> "Bangladesh does not consider as binding upon itself the provisions of article 2, as they conflict with *Sharia* law based on the Holy Quran and Sunna".[425]

Egypt has entered a general reservation on Article 2 and clearly states that:

> "...[t]o comply with the content of this article, provided that such compliance does not run counter to the Islamic *Sharia*".[426]

---

423 CEDAW, General Recommendation No. 28, para. 41

424 CEDAW, General Recommendations No. 28, para. 41-42
In the Paragraph 42 of General Recommendation 28, the Committee has acknowledged that: "The fact that a State party has entered a reservation to article 2 or to subparagraphs of article 2 does not remove the need for that State party to comply with its other obligations under international law, including its obligations under other human rights treaties that the State party has ratified or acceded to and under customary international human rights law relating to the elimination of discrimination against women. Where there is a discrepancy between reservations to provisions of the Convention and similar obligations under other international human rights treaties ratified or acceded to by a State party, it should review its reservations to the Convention with a view to withdrawing them."

425 United Nations Treaty Collection, accessed at: https://treaties.un.org/Pages/ViewDetails.aspx?src=IND&mtdsg_no=IV-8&chapter=4&lang=en#EndDec

426 CEDAW, Declarations, reservations, objections and notifications of withdrawal of reservations relating to the CEDAW, Sixteenth meeting, CEDAW/SP/2010/2, 2010, p. 10

Morocco reads the following reservation to Article 2:

> "They do not conflict with the provisions of the Islamic Sharia. It should be noted that certain of the provisions contained in the Moroccan Code of Personal Status according to women rights that differ from the rights conferred on men may not be infringed upon or abrogated because they derive primarily from the Islamic Sharia, which strives, among its other objectives, to strike a balance between the spouses in order to preserve the coherence of family life".[427]

Malaysia has entered a general reservation and referring to Sharia provision and the Federal Constitution:

> "[t]he provisions of the Convention do not conflict with the provisions of the Islamic Sharia law and the Federal Constitution of Malaysia. With regards thereto, further, the Government of Malaysia does not consider itself bound by the provisions of articles 2 (f) of the aforesaid Convention".[428]

In general, the reservations to any article of the CEDAW should be described, and their continued maintenance justified by the reserving state. Also, general reservations, especially to Article 2, should explain the interpretation of reservations and their effect on the integrity with regards to other human rights treaties.[429]

As mentioned above, these types of reservations to Article 2 lack any motive or reasons for formulating them, thus they encompass a more unlimited character.[430] For example, Egypt's reservation to Article 2 is linked to Sharia without

---

427 Ibid, p. 19

428 CEDAW, Sixteenth meeting, CEDAW/SP/2010/2, 2010, p. 16
Other reservations by Islamic Countries to Article 2: Iraq: "Approval of and accession to this Convention shall not mean that the Republic of Iraq is bound by the provisions of article 2........ [t]he reservation to this last-mentioned article shall be without prejudice to the provisions of the Islamic Shariah according women rights equivalent to the rights of their spouses so as to ensure a just balance between them.
Libyan Arab Jamahiriya: "Article 2 of the Convention shall be implemented with due regard for the peremptory norms of the Islamic Shariah relating to determination of the inheritance portions of the estate of a deceased person, whether female or male."
Syrian Arab Republic: "..... subject to reservations to article 2...... [T]his provision is incompatible with the provisions of the Islamic Shariah."

429 UN. Committee on the Elimination of Discrimination against Women, Compilation of Guidelines on the Form and Content of Reports to Be Submitted by States Parties to the International Human Rights Treaties, HRI/GEN/2/Rev.1/Add.2, para. C.2

430 Yahyaoui Krivenko, Ekaterina, Women, Islam and International Law: Within the Context of the Convention on the Elimination of All Forms of Discrimination Against Women (BRILL, 2009). p. 124

any explanation for its justification to preserve inequality, and also a refusal to examine reinterpretation.[431] Another type of reservation to article 2 is concerning the Family Code by Sharia in the case of Morocco.[432] It seems that reservations to Article 2, which "challenge the central principle of the Convention are contrary to the provisions of the Convention and general international law".[433] Paragraph 2 of Article 28 (CEDAW) states the generally worded reservation is incompatible with the object and purpose of the convention because it negatively affects an essential element of the Convention. Furthermore, being subject to the Sharia provisions raises doubts as to the degree of commitment of reserving state to implement Convention. Such reservations should determine the extent of Sharia; otherwise, based on international law, they bear unlimited scope, and their reservations should be removed, modified, or withdrawn.

c) Objection to Reservation

As a next step, objections to the CEDAW will be considered to reservations based on religious reasons that have been entered by Islamic countries that have such reservations. As already cited above, they are incompatible with the object and purpose of the Convention.[434] The following are some reactions of states objections regarding reservations to Article 2.

Denmark stated in its objection to Saudi Arabia's reservation to Article 2, in 2001:

> "The general reservation with reference to the provisions of Islamic law are of *unlimited scope and undefined character*. Consequently, the said reservations as being incompatible with the object and purpose of the Convention...and recommends to reconsider its reservations to the CEDAW".[435]

---

431 Freeman, Marsha A., RESERVATIONS TO CEDAW: AN ANALYSIS FOR UNICEF, United Nations Children's Fund (UNICEF), Gender, Rights and Civic Engagement Section, Division of Policy and Practice, New York, 2009, p. 14

432 For example Algeria's reservation to Article 2: "The Government of the People's Democratic Republic of Algeria declares that it is prepared to apply the provisions of this article on condition that they do not conflict with the provisions of the Algerian Family Code."

433 Ziemele, Reservations to Human Rights Treaties and the Vienna Convention Regime. p. 25

434 Compare also Ziemele, p. 25
These reservations subjecting the application of human rights treaties to domestic law are contrary to the object and purpose of human rights treaties.

435 United Nations Treaty Collection, accessed at: https://treaties.un.org/Pages/ViewDetails.aspx?src=IND&mtdsg_no=IV-8&chapter=4&lang=en#EndDec

France emphasized in its objections to the general nature of Bahrain's reservation that:

> "by making the implementation of articles 2 and 16 of the Convention subject to respect for the Islamic Sharia..... [a] *general and indeterminate scope* that it is not possible to ascertain which changes to obligations under the Convention they are intended to introduce".[436]

Germany's objection to the reservation of the United Arab Emirates expressed that:

> "to Article 2 (f)........., which give a specific legal system, the Islamic Sharia, precedence as a rule over the provisions of the Convention, it is *unclear to what extent the UAE feels bound by the obligations of the Convention*.... reservations that are incompatible with the object and purpose of the present Convention shall not be permitted".[437]

Thus, an objection is a statement that is made by one state to express their views on particular reservations entered by another state. The reasons for states objecting to the reservations to Article 2 under the general character of Islamic law provisions have broken the obligations under Article 2. Therefore are reported as being incompatible with the object and purpose of the Convention. In this regard, objecting states recommend identifying the extent of such reservations on relevant issues, hence opening an opportunity for dialogue toward the possibility of modifying its reservation.

C.3.1.2 Article 9

Article 9 of CEDAW provides granting gender quality in nationality laws, but before considering Article 9, should point out a brief overview of nationality and the consequences of the application of equal rights in nationality.

a) The General Principle of Nationality

The subject of international law is traditionally concerned with states and thus does not bear on individuals as international law subjects. However, nationality creates a link between individuals and state, and thereby, a state risks its interference with the violation of another state's sovereignty. Therefore, nationality plays a crucial role in international law because of a state yielding its jurisdiction and its national protection over other states. For example, today, significant numbers of people live outside their states of nationalities as refugees, workers, students,

436 Ibid
437 Ibid

and for family reasons and others. As a result, they need to be granted their rights within a state. Therefore, nationality has assumed even greater importance in relation to other states. One of the other functions of nationality in international law is "the duty of state to admit its nationals and allow them to reside within its territory". Subsequently, each state can determine under international legal obligations "who its nationals are" within their domestic law.[438]

There are two principles to granting access to nationality at birth *jus sanguinis* and *jus soli*. Accordingly, *jus sanguinis* is to acquire a nationality is determined by descent from a nation that usually one or both parents who have the nationality of a state. Historically, this principle may go through the father's line to acquire an individual's nationality, which in some countries is still preserved in its national law.[439] *Jus sanguinis* is "the preferred method of the conferral of nationality". Other individuals' nationality may work through *jus soli* by birthplace, which refers to being born in a state's territory, regardless of the parents' nationalities. This method is recognized in the law of many states because it performs "as a safeguard against statelessness".[440] However, the majority of states have adopted a combination of these principles, too.

Besides, nationality can be acquired by *naturalization* through marriage to a foreign national or a period of continuous residence or other conditions under domestic law.[441] In this regard, the Inter-American Court of Human Rights states that: "nationality no longer depends on the fortuity of birth in a given territory or on parents having that nationality; it is based rather on a voluntary act aimed at establishing a relationship with a given political society, its culture, its way of life and its values".[442] Therefore, a nationality acquired by naturalization is often

438 International Law Association, Committee on Feminism and International law, Final Report on Women's Equality and Nationality in International Law, in Report of the Sixty-Ninth Conference, London Conference, 2000, p. 10-11
Moreover, in this context International Court of Justice (ICJ) in the case of Nottebohm (Liechtenstein v. Guatemala, 1995) noted that: "the character thus recognized on the international level as pertaining to nationality is in no way inconsistent with the fact that international law leaves it to each State to lay down the rules governing the grant of its own nationality."

439 For example, in Iranian Civil Code in subparagraph (2) of Article 976 states:" Those born in Iran or outside whose fathers are Iranian."

440 Human Rights Council, Report of the Secretary-General, Human rights and arbitrary deprivation of nationality, Twenty-fifth session A/HRC/25/28, 2013, para. 28

441 UNHCR-OHCHR, Meeting Report, Regional Expert Meeting on the Human Rights of Stateless Persons in the Middle East and North Africa, 2010, p. 30

442 Final Report on Women's Equality and Nationality in International Law, p. 15

less safe because a state entity controls which will be eligible to be national. Many factors, such as the absence of appearance, ordinary crime, and fraud often recognized as grounds for the loss or deprivation of nationality conferred by naturalization.[443] Thus, nationality may be acquired, changed, retained, or prohibited due to nationality's arbitrary deprivation.

Today, in an increasingly globalized world with economically-motivated migration, persons who find themselves without a nationality are in an extremely vulnerable situation.[444] In other words, nationality use as a means for individuals "to become full members of the societies in which they find themselves or to obtain assistance in returning to the societies they voluntarily or involuntarily left".[445] Hence, nationality is a right that impacts the achievement of other fundamental human rights.

b) Gender Equality in Nationality Laws

The right to nationality is a fundamental human right for every man, woman, and child, which affirms in a series of human rights instruments.[446] Gender equality in nationality is "an essential dimension of ensuring women's human rights and crucial to preventing statelessness".[447]The Resolution of Human Rights Council (A/HRC/RES/20/4) prohibits any elimination and discrimination in nationality laws based on "race, colour, sex, language, religion, political or other opinion, national or social origin, property, birth, disability or other status".[448]

Gender discrimination in nationality results in significant human rights violations. Hence, one of the equality basics is eliminating the principle of dependent nationality because nationality is preliminary to achieve other rights. More importantly, women can able to participate with an independent nationality in their public and social lives, such as enjoying the rights to pass, work,

443 Human Rights Council, A/HRC/25/28, para. 6

444 Human Rights Council, Report on discrimination against women on nationality related matters, including the impact on children, Report of the Office of the United Nations High Commissioner for Human Rights, Twenty-third session, A/HRC/23/23, 2013, para. 3

445 Final Report on Women's Equality and Nationality in International Law, p. 4

446 Human Rights Council, Resolution A/HRC/RES/20/4, Promotion and protection of all human rights, civil, political, economic, social and cultural rights, including the right to development The right to a nationality: women and children, Twentieth session, 2012, para. 1

447 Human Rights Council, A/HRC/23/23, para. 72

448 Human Rights Council, Resolution A/HRC/RES/20/4, p. 1

and travel; to access resources, property, healthcare, and social services; and, to access education. Through social and economic independence, women's empowerment enables them to end violent and abusive relationships of marriage or partnerships, thus preventing human trafficking and child marriage. Furthermore, non-discrimination based on gender as one of the leading causes of statelessness in nationality laws can avoid or reduce statelessness.[449] The link between women's empowerment and nationality has been established in General Recommendation No. 21, which states that: "Nationality is critical to full participation in society. Nationality can also be acquired because of settlement or granted for humanitarian reasons such as statelessness and without status as nationals or citizens, women are deprived of the right to vote or to stand for public office and may be denied access to public benefits and a choice of residence. .... "[450]

Initially, the development of women's nationality rights in international law started in the 1930s at The Hague Codification Conference. A campaign followed the League of Nations' issue for a separate treaty based on gender equality in nationality law. After that, the Inter-American Commission adopted a mandate at the Montevideo Convention on Women's Nationality in 1933 to earn equality in civil and political spheres. The primary sources in international law are recognized in articles 2, 7, and 15 of the UDHR,[451] which stresses the right to nationality and the principles of non-discrimination as a starting step of human rights treaties. The progress of women's nationality law was the Convention on the Nationality of Married Women in 1957, the first nationality convention, which affirms a married woman's independent nationality. Article 1 states "neither the celebration nor the dissolution of a marriage between one of its nationals and an

449 Human Rights Council, A/HRC/23/23, para. 7

450 CEDAW, General Recommendation No. 21, para. 6

451 Article 2 of the UDHR stated: "Everyone is entitled to all the rights and freedoms set forth in this Declaration, without distinction of any kind, such as race, colour, sex, language, religion, political or other opinion, national or social origin, property, birth or other status. Furthermore, no distinction shall be made on the basis of the political, jurisdictional or international status of the country or territory to which a person belongs, whether it be independent, trust, non-self-governing or under any other limitation of sovereignty".

Article 7: All are equal before the law and are entitled without any discrimination to equal protection of the law. All are entitled to equal protection against any discrimination in violation of this Declaration and against any incitement to such discrimination and Article 15: to which everyone has the right to a nationality and no one shall be arbitrarily deprived of his or her nationality.

alien, nor the change of nationality by the husband during marriage, shall automatically affect the nationality of the wife". Besides, CEDAW focused on women's nationality and covered the evolving standards of women's nationality in international law. It relates to Article 9 discrimination-based gender to nationality, thus seeking to eliminate discrimination for family members. Concerning family relations, Article 9 also reinforces Article 5 and 16 of CEDAW in private law, which require the "elimination of stereotypical attitude based on male superiority, and providing for equal roles and responsibilities in the family".[452] Hence, Article 9 is the main source in relating nationality based on gender in international law.[453]

c) Content of Article 9

Article 9 grants women's equality in nationality law and their children's nationality. Both paragraphs of Article 9 stress achieving equal nationality rights through imposing obligations on state parties to remove any discriminatory laws against women in the area of nationality, and confer nationality on their children.

Article 9 (1) recognizes that women have equal rights as men to 'acquire, change or retain their nationality'. In this context, General Recommendation No. 21 acknowledges that "nationality should be capable of change by an adult woman";[454] that is a right for adult women in independent choices to acquiring, changing or retaining their nationality.[455] Moreover, Article 9 (1) requires states parties to protect women from statelessness or forcing their husbands' nationality on them during the marriage. It also reaffirms Article 1 of the Convention on the Nationality of Married Women, which emphasizing married women's

---

452 Freeman, Rudolf, Chinkin, The UN Convention on the Elimination of All Forms of Discrimination Against Women, p. 237

453 Article 9 of the CEDAW states:

1) States Parties shall grant women equal rights with men to acquire, change or retain their nationality. They shall ensure in particular that neither marriage to an alien nor change of nationality by the husband during marriage shall automatically change the nationality of the wife, render her stateless or force upon her the nationality of the husband.
2) States Parties shall grant women equal rights with men with respect to the nationality of their children.

454 CEDAW, General Recommendation No. 21, para. 6

455 Freeman, Rudolf, Chinkin, The UN Convention on the Elimination of All Forms of Discrimination Against Women, p. 242

independent nationality.[456] For example, it may be possible that a woman loses her nationality upon marriage with a foreigner and thus becomes stateless if she cannot acquire the nationality of her husband or if her husband changes his nationality, or if there is any dissolution of the marriage.[457] Moreover, General Recommendation No. 21 stresses the preventing of women's statelessness during a marriage that "should not be arbitrarily removed because of marriage or dissolution of marriage or because her husband or father changes his nationality".[458]

Article 9 (2) focuses on gender equality "with respect to the nationality of children",[459] which was the first universal human rights treaty to recognize transmitting nationality to the children.[460] Since then, a significant number of states

456 Article 1 of the Convention on the Nationality of Married Women: "Each Contracting State agrees that neither the celebration nor the dissolution of a marriage between one of its nationals and an alien, nor the change of nationality by the husband during marriage, shall automatically affect the nationality of the wife".

457 CEDAW, General Recommendations No. 32: on the gender-related dimensions of refugee status, asylum, nationality and statelessness of women CEDAW/C/GC/32 2014. para. 60

458 CEDAW, General Recommendation No. 21, para. 6

459 Some international human rights instruments have provided child's right to acquire a nationality.

- Article 24 (3) of the International Covenant on Civil and Political Rights: every child has the right to acquire a nationality.
- Article 7(1) of the Convention on the Rights of the Child: The child shall be registered immediately after birth and shall have the right from birth to a name, the right to acquire a nationality and. as far as possible, the right to know and be cared for by his or her parents.

460 States that discriminate against mothers in their ability to confer nationality on their children: The Bahamas, Bahrain, Barbados, Brunei, Burundi, Iran, Iraq, Jordan, Kiribati, Kuwait, Lebanon, Liberia, Libya, Madagascar, Malaysia, Mauritania, Nepal, Oman, Qatar, Saudi Arabia, Sierra Leone, Somalia, Sudan, Swaziland, Syria, Togo, United Arab Emirates

- States that discriminate against unmarried fathers in their ability to confer nationality on their children: The Bahamas, Barbados, Madagascar, Malaysia, the United States
- States that discriminate in a women's ability to confer nationality to spouses and/or acquire, change and retain her nationality: Bahamas, Bahrain, Bangladesh, Barbados, Benin, Brunei, Burundi, Cameroon, Central African Republic, Comoros, Congo (Republic of), Egypt, Guatemala, Guinea, Iran, Iraq, Jordan, Kiribati, Kuwait, Lebanon, Lesotho, Libya, Madagascar, Malawi, Malaysia, Mauritania, Mauritius, Monaco, Morocco, Nauru, Nepal, Nigeria, Oman, Pakistan, Philippines, Qatar, Saint Lucia, Saint Vincent & Grenadines, Saudi Arabia, Sierra Leone, Singapore, Solomon

upon ratification or accession to CEDAW have entered reservations to all or part of Article 9.

d) eservation

Sixteen Islamic countries have made reservations to Article 9, particularly to 9 (2), which seems to be a problematic provision for Muslim states to the application of Islamic principles.[461] Reservations entered into Article 9 can be separated into three groups.

The first group of reservations, which are contradictory to the Islamic constitution, are linked generally with Sharia. The following countries' reservations are from this group.

Oman attached reservation to Article 9 (2) that indicates concerns with a specific area of personal status based on Islamic in Oman's domestic law:

> "All provisions of the Convention not in accordance with the provisions of the Islamic Sharia and legislation in force in the Sultanate of Oman; that Article 9, paragraph 2, is included".[462]

Saudi Arabia has made a general reservation based on Sharia that states as far as not consider bound by Article 9 (2):

> "In case of contradiction between any term of the Convention and the norms of Islamic law and does not consider itself bound by paragraph 2 of article 9 of the Convention".[463]

The second group of the reservation to Article 9 does not cite on Islamic principle, but they referred to their nationality code.

Egypt has entered a reservation to Article 9, which is a more practical reason to justify its reservation:

Islands, Somalia, Sudan, Swaziland, Syrian Arab Republic, Tanzania, Thailand, Togo, Tunisia, United Arab Emirates, Yemen
For see more, Global Campaign for Equal Nationality Rights, "The Problem", accessed at: http://www.equalnationalityrights.org/the-issue/the-problem.)

461 Yahyaoui Krivenko, Women, Islam and International Law, p. 126

462 United Nations Treaty Collection, accessed at: https://treaties.un.org/Pages/ViewDetails.aspx?src=IND&mtdsg_no=IV-8&chapter=4&lang=en#EndDec

463 Ibid
See more reservation by Syria basis on Sharia principle to Article 9(2): "subject to reservations to article 2; article 9, paragraph 2, concerning the grant of a woman's nationality to her children;......, inasmuch as this provision is incompatible with the provisions of the Islamic Shariah;...... "

> Concerning article 9: "Without prejudice to the acquisition by a child born of a marriage of the nationality of his father. This is in order to prevent a child's acquisition of two nationalities where his parents are of different nationalities, since this may be prejudicial to his future. It is clear that the child's acquisition of his father's nationality is the procedure most suitable for the child and that this does not infringe upon the principle of equality between men and women, since it is customary for a woman to agree, upon marrying an alien, that her children shall be of the father's nationality".[464]

Kuwait's reservation to Article 9 (2) does not refer to Islamic Sharia, inasmuch pointed out "runs counter to the Kuwaiti Nationality Act";

> "….reserves its right not to implement the provision contained in article 9, paragraph 2, of the Convention, inasmuch as it runs counter to the Kuwaiti Nationality Act, which stipulates that a child's nationality shall be determined by that of his father".[465]

The third type of reservation to Article 9 listed without explanation; but side by side reserved with other Articles; they cited Article 2 and Article16 to be incompatible with the Islamic Sharia. The link between reservations to Article 2 and reservations to other special parts of the CEDAW as well as Article 9 is of particular importance; hence in relation to Article 9, this may potentially affect equal nationality rights for women.[466]

Bahrain has entered a reservation to Article 9 (2) and no further comment that stated Article 2 and 16 are incompatible with Sharia.

---

464 CEDAW Sessions, accessed at: http://www.un.org/womenwatch/daw/cedaw/reservations-country.htm.

465 Ibid

See also reservation by Algeria to Article 9: Article 9, paragraph 2: its reservations concerning the provisions of article 9, paragraph 2, which are incompatible with the provisions of the Algerian Nationality code and the Algerian Family Code The Algerian Nationality code allows a child to take the nationality of the mother only when: (1) the father is either unknown or stateless;(2) the child is born in Algeria to an Algerian mother and a foreign father who was born in Algeria;(3) moreover, a child born in Algeria to an Algerian mother and a foreign father who was not born on Algerian territory may, under article 26 of the Algerian Nationality Code, acquire the nationality of the mother providing the Ministry of Justice does not object. Article 41 of the Algerian Family Code states that a child is affiliated to its father through legal marriage. Article 43 of that Code states that 'the child is affiliated to its father if it is born in the 10 months following the date of separation or death'."

466 Compare also, Yahyaoui Krivenko, Women, Islam and International Law.126 and Human Rights Council, Twenty-third session, A/HRC/23/23, 2013, para.11

The Kingdom of Bahrain makes reservations with respect to the following provisions of the Convention: "Article 2, in order to ensure its implementation within the bounds of the provisions of the Islamic Sharia; Article 9, paragraph 2; Article 15, paragraph 4; Article 16, in so far as it is incompatible with the provisions of the Islamic Sharia"; [467]

Jordan's reservation is also relevant to the provision of Islam and has made a reservation to Article 9 (2) without explaining the scope of it.

Jordan does not consider itself bound by the following provisions: "Article 9, paragraph 2; Article 15, paragraph 4; Article 16, paragraph (1) (c, d, g)".[468]

e) Objection to Reservation

Other states parties have examined the reservations to Article 9, and have objected to those reservations concerning national law or religious law that violate the essential element of CEDAW in nationality; therefore, they are contrary to the object and purpose of the Convention.

Finland stated after examining the contents of Bahrain's reservation to paragraph 2 of Article 9:

> "A reservation which consists of a general reference to religious or other national law without specifying its contents does not clearly define to other Parties to the Convention the extent to which the reserving State commits itself to the Convention and therefore creates serious doubts as to the commitment of the receiving State to fulfill its obligations under the Convention. Such reservations are subject to the general principle of treaty interpretation according to which a party may not invoke the provisions of its domestic law *as justification for a failure to perform its treaty obligations* are in contradiction with the object and purpose of the Convention".[469]

Ireland, concerning the reservation made by Saudi Arabia:

> "In respect of any divergence between the terms of the Convention and the norms of Islamic law...such a reservation aims to exclude one obligation of non-discrimination which is so important in the context of the Convention … as to render this reservation contrary to the essence of the Convention".[470]

Norway objected to Malaysia's reservation, which refers to general principles in national law or religious reasons.

---

467 CEDAW Sessions, accessed at: http://www.un.org/womenwatch/daw/cedaw/reservations-country.htm.

468 Ibid

469 Ibid

470 Ibid

"A statement by which a State Party purports to limit its responsibilities under the Convention by invoking general principles of internal or religious law may create doubts about the commitment of the reserving State to the object and purpose of the Convention. Under well-established international treaty law, a State is not permitted to invoke internal law as justification for its failure to perform its treaty obligations. Therefore, such reservation is contrary to the object and purpose of the Convention".[471]

In summary, making reservations to Article 9 indicates that reserving states do not accept the obligations created under this Article. Moreover, such reservations to Article 9 by the Muslim states have the same inherent reasons for the reservations' justification: incompatibility with their religious beliefs or contradiction to their domestic law due to the religious values rooted in the legislation of such countries. Definitely, any reservation to Article 9 should be modified or removed because removing reservations to Article 9 is essential to ensuring gender equality in nationality. Therefore, this should be followed by appropriate legal and policy reforms to achieve in practice the realization of rights.[472]

C.3.1.3 Article 15

a) Content of Article 15

Article 15 provides full legal capacity and to the choice of residence and domicile.[473] Article 15 (1) addresses 'equality before the law', which refers to equality and non-discrimination in the substantive context of the law, in other words, 'equal protection of the law'. Therefore, its coverages include all matters in civil,

471 Ibid

472 Human Rights Council, Twenty-third session, A/HRC/23/23, 2013, para. 59

473 Article 15:

1) States Parties shall accord to women equality with men before the law.
2) States Parties shall accord to women, in civil matters, a legal capacity identical to that of men and the same opportunities to exercise that capacity. In particular, they shall give women equal rights to conclude contracts and to administer property and shall treat them equally in all stages of procedure in courts and tribunals.
3) States Parties agree that all contracts and all other private instruments of any kind with a legal effect which is directed at restricting the legal capacity of women shall be deemed null and void.
4) States Parties shall accord to men and women the same rights with regard to the law relating to the movement of persons and the freedom to choose their residence and domicile.

criminal, and administrative courts.[474] Article 15, paragraphs 2 and 3 are closely connected; in general, they relate to 'equality in a legal capacity', and focus on the removal of obstacles imposed by a legal system. Moreover, those paragraphs ensure women's legal capacity to conclude contracts and administer the property in their possession. In this regard, the Committee stressed that "when a woman cannot enter into a contract at all, or have access to financial credit, or can do so only with her husband's or male relative's concurrence or guarantee, she is denied legal autonomy".[475]

Finally, paragraph 4 concerns the freedom of movement and women's freedom to choose their residence and domicile. In practice, the limitations on women's freedom of movement affect their education and employment opportunities. As a result, women also have different levels of influence depending on their property status; this also renders them powerless in negotiating within family life.[476] Therefore, an adult woman should be capable of changing her domicile at will "regardless of her marital status"; this means applying equality to married and unmarried women. The recognition of this right for women is essential because any restrictions on a woman's right to choose a domicile "may limit her access to the courts in the country in which she lives or prevents her from entering and leaving a country freely and in her own right".[477]

b) Reservation

Reservation to this Article goes to "the heart of women's legal capacity"; on the one hand, any reservation restricts women when making decisions for themselves and their family, especially concerning managing property ownership. On the other hand, the lack of legal capacity results in women becoming dependent on males and subject to male authority, rendering them powerless in the family and having no recourse outside the family.[478] Hence, the Committee states that any limitation on women's legal capacity by-laws would be "denying women their rights to be equal with men and restricting women's ability to provide for themselves and their dependants".[479]

---

474 Freeman, Rudolf, Chinkin, The UN Convention on the Elimination of All Forms of Discrimination Against Women, p. 391
475 CEDAW, General Recommendation No. 21, para. 7
476 Freeman, RESERVATIONS TO CEDAW: AN ANALYSIS FOR UNICEF, p. 9
477 CEDAW, General Recommendation No. 21, para. 8
478 Freeman, RESERVATIONS TO CEDAW: AN ANALYSIS FOR UNICEF, p. 9
479 CEDAW, General Recommendation No. 21, para. 8

Eight Islamic countries entered reservations to article 15, exclusively to paragraph 4, which provides equality in choice of residence and domicile and freedom of movement. In general, in Muslim countries, the husband or male head of the household determines the choice of residence and domicile. These reservations to Article 15 (4) refer to the incompatibility with the civil law of reserving states (such Morocco, Tunisia), and also refer to Islamic Sharia which it is not compatible (such Jordan, Bahrain).[480]

Morocco entered a reservation to Article 15 (4) that the Code of Personal Status confirms the principle of the primacy of the husband/household in the administration of his household and the choice of place of residence.[481] Morocco states in its reservation to Article 15(4) that:

> "…it can only be bound by the provisions of this paragraph, in particular, those relating to the right of women to choose their residence and domicile, to the extent that they are not incompatible with articles 34 and 36 of the Moroccan Code of Personal Status".[482]

Tunisia also made a reservation to Article 15 (4), in which it states that:

> ".....the free choice of the woman's residence could only be curtailed in the light of her custody duties for a child of school age; therefore, it must not be interpreted in a manner which conflicts with the provisions of the Personal Status Code on this subject".[483]

Jordan has attached a reservation to Article 15 (4) that:

> ".....are not conferred on women in Jordan, since Jordan is an Islamic country and such rights may not be conferred on women, as this would be contrary to the teaching of Islam….women are forbidden to travel alone…. they must be accompanied by either a close male relative……therefore not possible to grant such a right or the freedom to choose a place of residence, in view of the fact that the State religion views a woman as belonging to her husband, and as unable, whether married or single, to make an independent choice of dwelling place".[484]

Bahrain stated in its reservation regarding Article 15 (4) that:

---

480 Moreover, other Muslim majority States have entered reservation to Article 15(4): Algeria, Oman, Syria and the UAE.

481 CEDAW, Second periodic report of States parties, Morocco, February 2000, CEDAW/C/MOR/2, p. 56

482 United Nations Treaty Collection, accessed at: https://treaties.un.org/Pages/ViewDetails.aspx?src=IND&mtdsg_no=IV-8&chapter=4&lang=en#EndDec

483 CEDAW, Combined initial and second periodic report of Tunisia, Fourteenth session, 16 January – 3 February 1995, CEDAW/C/TUN/1-2, para. 248

484 CEDAW, Initial reports of States parties, Jordan, November 1997, CEDAW/C/JOR/1, p. 23-24

> "…the implementation of para. 4 of Article 15 will be without breaching the provisions of the Islamic Sharia".[485]

c) *Objection to Reservation*

Other states parties have examined the reservations to Article 15 and objected to those which influence the effectiveness of women's rights.

Spain objected to the contents of Qatar's reservation to Article 15:

> " …..since their intent is to exempt Qatar from committing itself to the elimination of specific forms of discrimination against women in such areas as equality with men before the law, free movement and residence, These reservations *affect essential obligations* arising from the Convention and their observance is necessary in order to achieve the purpose of the Convention".[486]

Austria, with regard to the reservation made by the Syrian Arab Republic to Article 15 (4) states that:

> "…this is contrary to the object and purpose of the Convention".[487]

The Netherlands considers the reservation by Morocco regarding article 15 (4) to be incompatible with the object and purpose of the Convention.[488]

C.3.1.4 Article 16

a) *Content of Article 16*

Article 16 relates to equality in marriage and divorce.[489] Article 16 (1) covers gender equality rights in all aspects of marriage and the dissolution of marriage.

---

485 United Nations Treaty Collection, accessed at: https://treaties.un.org/Pages/ViewDetails.aspx?src=IND&mtdsg_no=IV-8&chapter=4&lang=en#EndDec

486 Sixteenth meeting, June 2010, CEDAW/SP/2010/2, p. 36

487 United Nations Treaty Collection, accessed at: https://treaties.un.org/Pages/ViewDetails.aspx?src=IND&mtdsg_no=IV-8&chapter=4&lang=en#EndDec

488 Eleventh meeting, August 2000, CEDAW/SP/2000/2, p. 65

489 Article 16:

1) States Parties shall take all appropriate measures to eliminate discrimination against women in all matters relating to marriage and family relations and in particular shall ensure, on a basis of equality of men and women:
   (a) The same right to enter into marriage;
   (b) The same right freely to choose a spouse and to enter into marriage only with their free and full consent;
   (c) The same rights and responsibilities during marriage and at its dissolution;

On the one hand, it provides "the same rights and responsibility" for women and men as spouses, partners, and the guardianship of children during marriage and the dissolution of marriage.[490] On the other hand, it protects women's equal access to their household resources (same property and inheritance rights), and legal protection to administrate their property. Article 16 (2) prohibits child marriages that negatively affect the female and obliges states parties to institute a minimum age for marriage. Therefore, it requires states parties to comply with their provisions in this context; moreover, it requires "the registration of all marriages whether contracted civilly or according to custom or religious law".[491] In general, the issues in Article 16 include forced marriages, polygamous marriages, the attribution to the husband of the status of head of household and primary decision-maker, and the denial of legal protection to *de facto* unions and rights of parents of children born in such unions. They also include forced pregnancies, abortions or sterilization, the obligation for a woman to change her name upon marriage or at its dissolution, and the granting to men a more significant share of property upon dissolution of marriage.[492]

(d) The same rights and responsibilities as parents, irrespective of their marital status, in matters relating to their children; in all cases the interests of the children shall be paramount;
(e) The same rights to decide freely and responsibly on the number and spacing of their children and to have access to the information, education and means to enable them to exercise these rights;
(f) The same rights and responsibilities with regard to guardianship, wardship, trusteeship and adoption of children, or similar institutions where these concepts exist in national legislation; in all cases the interests of the children shall be paramount;
(g) The same personal rights as husband and wife, including the right to choose a family name, a profession and an occupation;
(h) The same rights for both spouses in respect of the ownership, acquisition, management, administration, enjoyment and disposition of property, whether free of charge or for a valuable consideration.

2) The betrothal and the marriage of a child shall have no legal effect, and all necessary action, including legislation, shall be taken to specify a minimum age for marriage and to make the registration of marriages in an official registry compulsory.

490 Freeman, Rudolf, Chinkin, The UN Convention on the Elimination of All Forms of Discrimination Against Women, 2012. p. 416

491 CEDAW, General Recommendation No. 21, para. 38.39

492 Yahyaoui Krivenko, Women, Islam and International Law, p. 129

The Committee, with General Recommendation No. 21 in Articles 9, 15 and 16, considers that "these three articles in the Convention that have special significance for the status of women in the family". In fact, CEDAW "goes further" than earlier human rights treaties concerning women's personal status,[493] by "recognizing the importance of culture and tradition in shaping the thinking and behavior of men and women and the significant part they play in restricting the exercise of basic rights by women".[494]As a result, the implementation or non-implementation of Article 16 has significant consequences on women's lives; therefore, the Committee recognizes that Article 2 and 16 are 'the core provisions' of the CEDAW. In other words, these articles create fundamental women's human rights and oblige states parties to take necessary measures to eliminate obstacles to their adoption and implementation.

b) Reservation

Thirty-four states parties have entered reservations to this Article, sixteen of which are from Islamic countries. This Article has the highest number of reservations. However, the Committee has made clear that the states parties with reservations to Article 16 "relegate laws and practices that critically affect women's human rights to a system that is unreachable by and unaccountable to international norms".[495] The reservations to Article 16 are justified under the name of "cultural, religious beliefs or on the country's economic or political status"[496] even though reservations to Article 16 are impermissible, regardless of the content of the reservations. Most Islamic countries have entered a general reservation to the whole of Article 16 or a specific paragraph of Article 16. It must add that the scope of reservations by Islamic countries is quite different; some refer to the conflict with Sharia law, and others reject it on the grounds of their Personal Status, which considers in the following.

Egypt refers to the whole of Article 16 and states that it cannot be implemented "without prejudice to the Islamic sharia provisions".

> "....concerning the equality of men and women in all matters relating to marriage and family relations during the marriage and upon its dissolution, without prejudice to the Islamic sharia provisions whereby women are accorded rights equivalent to those of

493 Freeman, Rudolf, Chinkin, The UN Convention on the Elimination of All Forms of Discrimination Against Women, p. 415

494 CEDAW, General Recommendation No. 21, para. 3

495 Freeman, RESERVATIONS TO CEDAW: AN ANALYSIS FOR UNICEF, p. 6

496 CEDAW, General Recommendation No. 21, para. 41

> their spouses so as to ensure a just balance between them. *This is out of respect for the sacrosanct nature of the firm religious beliefs which govern marital relations in Egypt* and which may not be called in question and in view of the fact that one of the most important bases of these relations is an equivalency of rights and duties so as to ensure complementarity which guarantees true equality between the spouses, not a quasi-equality that renders the marriage a burden on the wife".[497]
>
> Egypt's representative explained concerning the impact of Article 16 that "Islamic law had given a prominent position to all women and liberated them from any form of discrimination. Except for certain rights and responsibilities during marriage and at its dissolution, Islamic law had given women all the necessary rights even before the ratification of the Convention with regard to rights and responsibilities during marriage, and at its dissolution, a certain difference existed between the Convention and Islamic law".[498]

The view of Egypt's reservation to Article 16 argues that women's necessary rights have already been provided for under Sharia, and other additional rights are not essential. Also, Egypt's representative appears to be saying that the promotion of the CEDAW in Egypt is unnecessary with the expectations that promote women's place is in the home.[499]

Morocco made a general reservation to Article 16 and cited the incompatibility of the equality provisions with Islamic Sharia.

> "...equality of this kind is considered incompatible with the Islamic sharia, which guarantees to each of the spouses the rights and responsibilities within a framework of equilibrium and complementarity in order to preserve the sacred bond of matrimony".[500]

Algeria, regarding its reservation to Article 16, declares that:

> "...the provisions of article 16... in all matters relating to marriage, both during marriage and at its dissolution, should not contradict the provisions of the Algerian Family Code".

In this regard, it must be mentioned that Algeria's Family Code is based on the Constitution, which stated that Islam was the religion of the State. Algeria's representative clearly stated that "those reservations did not impede the exercise by

497 United Nations Treaty Collection, accessed at: https://treaties.un.org/Pages/ViewDetails.aspx?src=IND&mtdsg_no=IV-8&chapter=4&lang=en#EndDec

498 CEDAW, Report of the Committee on the CEDAW, Third session, Volume II, No. 45 (A/39145), 1984, para. 215-216

499 Michele Brandt; Jeffrey A. Kaplan, The Tension between Women's Rights and Religious Rights: Reservations to Cedaw by Egypt, Bangladesh and Tunisia, JOURNAL OF LAW & RELIGION, 1995, p. 121

500 CEDAW, Sixteenth meeting, CEDAW/SP/2010/2, p. 20

women of their economic, social, cultural, civil and political rights who enjoyed de facto equality in almost every area of public life. The difficulties encountered were largely in the area of women's personal status." Furthermore, the representative explained that Article 16 was "problematic for Muslim countries in which legislation on personal rights was guided by Sharia law. The time was not right at present for the radical changes that would be required to bring Algeria's Family Code into line with the Convention".[501]

Malaysia has made a number of reservations in the first accession to the Convention, in 1995, and expressed that it does "not consider itself bound by the provisions of Article 16, paragraph 1 (a), (c), (f) and (g), and paragraph 2 of the aforesaid Convention".[502]

Malaysia's family law consists of a combination of Civil, Sharia law, and customary laws; however, Malaysia reports that "the concept of women's equality in Malaysia is based on the culture and traditional beliefs of its various ethnic groups with the influence of religious values".[503] Therefore, Malaysia has taken steps to review reservations to Article 16. As a result, the reservations to 16 (b), (d), (e), and (h) were withdrawn, and Malaysia has expressed that the remaining reservations to the Articles are conflict with the provisions of the Islamic Sharia and the Federal Constitution of Malaysia. In this regard, Malaysia's representative has pointed out that there is no time frame to withdraw the reservation of Article 16 because the Government needs to negotiate with the conservative Islamic scholars.[504]

Kuwait declares that "it does not consider itself bound by the provision contained in article 16, paragraph 1 (f), inasmuch as it conflicts with the provisions of the Islamic sharia, Islam being the official religion of the State".[505]

It seems that the implantation of Article 16 in Islamic countries is problematic because they have not formulated merely general reservations to this Article, although the nature of such reservations is quite different. These differences

---

501 CEDAW, Consideration report, Initial report of Algeria, Twentieth session, CEDAW/C/SR.406, 2002, para 31-32

502 United Nations Treaty Collection, accessed at: https://treaties.un.org/Pages/ViewDetails.aspx?src=IND&mtdsg_no=IV-8&chapter=4&lang=en#EndDec

503 CEDAW, Combined initial and second periodic reports of States parties Malaysia, CEDAW/C/MYS/1-2, 2004, para. 380

504 CEDAW, Sixteenth meeting, CEDAW/SP/2010/2, p. 16
see also: CEDAW, Consideration of reports, Combined initial and second periodic report of Malaysia, Thirty-fifth session, CEDAW/C/SR.731, 2006, para. 38

505 CEDAW, Sixteenth meeting, CEDAW/SP/2010/2, p. 14

are due to what degree Islamic law is incorporated into their legislation and the different interpretations of Islamic law of each country.[506] Consequently, "the extent and nature of reservations based on Sharia" to Article 16 have different results when applied to this Article; furthermore, it could impact the 'constructive dialogue' with the Committee regarding the withdrawal or non-withdrawal of Article 16.

c) Objection to Reservation

Regarding the reservations to Article 16 for religious reasons, other states parties have entered objections.

Austria has examined the modification of the reservations made by Qatar; however, it states that:

> "….a reservation which consists of a general reference to constitutional provisions and Islamic Sharia law without specifying its implications does not do so. Moreover, the reservations to Article 16, if put into practice, would inevitably result in discrimination against women on the basis of sex. This is contrary to the object and purpose of the Convention".[507]

The Netherlands has examined the reservations made by the Government of Malaysia regarding Article 16 and objected.

> "…concerning the Islamic Sharia of Bahrain, reservations which seek to limit the responsibilities of the reserving State under the Convention by invoking the Islamic Sharia, may raise doubts as to the commitment of this State to the object and purpose of the Convention".[508]

Poland with regard to the reservations made by Oman upon accession objects that:

> "…..by making a general reference to the Islamic Sharia without indicating the provisions of the Convention to which the Islamic Sharia applies… does not specify the exact extent of the introduced limitations. Therefore, such reservations incompatible with the object and purpose of a treaty shall not be permitted".[509]

The increase of the objections to the reservations to Article 16 appears that the general character of Islamic reservations is unacceptable; also, the other states

506 Yahyaoui Krivenko, Women, Islam and International Law, p. 130

507 CEDAW, Sixteenth meeting, CEDAW/SP/2010/2, p. 33

508 United Nations Treaty Collection, accessed at: https://treaties.un.org/Pages/ViewDetails.aspx?src=IND&mtdsg_no=IV-8&chapter=4&lang=en#EndDec

509 Ibid

objected to the unclear commitment of reserving states to Article 16 as a core provision of the CEDAW. In this regard, the Committee has clearly stated that:

> "...neither traditional, religious or cultural practice nor incompatible domestic laws and policies can justify violations of the Convention. The Committee also remains convinced that reservations to article 16, whether lodged for national, traditional, religious, or cultural reasons, are incompatible with the Convention and, therefore, impermissible and should be reviewed and modified or withdrawn".[510]

C.3.2 Practice of the Committee

As mentioned above, the reservations do not permit that target the central principles of the Convention, especially those contained in Articles 2 and 16. Islamic countries have entered reservations on the grounds of national law, religion, culture or tradition, and justify the reservations for women's underlying discrimination. Thus, they are contrary to the provisions of the CEDAW and general international law.

This section will address the degree to which the Committee has accepted gender discrimination for religious reasons in practice. It will also deal with the future tendency of international law concerning the recognition of this particularity. Therefore, the Committee's role is essential to review such reservations, as a body of experts considering periodic reports, and opening a 'constructive dialogue' with the state party; consequently, it makes concluding comments/general recommendations thereon.

C.3.2.1 Constructive Dialogue and Concluding Comment

This procedure has led to the withdrawal of such reservations based on Islamic law, as in the cases of Algeria, Bangladesh, Egypt, Jordan, Malaysia, Tunisia, and Morocco. However, other Islamic reserving states still have not withdrawn or modified their reservations. Thus, the same strategy of the Committee has two different consequences, which considers in the following.

The first step addresses the Islamic countries that have withdrawn their reservations, including Algeria, Egypt, and Malaysia.

Algeria. Algeria issued reservations to articles 2, 9 (2), 15 (4), and 16 that are severe obstacles to implementing the obligation of the CEDAW.

---

510 CEDAW, General Recommendation No. 29: on article 16 of the Convention on the Elimination of All Forms of Discrimination against Women, CEDAW/C/GC/29, 2013, para. 54

Algeria submitted its initial report in 1998 and stated that since accession to CEDAW, the government had taken positive measures to envision amendments to the Family Code. However, those reservations would be removed if they occur in favor of gradual changes in the country.[511] The most important one is "to the place and role of Islamic law among the legal instruments and jurisprudence of Algeria". Algeria representatives also asserted that "fundamentalist Islamic movements used the status of women as a symbol for the type of society they wished to create. Those opposed to such a society must, therefore, promote women's rights with even greater vigor and urgency; the Government of Algeria must continue to be uncompromising and consistent in the implementation of the Convention in all areas, especially family law..." [512]

Regarding those reservations, the members of the Committee noted that the Algerian Government "intended to improve the Family Code in the teeth of conservative fundamentalism"; therefore, as the first step, Algeria would be lifting its reservations to the Convention and following international standards about women's human rights.[513] Moreover, Islam should not be used "as an excuse for depriving women of their rights".[514] Thus, the Committee recommended that Sharia "must be reinterpreted in light of an understanding of the circumstances that had prevailed at the time of its revelation".[515] Moreover, the state had a responsibility to show that "Islam could be adapted to take into account women's rights.... the Government would show the necessary will to implement the Convention, with a view not only to guaranteeing women's rights but also to taking a major step towards freeing Muslims from being held hostage by fundamentalist groups".[516]

Hence, Algeria, in 2002, reformed the Code of Algerian Nationality that allows women equal rights concerning the transmission of their nationality to their children. As a result, Algeria has withdrawn only its reservations to Article 9 (2). While welcoming the withdrawal of the reservation, the Committee emphasized that "the numerous discriminatory provisions of the Family Code and the persistence of prejudice and patriarchal practices conflict *de facto*

---

511 CEDAW, Initial reports of States parties, ALGERIA, CEDAW/C/DZA/, 1 1 September 1998, para. 30

512 Ibid, para. 45

513 CEDAW, Initial report of Algeria (continued), CEDAW/C/SR.412, 6 February 2002, para. 54

514 CEDAW, Initial report of Algeria, CEDAW/C/SR.407, 1 February 2002, para. 2

515 Ibid, para. 39

516 CEDAW, Initial report of Algeria, CEDAW/C/SR.406, 5 February 2002, para. 45

with the principles of the Convention", therefore, other reservations must also withdraw.[517]

In the second periodic report (2005), the Algerian representative acknowledged concerning other reservations that the "family had evolved from a patriarchal structure headed by the husband to one that was based on family solidarity. It had proposed modifications ....and were currently being debated in the society....would be brought before the National Assembly in the near future".[518] However, On 8 March 2004, the President requested the Government "to take the necessary steps to bring the national legislation into line with developments in international law and to review the appropriateness of the reservations that Algeria had entered when it ratified the Convention".[519]

After examining the reports, the Committee made its Concluding Comments. In Concluding Comments (2005), the Committee argued that Algeria had taken some reform in the legislative area, as far as proceeding to withdraw its reservation to CEDAW. They emphasized the revision of the Code of Algerian Nationality to remove discriminatory Nationality provisions in which women do not have equal rights in the transmission of nationality. However, there are still obstacles to progress in revising the discriminatory Family Code that, in particular, does not abolish polygamy, women's legal guardianship, nor inheritance law. Moreover, in the Concluding Comments (2012), the Committee stated that Algeria must expedite legislative reforms to withdraw its reservations to articles 2, 15, paragraphs 4 and 16 of the Convention within a specific time frame. The Committee re-emphasized that the reservations to articles 2 and 16 are contrary to the object and purpose of the Convention, and thus they are impermissible.[520] In this regard, the Committee recommended the government must "take systematic measures to engage the media, community and religious leaders and NGOs in combating negative stereotyping and societal attitudes".[521]

Despite the Concluding Comments that encouraged Algeria to withdraw its reservations to articles 2, 15 (4), and 16, they still have not been lifted.

---

517 Ibid, para. 68

518 CEDAW, Thirty-second session, Report of the Chairperson of the pre-session working group Second periodic report of Algeria, CEDAW/C/SR.667, 2005, para. 17

519 CEDAW, Concluding Comments: Algeria, CEDAW/C/DZA/CC/2, 11 January 2005, para. 9

520 CEDAW, Concluding Observations: Algeria, CEDAW/C/DZA/CO/3-4, 23 March 2012, para. 13 and 14(b)

521 Ibid, para. 28(b)

Egypt. Egypt explained that the reservations to articles 2, 9 (2), and 16 are "without prejudice to the prescriptions of Islamic law". However, the reservation to Article 16 is concerning "the prescriptions of Islamic religious law", because Islamic law had given women a prominent position without any discrimination.[522] Furthermore, the representative in the third report (2001) mentioned that the Government intended to eliminate discrimination against women, but sometimes cultural constraints and traditions, which are rooted in Egyptian and Islamic culture, prevent this. They create obstacles to achieve equality between women and men. More importantly, Egypt must "clarify misinterpretations of religious concepts and demonstrate that the principles of Sharia provide for the full equality of women with men".

Regarding Egypt's reservations to the Convention, the representative stated that the report on the Islamic Sharia, which Government required, had concluded that there is no conflict between the Sharia and the principles of equality and non-discrimination; however, the general reservation to Article 2 was "purely precautionary". Therefore, it should be withdrawn.[523] Also, withdrawing the reservation is closely linked to the reform of the laws. In this context, the Government had established, on the one hand, a Committee to review those reservations. The Committee asserted that the reservation to article 2 should be withdrawn because its existence cannot justify under Sharia or another legal system. On the other hand, The National Committee for Women (founded in 1992) has pursued Parliament to withdrawing reservations with the support of *Al-Azhar* University and the lobby of Sharia law professors in religious institutions. However, the reform in the nationality law is especially still under consideration.[524]

After the report by Egypt's representative, the Committee members acknowledged that the report addressed more the patriarchal mentality, which was often justified under Islamic law. The members of the Committee recommended that measures and policies for eliminating gender discrimination must clearly and openly be related to the concept of universal norms of women's rights that would

522 CEDAW/C/SR.492 and 493, 19 January 2001, para. 318, CEDAW, Report of the Committee, Third session, Volume II, No. 45 (A/39/45), 26 March 1984, para. 183-186 and 215

523 CEDAW, Third and combined fourth and fifth periodic reports of Egypt, CEDAW/C/SR.492, 26 March 2001, para. 8

524 CEDAW, Third and combined fourth and fifth periodic reports of Egypt, CEDAW/C/SR.492, 26 March 2001, para. 17 and 19

seek to withdraw the reservations to the substantive articles of the Convention. Moreover, the Egyptian Government would ratify the Optional Protocol, as full implementation of the universal rights of women.[525] *Ms. Schöpp-Schilling*, another member of the Committee, requested clarification on the influence of the National Council for Women, as well as its commitment to communicate the Committee's conclusions to the Government. Finally, she suggested that a study on the relationship between the Sharia and the Convention should be provided to the Committee.[526]

After the negotiation with the Committee, the campaign of Egyptian women's groups formed to implement the CEDAW for Egyptian women with association with other NGOs. The campaign focused on the impact of nationality restrictions on Egyptian women and children. As a result, the Nationality Law was reformed in June 2004, which establishes gender equality in the transmission of women's nationality to the children. Therefore, Egypt withdrew only the reservation to Article 9 (2) in January 2008.[527]

Furthermore, Egypt explained in its report (2008) that Egypt seeks intensive efforts to withdraw the reservation to Article 2, which is not incompatible with Egypt's Constitution or laws.[528] In this regard, the Egyptian Foreign Ministry also has formed "a high-level Committee to study the withdrawal of Egypt's reservation to Article 2, which does not conflict with Egypt's Constitution and legislation".[529] Regarding Article 16, negotiations are currently underway to withdraw Egypt's reservation of Article 16.[530] However, there is "the minimal nature of this change," in this regard. The CEDAW Committee noted that the law was a "major step forward towards withdrawal"; Egypt still has not withdrawn its reservation to articles 2 and 16.[531]

Malaysia. Malaysia ratified the CEDAW in 1995, and with the first accession, made some reservations to articles 9 (2), 16 (1) paragraphs (a, c, f, g), and

---

525 Ibid, para. 29-30

526 CEDAW, Third and combined fourth and fifth reports of Egypt, CEDAW/C/SR.493, 27 March 2001, para. 20

527 Freeman, RESERVATIONS TO CEDAW: AN ANALYSIS FOR UNICEF, p. 204

528 CEDAW, Combined sixth and seventh periodic reports of States parties: Egypt, CEDAW/C/EGY/7, 5 September 2008, p. 15

529 Ibid, p. 16

530 Ibid, p. 76

531 Freeman, RESERVATIONS TO CEDAW: AN ANALYSIS FOR UNICEF, p. 16

paragraph 2 of Article 16. Malaysia referred that those provisions as contrary to Sharia law and the Federal Constitution of Malaysia. At the Fourth World Conference on Women in Beijing, the head of the Malaysian delegation stressed their commitment to gender-equal rights and implementation of the Beijing Platform for Action. Hence, the creation of the reservations must be reviewed.[532] As a result, Malaysia withdrew the reservations to articles 2 (f), 9 (1), 16 (1) paragraphs (b, d, e, h), in 1998. However, the remaining reservations were based on the conflict between Islamic law and the Federal Constitution of Malaysia.[533] The representative of Malaysia presented the initial and second periodic report (2006) and noted that Islamic family law is within the jurisdiction of the Federal Government.[534] Therefore, recognizing that the Islamic Family law is for "the sensitivity and complexity of matters relating to conversion and in view of the sentiments expressed by various groups in that regard, (the Government) was taking steps to ensure a holistic approach to the issue in order to avoid dissatisfaction within the Malaysian community". Hence, it is not the time for lifting the reservation of Article 16, but the Government was still negotiating with the relevant stakeholders. Moreover, the Government has established the Inter-Ministerial Committee to review for remaining reservations to CEDAW.[535]

The members of the Committee considered these reports from Malaysia and opened a dialogue to clarify the place of Sharia law in Malaysia's laws. Member *Ms. Khan* stated that "a narrow interpretation of the sharia had been used as a basis for amendments to laws..... It would be interesting to know what further action the Government might be planning to bring Malaysian legislation more closely into line with the Convention".[536] *Ms. Schöpp-Schilling* also welcomed that Malaysia was reviewing some reservations; however, she asked that the clarification of the reservation be extended to a general interpretation of those articles. Moreover, she noted that the Government assumed "responsibility for ensuring consistency in harmonizing Islamic sharia law". As a result,

---

532 CEDAW, Combined initial and second periodic reports of States parties: Malaysia, CEDAW/C/MYS/1-2, 12 April 2004, para. 68

533 Ibid, para. 69,

534 CEDAW, Consideration of reports, Combined initial and second periodic report of Malaysia, CEDAW/C/SR.731, 20 June 2006, para. 4

535 CEDAW, Consideration of reports, Combined initial and second periodic report of Malaysia, CEDAW/C/SR.731, 20 June 2006, para. 13 and 38

536 CEDAW, Consideration of reports, Combined initial and second periodic report of Malaysia, CEDAW/C/SR.731, 20 June 2006, para. 6

the Government must be transparent in contrast to Malaysia's constitutional and Sharia law relating to the substantive equality of women.[537]

Besides, the Committee, in its Concluding Comment (2006), communicated that laws in Malaysia based on Sharia interpretation must be reformed,[538] especially Islamic Family Law, which impacts women's equality rights the most.[539] In this context, the Committee argued that Malaysia undertakes "a process of law reform to remove inconsistencies between civil law and Islamic law". Accordingly, the Committee encouraged the Government to take the necessary steps to increase support for law reform through collaboration with Islamic jurisprudence research organizations, civil society organizations, women's non-governmental organizations, and community leaders.[540] The Committee also urged that Malaysia review all its remaining reservations to withdraw them, especially the reservations to article 16, which are contrary to the object and purpose of the Convention.[541]

Consequently, as a follow-up to the constructive dialogue with the Committee, women's rights activists (SUHAKAM) sat on the interagency coordinating meeting to review the reservations with the various group, including religious scholars. It included the removal of the reservations based on the Sharia laws in 2008. Also, SUHAKAM focused on withdrawing the reservation to Article 16 (1) (a) to seek to better implementation of Article 16. Consequently, the Ministry of Women, Family, and Community Development withdrew its reservations made to Articles 5 (a), 7 (b) and 16 (2) of the Convention on 6 July 2010. However, the reservation to 16 (1) (a) has not withdrawn. This decision was taken based on the terms of the Islamic perspective.[542] Additionally, SUHAKAM pursued to adopt OP-CEDAW to strengthen the implementation of CEDAW. In this regard, SUHAKAM explained that the OP is not inconsistent with religious reasons nor cultural sensitivity; therefore, the Government cannot justify their action to accede to the Protocol.[543]

537 Ibid, para. 14-16

538 CEDAW, Concluding comments: Malaysia, CEDAW/C/MYS/CO/2, 31 May 2006, para. 9

539 Ibid, para. 13

540 Ibid, para. 14

541 Ibid, para. 10

542 Suhakam's Report on the Status of Women's Rights in Malaysia, SUHAKAM, 2010, p. 11-12

543 Ibid, p. 79

Malaysia, in its recent report (2016), explained that the Government was committed to implementing laws and policies on matrimony gender equality in family law in both civil and Sharia systems. Nevertheless, the remaining reservations to articles 16 (1) paragraphs (a, c, f, g) are based on Islamic law. On the one hand, the Government has upheld the promotion of the rights of Muslim women, as sanctioned by Islamic law. On the other hand, it has to be proven that before lifting those reservations, the laws such as the Islamic Family Law Act, Rules and Regulations, and Practice Directions of Islamic courts must be reviewed to remain consistent within the continuing measures of Government.[544]

The Committee welcomes the progress achieved after reviewing the combined initial and second periodic reports (2006). In particular, the legislative amendments to civil law ending discrimination against women in marriage and the family, as far as the jurisdiction of civil courts is over matters of Islamic law. However, the Committee notes with concern the remaining reservations to some paragraphs of Article 16, which are contrary to the object and purpose of the Convention.[545] Thus, the State of Malaysia cannot justify its position on the grounds of incompatibility with the Federal Constitution and Islamic provisions. The Committee, in its Concluding recommendation (2018), acknowledged that Malaysia provides capacity-building on gender equality to law enforcement officials, members of the judiciary, and members of religious institutions.[546] In this regard, the adoption of *fatwas* by religious institutions would guarantee gender equality in family laws, as well as providing conditions to withdraw remaining reservations.[547] However, the reservations still maintain on Articles 9 (2) and Articles 16 (1) (a) (c) (f) and (g).

It must add that other Islamic countries have withdrawn their reservations: Bangladesh to Article 16 paragraph 1(f), Jordan to Article 15 (4), and Tunisia to articles15 (4), 9 (2), 16 (c), (d), (f), (g), (h), and Morocco to articles 9 (2) and 16.

Other Islamic countries have still not withdrawn their reservations to the Convention. In this regard, the cases of Saudi Arabia and Pakistan will be addressed.

---

544 CEDAW, Combined third to fifth periodic reports of States parties due in 2012: Malaysia, CEDAW/C/MYS/3-5, 17 October 2016, para. 183-185

545 CEDAW, Concluding observations on the combined third to fifth periodic reports of Malaysia, CEDAW/C/MYS/CO/3-5, 14 March 2018, para. 9 and 53

546 Ibid, para. 50

547 Compare also, Concluding observations on the combined third to fifth periodic reports of Malaysia, CEDAW/C/MYS/CO/3-5, 14 March 2018, para. 49-50

Saudi Arabia has a conservative interpretation of Islam, resulting in women's rights not being developed; however, Saudi Arabia accessed the CEDAW by placing a general reservation. In Pakistan, on the one hand, women's rights have developed as a whole; on the other hand, Pakistan entered the general declaration on the CEDAW and has not yet withdrawn it.

Saudi Arabia. Saudi Arabia ratified the Convention in 2000, and stated that "contradiction between any term of the Convention and norms of Islamic law".

Saudi Arabia, in its initial and secondary reports, introduced the Government's position about the reservations. The representative admitted that the Kingdom was eager to increase women's role but within "a clear and just Islamic philosophical framework".[548] In fact, the protection of human rights shall be under Islamic law.[549] Thus, on the one hand, the majority of society has accepted Islamic law, and the reservation must be understood in this light. On the other hand, there are various interpretations of Islamic jurisprudence that have been taken into account, especially the personal status laws derived from the Sharia.[550] Therefore, the general reservations were mere "a precautionary measure against possible interpretations of the Convention that might contradict legal provisions in force in the kingdom".[551] However, the general reservation did not impact the core of the general principles of the Convention; instead, it referred to the potential conflict between provisions of the CEDAW and the norms of Islamic law. Hence, being a reservation relating to the application of CEDAW, it must not contradict the principles of Sharia.[552] In general, the Government has taken several measures to facilitate a more positive image of Islam, particularly in the educational sphere. Moreover, the King established a high-level scholarly panel, including the various schools of jurisprudence, to clarify the provisions of Islamic law and CEDAW, but it will not change overnight.[553]

548 CEDAW, Consideration of reports combined initial and second periodic reports of Saudi Arabia, CEDAW/C/SR.815, 15 February 2008, para. 5

549 CEDAW, Combined initial and second periodic reports: Saudi Arabia, CEDAW/C/SAU/2, 29 March 2007, para. 11

550 CEDAW, Consideration of reports combined initial and second periodic reports of Saudi Arabia, CEDAW/C/SR.815, 15 February 2008, para. 22 and 24

551 Ibid, para. 12

552 CEDAW, Combined initial and second periodic reports: Saudi Arabia, CEDAW/C/SAU/2, 29 March 2007, para. 7

553 CEDAW, Consideration of reports combined initial and second periodic reports of Saudi Arabia, CEDAW/C/SR.815, 15 February 2008, para. 22 and 60

The Committee concluded that Saudi Arabia had made those reservations within the framework Sharia, which gives precedence to Islamic law in meeting provisions of the CEDAW.[554] Additionally, the Committee urges that the Government considers the withdrawal of its general reservation, particularly in light of the fact that "the delegation assured that there is no contradiction in substance between the Convention and Islamic Sharia".[555]

However, Saudi Arabia has not withdrawn its reservation, which appeared in further reports (the third and fourth periodic reports) in 2018. The representative stated that the Government has endeavored to eliminate negative gender stereotypes that would lead to discrimination against women. However, the most recent review established that the reservation to article 2 did not influence its compliance with the Convention.[556] As a result, the Committee contended that the general reservation is incompatible with the object and purpose of the Convention and also recommended that the State party review its general reservation. In this regard, it is advised to open a participatory dialogue with leaders of religious communities and women on women's human rights in Islam, with a view to withdrawing the reservations, and "taking into consideration the best practices of countries that are members of the Organization of Islamic Cooperation and have similar cultural and religious backgrounds and legal systems".[557]

Pakistan. In 1996, Pakistan ratified the CEDAW and made a general declaration that states: the accession by Pakistan to the Convention is subject to the provisions of the Constitution of the Islamic Republic of Pakistan. The general nature of this declaration refers to Pakistan's domestic laws, hence raising doubts about Pakistan's obligations toward the implementation of the CEDAW.

Pakistan submitted its first report in 2005. Their representative explained that the subject of this declaration regarding the implementation of the Convention was a sensible course of action. In other words, the declaration is not against the purpose of the CEDAW, but rather a means of assuaging the concerns of those

554 CEDAW, Combined initial and second periodic report of Saudi Arabia, CEDAW/C/SAU/2, 17 January 2008, para. 19

555 CEDAW, Concluding comments: Saudi Arabia, CEDAW/C/SAU/CO/2, 8 April 2008, para. 10

556 CEDAW, Consideration of reports Combined third and fourth periodic reports of Saudi Arabia, CEDAW/C/SR.1582, 2 March 2018, para. 28

557 CEDAW, Concluding observations on the combined third and fourth periodic reports of Saudi Arabia, CEDAW/C/SAU/CO/3-4, 14 March 2018, para. 10 and para. 16(a)

who had misgivings about the Convention.[558] After independence in 1947, Pakistan had become an Islamic republic, grounded in the principle of Islamic law. Thus, the Government tends "to be highly patriarchal and conservative", and the result of placing this declaration is that the State has given itself a safeguard by deciding to choose when any provision of the Convention contrasts with the Constitution.[559] However, seven articles of the Constitution contain specific prohibitions against discrimination, which are neither in conflict with the Convention nor Islamic law. In fact, Pakistan faces other challenges in the promotion of women's rights, such "as a serious impoverishment of resources", and "lack of awareness and entrenched societal attitudes relating women's rights". In this regard, various programs have been launched, and some positive changes have occurred for Pakistani women.[560] However, several stereotypes still prevail, and so far, legal guarantees against discrimination have not been fully implemented; indeed, CEDAW has reported that "at times actions, which have no religious sanction, are justified based on tenets of Islam".[561] Nevertheless, Pakistan has seriously committed its international obligations; thus, the Ministry of Women Development's request that the National Commission on the Status of Women to withdraw Pakistan's declaration, and ratify the Protocol is under careful review.

Mr. *Flinterman*, a member of the Committee, pointed out that the Declaration referred to in the report was not a reservation, and was "aimed at curtailing Pakistan's related obligations but merely a declaration…with the spirit of the Constitution of Pakistan and Islamic law…..so, the Declaration was not necessary".[562] Furthermore, he said that the declaration is contrary to international law and prescribed the conditions under which it might be withdrawn.[563] Moreover, The Chairperson noted that Pakistan had withdrawn its reservation (1997) on acceding to the Convention on the Rights of the Child, which was grounded

558 CEDAW, Combined initial, second and third periodic reports: Pakistan, CEDAW/C/PAK/1-3, 3 August 2005, para. 3

559 Zia, Maliha; Butt, Riffat, Pakistan NGO Alternative Report on CEDAW 2005-2009, Aurat Publication and Information Service Foundation (AF), 2012, p. 17

560 Compare also, CEDAW, Combined initial, second and third periodic report of Pakistan, CEDAW/C/SR.781, 19 July 2007, para. 23, 44 and 47

561 CEDAW, Combined initial, second and third periodic reports: Pakistan, CEDAW/C/PAK/1-3, 3 August 2005, para. 49

562 CEDAW, Combined initial, second and third periodic report of Pakistan, CEDAW/C/SR.782, 18 July 2007, para. 55

563 CEDAW, Combined initial, second and third periodic report of Pakistan, CEDAW/C/SR.781, 19 July 2007, para. 13

in the principles of Islamic laws. Therefore, it could pursue that example concerning CEDAW. However, the Committee wanted to "know what mechanisms were available to challenge laws, not in line with the Constitution or with the Convention".[564]

The Committee made its first Concluding Comment on the report of Pakistan in 2007. The Committee welcomed that the declaration did not place any restrictions upon its obligations to implement the Convention; however, the Committee urged that Pakistan must withdraw its declaration without delay. Since the Constitution does not contain gender discrimination, neither does legislation include a definition of discrimination under article 1 of the Convention, furthermore, nor are there provisions on the equality of women with men in line with article 2 (a) of the Convention.[565] In this regard, Pakistan should modify stereotypical attitudes and traditional norms to strengthen societal support for equality between women and men. Most importantly, the efforts of NGO actors and religious leaders could be counteracting the misinterpretation of Islam.[566]

In the fourth periodic report, Pakistan's representative revealed that the declaration still had not been withdrawn because only 21 percent supported (from all relevant Federal Ministries and the Provincial Women's Development Department) the withdrawal of this declaration. This comment was received from all related Federal Ministries and the Provincial Women's Development Departments concerning the withdrawal of the declaration, and a consensus was not reached. Additionally, the declaration did not impact the legislative processes to eliminate gender discrimination, and the commitment of the State to implement the Convention.

On the other hand, the Government has taken measures to counteract the extremists' influence, which has exerted effort to restrict women's rights. In this regard, the media and religious leaders made strong statements about the misrepresentation of Islam, which these groups propagate.[567] However, in the second Concluding Comment in 2013, the Committee welcomed that Pakistan had enacted several legal provisions toward eliminating gender discrimination since combined initial, second, and third periodic reports. Nonetheless, the Committee argued that Federal Ministries did not support the withdrawal of the

564 Ibid, para. 18

565 CEDAW, Concluding comments: Pakistan, CEDAW/C/PAK/CO/3, 11 June 2007, para. 13 and 14

566 Ibid, para. 29

567 Ibid, para. 180

declaration, and recommends State party strengthen its efforts to the withdrawal of the declaration and reiterates its recommendation to do so without delay.[568]

It is interesting to note that in two concluding comments, the Committee did not state that the declaration is contrary to the Convention's subject and purpose; however, the Committee recommends withdrawing the declaration.

C.3.2.2 General Recommendation

After examining reports, the Committee makes its interpretation within a general recommendation (Article 21). Whereby, the Committee clarifies the substantive provisions as well as the Committee's approaches to implementing CEDAW's obligations. General recommendations No. 21 and 29 are the most crucial Committee view, which clarifies to what degree the Committee accepts gender discrimination for religious reasons.

In General Recommendation No. 21 the Committee states that "….**whatever the legal system**, **religion**, custom or tradition within the country, the treatment of women in the family both at law and in private must accord with the principles of equality and justice for all people, as article 2 of the Convention requires".[569] Moreover, the Committee affirms that "….whether their laws comply with the principles of articles 9, 15 and 16 and where, **by reason of religious** or private law or custom, compliance with the law or with the Convention **is impeded**".[570] Therefore, the Committee encourages that states parties take necessary steps to comply with the Convention, in particular in order to comply with articles 9, 15, and 16.[571] In this regard, states parties also "should introduce measures directed at encouraging full compliance with the principles of the Convention, particularly where religious or private law or custom conflict with those principles".[572]

Additionally, the examination of the reports of states parties indicate that inequality in the family is often justified in the name of religion, tradition, and culture; for these reasons, many states parties have entered reservations to all or parts of articles 2 and 16 to maintain their legal arrangements, but the extent of such reservations are not compatible with the object and purpose of the CEDAW.[573] On the other hand, the constitutions of a number of states parties

568 CEDAW, Concluding observations on the fourth periodic report of Pakistan, CEDAW/C/PAK/CO/4, 27 March 2013, para. 9-10

569 CEDAW, General recommendation No. 21, para. 15

570 CEDAW, General recommendation No. 21, para. 48(b)

571 CEDAW, General Recommendation No. 21, para. 49

572 CEDAW, General Recommendation No. 21, para. 50

573 CEDAW, General Recommendation No. 29, para. 2-3

recognize equal protection and non-discrimination provisions but "have not revised or adopted legislation to eliminate the discriminatory aspects of their family law regimes, **whether they are regulated by civil code, religious law,** ethnic custom or any combination of laws and practices. All these constitutional and legal frameworks are discriminatory, **in violation of article 2 in conjunction with articles 5, 15 and 16 of the Convention**".[574]

General Recommendation No. 29 makes the crucial point that "neither traditional, religious or cultural practice nor incompatible domestic laws and policies can justify violations of the Convention. The Committee also remains convinced that reservations to article 16, whether lodged for national, traditional, religious or cultural reasons, are incompatible with the Convention and therefore impermissible and should be reviewed and modified or withdrawn".[575]

As a result of the Committee's recommendations, several states parties have modified their family laws and provided equality on the whole; consequently, they have withdrawn their reservation relating to Islamic laws. Accordingly, other states parties should take "into consideration **the experiences of countries with similar religious backgrounds** and legal systems that have successfully accommodated domestic legislation to commitments emanating from international legally binding instruments, with a view to withdrawing reservations".[576]

C.3.2.3 Conclusion

By and large, the reservation issue is high on the Committee's agenda, in which the assessment of a reservation has appeared in its general recommendations and concluding comments statements. Above all, the Committee formulates a robust approach when the reservation targets the core provisions of the CEDAW (general recommendations No. 28, 29, and 21). In this case, the Committee emphasizes time and again that the reservation on any grounds to Article 2 and 16 are incompatible. In addition, the Committee's procedure regarding the incompatibility of a reservation has had a positive impact on other states parties. It defines the scope of the reservation's incompatibility for other states; thus, many reservations have been withdrawn or modified since the 1990s. However, the

574 CEDAW, General Recommendation No. 29, para. 10
575 CEDAW, General Recommendation No. 29, para. 54
576 CEDAW, General Recommendation No. 29, para. 55

question remains that the Committee has not addressed the legal consequences of impermissible reservations.[577]

For the most part, a general reservation is incompatible, especially when the reservation is created based on religious reasons. In this context, *Professor Pellet* (the Reportage of the International Law Commission) asserted that Islamic reservations are not a problem because they refer to religious law; rather, the problem is the vagueness of such reservations. It means that the meaning is unclear, and therein lies its incompatibility with the object and purpose of the treaty.[578] In fact, a form of gender inequality is read into the Islamic reservation; they have systematic legal protection because Islamic jurisprudence is recognized as a source of law in the constitutions of Islamic countries. Hence, Islamic reservations pursue a potential source of gender inequality and create obstacles to implementing CEDAW, which is related entirely to women's rights.[579]

In general, the dialogue between the Committee and Islamic countries has been problematic concerning gender discrimination, religion, and the state party's international obligations. On the one hand, the Committee has maintained a pragmatic attitude, and considered side by side the link between gender discrimination and Sharia as a fact in Islamic society. The Committee has found that the Islamic governments are a part of the process of women's human rights development because religion or Islam is intertwined in cultural, traditional, custom, legal and political structure, but in different variations among Islamic countries. Therefore, the Committee has encouraged Islamic governments to lobby religious-liberal communities or Sharia scholars to find harmony between CEDAW's obligations and Islamic law.

On the other hand, the Committee has a role as an international monitory mechanism. Hence, the Committee must attend to the compatibility of the state's obligations with CEDAW's object and purpose, regardless of any grounding in domestic laws, culture, or religion. In fact, states by ratifying CEDAW recognizes the principle of equality and non-discrimination against women, and by

577 Compare also, De Pauw, Marijke, Women's rights: from bad to worse? Assessing the evolution of incompatible reservations to the CEDAW Convention, Merko urios - Gender in European and International Law - Vol. 29/77, 2013, p. 64

578 Monforte, Tanya, BROAD STROKES AND BRIGHT LINES: A RECONSIDERATION OF SHARI'A BASED RESERVATIONS, Columbia Journal of Gender and law, 2017, p. 13

579 Compare also, Monforte, BROAD STROKES AND BRIGHT LINES, p. 51

entering an Islamic reservation might be disturbing the integration of CEDAW's provisions.

Thus, the Committee has taken precautions to discuss Islam and women's human rights in a constructive dialogue, but in its final analyses (concluding comments or general recommendations), it must emphasize compliance with international women's standards. It seems that the Committee has not had any tendency to recognize reservations based on religion. Accordingly, in the Committee's view, the remaining Islamic reservations have resulted in inequality for women. Additionally, the Committee does not accept religious reasons for justification for violating international obligations. In this regard, the Committee emphasizes expressly that "domestic laws may never be used as justification for failures by States parties to carry out their international obligations". [580]

Simultaneously, the Committee must seek to implement the CEDAW's provisions and show it has made a serious attempt in this regard. For this reason, it is recommended that the Committee push the Islamic countries to be transparent in their interpretation of Sharia so that they be held accountable for them. Furthermore, the Committee must examine whether gender inequalities have been reformed in the states' legal structures. For instance, some Islamic countries have taken steps to improve women's rights that have resulted in withdrawing part of the Islamic reservation. In this way, the Committee can highlight such reformations in its dialogue and dialogue with similar religious backgrounds; this could lead to withdrawing the remaining Islamic reservations or transferring to a specific reservation without a vague understanding.

D. Monitoring Mechanisms of the International Covenants

D.1 Human Rights Committee

The Human Rights Committee monitors the implementation of the International Covenant on Civil and Political Rights (ICCPR), which embodies eighteen independent experts (Article 28). The monitoring mechanisms include examining the state's report (Article 40, usually every four years), formulating the General Comment (Article 40, paragraph 4), and, considering inter-state complaints of any of the rights in the ICCPR (Article 41). Furthermore, the First Optional Protocol (1976) provides the competence for the Committee to examine individual complaints about alleged violations of the Covenant by states parties. Also, the Second Optional Protocol (1989) gives the Committee full competence to

580 CEDAW, General Recommendation No. 28, para. 33

abolition the states' death penalty. It must note that the Committee will consider communication when a state becomes a party to the Ops, not a state party to the Covenant. In doing so, they recognize the Committee's competence to receive and consider communications from individuals (Article 1 of the First-OP). However, both inter-state and the individual complaints procedures "were optional" and to be decided after "a purely written procedure by means of legally non-binding final views".[581]

Most Islamic countries have ratified the Covenant, but only Algeria and Tunisia have ratified the First-OP,[582] and none of the Islamic countries has ratified the Second-OP, as of 2019.[583] It means that Islamic countries are not accountable before the HRC for violating ICCPR's rights; neither can other states parties lodge such communications against them. As a result, the HRC only monitors the obligations of Islamic countries by considering their reports and concluding observations thereon.

D.1.1 The Scope of the Consideration of Gender Discrimination under HRC

The World Conference on Human Rights (1993) determined the scope of the work of the HRC and the CESCR. Both committees consider discrimination against women that affects women's physical integrity, which such discrimination against women regards as the root cause of human rights abuses and constraints. The issues of discrimination referred to articles 2 and 3 of both covenants, which are substantive provisions of non-discrimination and equality principles. Consequently, the HRC and the CESCR address the specific experience of women in an integrated manner, under Article 3 (gender equality rights) in both covenants. In other words, the HRC does not expressly operate on the issues of discrimination against women in society; instead, the HRC considers harmful gender ideologies in the context of physical violence against women.[584]

---

581 Nowak, Manfred, Comments on the UN High Commissioner's proposals aimed at strengthening the UN human rights treaty body system, Netherlands quarterly of human rights / Studie- en Informatiecentrum Mensenrechten <Utrecht> 31, Nr. 1 (2013): 3–8, p. 3

582 United Nations Treaty Collection, accessed at: https://treaties.un.org/Pages/ViewDetails.aspx?src=IND&mtdsg_no=IV-5&chapter=4&clang=_en

583 United Nations Treaty Collection", accessed at: https://treaties.un.org/Pages/ViewDetails.aspx?src=IND&mtdsg_no=IV-12&chapter=4&clang=_en

584 Leeuwen, Fleur van, Women's rights are human rights: the practice of the United Nations Human Rights Committee and the Committee on Economic, Social and Cultural

In doing so, the HRC considers physical violence against women, which are most of the issues discussed in General Comment No. 28. These call more considerable attention to rape, domestic violence, trafficking in women, and sexual harassment even though Article 3 concentrates on the right to equality of men and women.[585]

However, the CEDAW Committee, as a body of experts on women's rights, directs its attention to any underlying discrimination of women in society and addresses, in varying degrees, the existence of stereotyped conception of women owing to socio-cultural factors.[586]

D.1.2 HRC and Religious Reasons

ICCPR focuses on everyone's civil and political rights, even though it sets out several articles specifically regarding women. Some Islamic countries such as Bahrain, Pakistan, and Qatar have entered declarations or reservations on the grounds of Sharia.[587] Such reservations deal mainly with Article 3 (gender equality rights) and Article 23 (equal rights of spouses within marriage and its dissolution), which have a 'far-reaching' effect on the other articles of the ICCPR. As a result, this situation has led to discriminatory application of the provisions of the ICCPR, principally toward women.[588]

However, the HRC examines the periodic reports and comments on them. For example, the HRC expressed its dissatisfaction with Kuwait's lack of progress by its creation of discriminatory provisions, as the HRC illustrated in the third

---

Rights, School of Human Rights Research series / School of Human Rights Research <Utrecht>. - Antwerpen [u.a.] : Intersentia, 1999- 36 (Antwerp [u.a.]: Intersentia, 2010), p. 40-41

585 Ibid, p. 143

586 Ibid, p. 39

587 The reservation of Bahrain: Article 3, (18) and (23) as not affecting in any way the prescriptions of the Islamic Sharia.
The declaration of Pakistan: Articles 3 shall be so applied to the extent that they are not repugnant to the Provisions of the Constitution of Pakistan and the Sharia laws.
Qatar made this reservation that: Article 3 with regard to provisions related to the inheritance of power, for it contravenes the provisions of article 8 of the Constitution. Moreover, Article 23.4 is contravenes the Islamic Sharia,
See also United Nations Treaty Collection, accessed at: https://treaties.un.org/Pages/ViewDetails.aspx?src=TREATY&mtdsg_no=IV-4&chapter=4&clang=_en.

588 Baderin, Mashood A.; Ssenyonjo, Manisuli, Hrsg., International human rights law: six decades after the UDHR and beyond (Farnham [u.a]: Ashgate, 2010), p. 344

periodic report of Kuwait (2016) regarding the reservation to articles relevant to gender discrimination. The Committee was also concerned with the primacy of Sharia law over conflicting or contradictory provisions of the Covenant. Furthermore, the HRC recommended that Kuwait take all necessary steps to withdraw the declarations on articles 2.1, 3, and 23.[589] Moreover, concerning Bahrain's reservation, the Committee mentioned that the overly broad reservations to articles 3, 18, and 23 apply only to the extent of those articles, and do not affect the provisions of Sharia. Nevertheless, those reservations are incompatible with the object and purpose of the Covenant.[590]

Furthermore, HRC has formulated two general recommendations No. 4 and 28, regarding Article 3 (equal rights basis on sex). General Comment No. 4 concerns articles 3, 2 (1) and 26, that in general, require affirmative action to ensure the positive enjoyment of the ICCPR rights and that states parties undertake legislative or administrative measures to regulate matters that may negatively affect the rights provided for in the Covenant.[591] Thus, in General Comment No. 4, the Committee explicitly states that affirmative action should also be taken to ensure the positive enjoyment of the rights in the ICCPR.

Moreover, General Comment No. 28 (2000) is the most important in explicitly stating HRC's view regarding gender equality rights, which replaces General Comment No. 4. It reflects the experience the Committee has gathered from its activities over the last 20 years. This General Comment provides some of the factors that impact the enjoyment of gender equal rights within the ICCPR. Besides, this General Comment mentions the influence of religion, traditions, and culture on the equal treatment of women, which can seriously impair the equal enjoyment by women of their rights. The Committee states that "inequality in the enjoyment of rights by women throughout the world is deeply embedded in tradition, history, and culture, including religious attitudes.....States parties should ensure that **traditional, historical, religious or cultural attitudes are not used to justify violations of women's equal right to equality** before the law and to equal enjoyment of all Covenant rights".[592]

589 HRC, Concluding observations on the third report of Kuwait, CCPR/C/KWT/3, 11 August 2016, para. 6

590 HRC, Concluding observations on the initial report of Bahrain, CCPR/C/BHR/CO/1, November 2018, para. 7

591 CCPR, General Comment No. 4: on Article 3 (Equal Right of Men and Women to the Enjoyment of All Civil and Political Rights) U.N. Doc. HRI/GEN/1/Rev.1, 1981, para. 2-3

592 CCPR, General Comment No. 28, para. 5

Hence, according to the Committee's attitude, tradition, culture, and religious grounds cannot constitute a justification for discrimination against women. In the case of *Müller and Engelhard v Namibia* (gender discrimination in spouses in Namibian Law), the Committee asserts that: "in the view of the importance of the principle of equality between men and women, the argument of a long-standing tradition cannot be maintained as a general justification for different treatment of men and women, which is contrary to the Covenant".[593] In this case, the Committee decided that a 'long-standing tradition' cannot be used as a justification to discriminate against women. It can be concluded, in case of a clash between the equal enjoyment by women of their rights and religious norms, traditions and cultural preference will be given to the equal enjoyment by women of their rights. Even about freedom of thought, conscience, and religion, tradition may not be relied upon to justify discrimination against women.[594]

D.2 Committee on the ICESCR

The Committee on Economic, Social and Cultural Rights (CESCR) is the body of eighteen independent experts that monitors the implementation of the ICESCR. States parties undertake to submit periodic reports to the Committee, within two years of the Covenant's entering into force, and after that every five years. The Committee examines each report and submits recommendations to the state party in the form of 'concluding observations' (Article 16-18). Further, the Committee makes a General Comment that is its interpretation of the provisions of the Covenant (Article 19). Additionally, the ICESCR has an OP that was adopted in 2008 and establishes complaint and inquiry mechanisms for the ICESCR.[595]

As requested by the World Conference on Human Rights (1993), the CESCR takes into account the gender-specific form and circumstances of the human rights abuses. Therefore, the CESCR addresses sexual harassment and honor crimes that are explicitly relevant to women's deep-rooted discrimination in

593 Conte, Alex; Burchill, Richard, Defining civil and political rights: the jurisprudence of the United Nations Human Rights Committee, 2. Aufl. (Farnham [u.a.]: Ashgate, 2009), p. 240

594 Oostland, Rolanda, Non-discrimination and Equality of Women, A comparative analysis of the interpretation by the UN Human Rights Committee and the UN Committee on the Elimination of Discrimination against Women, Oostland, 2006, p. 53 and 64

595 As of 2019, none of Islamic countries ratified OP-ICSCR.
See also: United Nations Treaty Collection, accessed at: https://treaties.un.org/Pages/ViewDetails.aspx?src=TREATY&mtdsg_no=IV-3-a&chapter=4&clang=_en.

society. In general, the CESCR does not request states parties to tackle the root or manifestations of violence against women by addressing discrimination of women; instead, it addresses physical violence against women for criminalization and prosecution of these acts.[596]

In spite of the fact that most Islamic countries have ratified the ICESCR, some of them have entered Islamic reservations to articles 2 (2) and 3,[597] which provide the equal right women and men to the 'enjoyment' of ICESCR rights. In general, an analysis of the CESCR's concluding observations (1993-2001) indicates that under the Committee's approach, "the centrality of cultural and traditional practices, attitudes and beliefs to the persistence of sex discrimination".[598] Moreover, CESCR adopted General Comment No. 16 (2005) that provides a "general approach to substantive gender equality rights" to the enjoyment of economic, social and cultural rights. It must add that this General Comment is considered a gender equality comment; it does not address the structural barriers that are rooted in social norms, cultural, traditional, and religious beliefs, where women's inequality is institutionalized. Article 3 and its general comment, in particular, promote the substantive understanding of gender equality and non-discrimination, and for realizing requests a range of measures to implement the Convent's rights.[599]

E. Conclusion

In fact, both international covenants adopt a substantive approach to gender equality and promote a 'gender-inclusive interpretation' of their treaty provisions.[600] Moreover, as mentioned above, both committees address discrimination

596 Oostland, Non-discrimination and Equality of Women, p. 4

597 For example, the declaration of Kuwait regarding article 2, paragraph 2, and article 3 that states as consistent with the provisions of the Kuwait Constitution in general. The reservation of Qatar that states: "not consider itself bound by the provisions of Article, for they contravene the Islamic Sharia with regard to questions of inheritance and birth."
See also: United Nations Treaty Collection, accessed at: https://treaties.un.org/Pages/ViewDetails.aspx?src=TREATY&mtdsg_no=IV-3&chapter=4&clang=_en"

598 Otto, Dianne, Gender Comment': Why Does the UN Committee on Economic, Social and Cultural Rights Need a General Comment on Women?, Canadian Journal of Women and the Law, 2002, p. 41

599 Ibid, p. 52

600 Ibid, p. 51

of women as a root cause of human rights abuses and constraints that affect women's physical integrity. But, the CEDAW reiterates the existence of stereotypes rooted in socio-cultural factors, which are the structural barriers to the enjoyment of women's equality rights. Hence, it would recommend that both committees must promote their 'gender equality comments', that address the deeply structural inequality in the cultural, traditional, and religious contexts, which are the leading cause of the persistence of sex discrimination, regardless as requested on the World Conference on Human Rights for both committees. On the one hand, in general, there is not a solemn commitment of states to the CEDAW, which creates a marginalized status for the CEDAW; as a result, the CEDAW's general recommendations have had little effect in comparison with that of the ICCPR and ICESCR.[601] Therefore, concerning both committees' recognition of the existence of stereotyping in gender issues, it can complement the CEDAW's general recommendations. On the other hand, the ICCPR and ICESCR have not openly confronted Islamic reservations in gender equality articles than the CEDAW; hence, this could potentially induce both committees to collaborate on gender issues within this context.

601 Ibid, p. 21

Final Remarks

The emphasis on gender discrimination in general and in specialized international human rights treaties demonstrates that "gender- sensitivity" is an essential issue in the view of international law. International covenants (UDHR, ICCPR, and ICESCR) provide a general approach to 'substantive gender equality rights' to enjoy their treaty provisions. CEDAW goes further and addresses the details of equality rights by 'eliminating any discrimination against women'. In general, these conventions design a framework for implementing gender equality rights and non-discrimination by imposing legal obligations on states parties; it must be guaranteed in their law (*de jure*) and state practice (*de facto*). Therefore, states parties have the primary responsibility to implement gender equality rights and non-discrimination.

Thus, a state's jurisdiction plays an essential role in promoting or hindering the principle of gender equality rights and non-discrimination, and the degree to which a state's jurisdiction of gender equality rights is compatible with international law. For instance, the Western construct engages more with an international standard of gender equality rights; hence, there are not serious inconsistencies in gender issues between Western countries and international law. Whereas, non-Western countries may be uncomfortable with this dynamic; that due to diversity in culture, religion, traditional, political, and socio-economic aspects. Moreover, if a state's jurisdiction is not compatible with international standards in gender issues, it has to take a series of legislative and policy reforms. So, a state will be considered whether culture, religion, traditional, political, and socio-economic fields have the capacity to accept and comply with international law.

Therefore, with respect to diversity in the international community, the realization of international gender equality rights may be challenged. Thus far, there is a gap between the theory and the practice of gender equality rights and non-discrimination because, on the one hand, it depends on the extent to which degree states parties have reconciled it. On the other hand, international law sets out legal obligations on states parties to protect and promote gender equality rights and non-discrimination, without considering the legal consequences for violating or ignoring women's human rights standards. However, the monitoring mechanisms can fill this legal gap, on the whole, which can identify the obstacles to realizing gender equality rights and non-discrimination.

As considered in Chapter two, religion might be used as justification to ignore women's human rights. In Islamic countries, Islam creates an 'identity', which is often deeply entrenched in society. Thus, it prioritizes its doctrines in the national constitution and other domestic laws. Religious scholars, who are exclusively male, have the competence to interpret Islamic law, assuming unequal rights for women compared to men. Therefore, their jurisprudential interpretation of Islam often heavily influences many different aspects of women's rights in politics, society, and private life. As a result, gender discrimination for religious reasons defines for women.

In fact, this form of gender discrimination is usually a 'unilateral statement' by religious clerics, which often continues in legal structures, resulting in women facing severe legal obstacles institutionalized in domestic laws. In doing so, there exists the practice of illegal discrimination while claiming a form of legality. Furthermore, the *Imams* may promote non-legal gender discrimination, which manipulates customary-cultural norms and patriarchal structures impose discrimination on women. In general, this form of gender discrimination is a more 'practical instrument' for maintaining discrimination against women.

However, religious proscriptions or *fatwas* are open to interpretation; respect to social and political development can also be re-interpreted. This dynamic status of Islamic law has led to a division between traditional and liberal interpretations of Islam. Thus, women have benefited from this division, and some of the women's rights have improved in line with liberal interpretations of Islam. But, these reformations have occurred more during participation in decision-making processes, than in family law. This is because, on the one hand, the backing of political power structures had played a vital role in practice when they initiated the process of reformations; thus, the presence of women in public decision-making processes is more visible and can be used as a message toward liberal positions in public and the international community. On the other hand, it seems that reform or more reform in family law may provoke the anger of the religious conservatives-line, especially regarding property rights. It appears that they want to preserve their patriarchal structure in the family relations, but when this is threatened, they can mobilize civil regimes to oppose the government. Consequently, Islamic governments do not tend to pursue the reformations of unequal gender rights in family law; in fact, they benefit from a reinterpretation of Islam to suit their purposes.

Nevertheless, the majority of Islamic countries have ratified international human rights treaties because they do not want to be isolated from the human rights system. But by placing reservations based on Islam, they are safeguarding themselves to choose any provision of the conventions when it contrasts with Islamic law. Nonetheless, there is, in fact, gender discrimination in the form of 'Islamic reservations' when Islamic countries want to engage with international mechanisms, and excluding the legal effect of specific provisions in their obligations at the international level. In other words, an Islamic reservation is "the way to maintain some semblance of coherence between international commitments",[602] which in practice, they highlight their jurisdiction of Islamic law over women's human rights. What is even more challenging is the unlimited character and vague meaning of such reservation, thus leading to extending a general interpretation of gender equality rights within Sharia. As a result, many objections have been raised by other states parties to those reservations, which are made on the grounds of the incompatibility with the object and purpose of the treaty.

As considered in Chapter three, reservations based on Islam target more the CEDAW specifically articles 2, 9, 15 and 16, which are key provisions of the CEDAW. Moreover, some reservations based on Islam has been entered to articles 2 (2) and 3 of the ICCPR and ICESCR (the substantive provisions of the gender equality rights). This category of Islamic reservations to gender equality articles indicates that gender equality rights are a sensitive topic in Islamic countries, mostly about family law, where the conflict is more apparent between women's Islamic law and women's human rights than women's participation in public life.

However, the CEDAW-Committee has maintained a pragmatic attitude toward discussing Islam and women's human rights in a constructive dialogue. But the CEDAW-Committee has clarified that international law does not recognize religion as a justification for discrimination against women in their final analyses (concluding comments or general recommendations). Furthermore, they continue to emphasize compliance with international women's standards through the withdrawal of such reservations. Both the HCR and CESCR, in their General Comments, have acknowledged the same view as the CEDAW.

A surprising fact is that some reservations based on Islam have been withdrawn, which was resulted from some legislative reforms in their respective countries. Thus, such improvements did not remain in the domestic area; they became apparent at the international level, which has led to compatibility in some contexts of gender equality between Islam and international law. Therefore, on the one hand, the withdrawal of some reservations indicates that Islamic jurisprudence has the potential towards recognition of women's human rights if an Islamic government strengthens its efforts to withdrawing such reservations. On the other hand, it opens up the committee's opportunity to employ dialogue

602 Monforte, BROAD STROKES AND BRIGHT LINES, p. 18

toward the possibility of withdrawing the remaining Islamic reservations in situations with similar religious, cultural, legal, and political backgrounds.

The Following Recommendations are the most important steps to promote Muslim women's rights at the national and international level:

A) At the national level

The promotion of women's rights through "soft religious measures" by the liberal-religious communities. Religious communities are influential stakeholders in improving women's rights because of such discrimination grounded on Sharia. Therefore, the liberal-religious communities play a prominent role in making a lobby with fundamentalists and traditionalists' religious communities, who are sanctioned as a result of any promotion of women's rights by Islamic law. Therefore, any discussion about promoting women's rights by the liberal-religious community can soften the conservative religious line.

The promotion of women's rights under the name of women's Islamic law: For Islamic countries, women's human rights are engaged more with Western values; thus, the promotion under the name of women's human rights may be labeled an anti-religious attitude, and be rejected by strong opposition from the dominant religious entities. Therefore, the improvement of women's rights under the name of women's Islamic law is a precautionary action to assure religious communities and the patriarchal structure that equality and non-discrimination are fundamental rights in Islamic law, not promoting Western values.

Thus, there is a great deal of potential in Islam; may utilize women to develop their rights under the name of Islam, which makes a compromise between religious communities and women, who understand the social and political dynamics, are ready to achieve a more effective role in society, more political participation, and improved family relations.

The highlight of the division between traditional and liberal interpretations of Islam to improve anti-discriminatory laws in the family. The dynamic status of Islamic law leads to a division between traditional and liberal interpretations of Islam; thus, the position of women in participatory decision-making processes is improved. Therefore, highlighting this division can contribute to the removal of discriminatory provisions in family law.

The joining of religious leaders with public campaigns on the issue of improving women's rights. When religious leaders join the campaigns on women's subjects, this could be with the approval of the religious authority over political structures to remove some legal discrimination against women. Otherwise, religious communities can propagate, through systematic media measures, the blocking of improvement on women's rights in the public discussion.

B) At the international level:

The withdrawal of some reservations indicates that Islamic law has the potential to recognize women's human rights. This provides an opportunity for human rights activism to promote an Islamic discourse in the framework of women's human rights, which could find harmony in gender issues between Islamic law and human rights.

The ICCPR and ICESCR must promote 'gender equality comments in structural barriers'. Both covenants must also address the structural inequality rooted in the cultural, traditional, and religious contexts, regardless as determined by the World Conference on Human Rights (1993) for both committees. On the one hand, in general, there is a serious commitment of states to both covenants, which are developed through UDHR, as the most important document on fundamental human rights. On the other hand, neither of the covenants openly confronts the reservations based on Islam in gender equality articles than the CEDAW. Therefore, this could potentially induce both committees to collaborate on gender issues and strengthen CEDAW's General Recommendations in this context.

Bibliography

A) Monographies

Alfredsson, Gudmundur, Hrsg., International human rights monitoring mechanisms: essays in honour of Jakob Th. Möller, The Raoul Wallenberg Institute human rights library / Raoul Wallenberg Institutet för Mänskliga Rättigheter och Humanitär Rätt. - Leiden [u.a.] : Nijhoff, 1997- ; ZDB-ID: 2026501-3 7 (The Hague [u.a.]: Nijhoff, 2001)

Alfredsson, Gudmundur; Eide, Asbjørn, The Universal Declaration of Human Rights: A Common Standard of Achievement (Martinus Nijhoff Publishers, 1999)

Alfredsson, Gudmundur; Grimheden, Jonas; G. Ramcharan, Bertrand, International Human Rights Monitoring Mechanisms: Essays in Honour of Jakob Th. Möller (Martinus Nijhoff Publishers, 2009)

Aust, Anthony, Modern Treaty Law and Practice, Third Edition, (Cambridge University Press, 2013)

Baderin, Mashood A.; Ssenyonjo, Manisuli, Hrsg., International human rights law: six decades after the UDHR and beyond (Farnham [u.a]: Ashgate, 2010)

Cavendish, Marshall, World and Its Peoples (Marshall Cavendish, 2006)

Conte, Alex; Burchill, Richard, Defining civil and political rights: the jurisprudence of the United Nations Human Rights Committee, 2. Aufl. (Farnham [u.a.]: Ashgate, 2009)

Conte, Alex; Davidson, Scott; Burchill, Richard, Defining civil and political rights: the jurisprudence of the United Nations Human Rights Committee, Repr (Aldershot [u.a.]: Ashgate, 2005)

Corten, Olivier; Klein, Pierre, The Vienna Conventions on the Law of Treaties: A Commentary (Oxford University Press, 2011)

Elie Alagha, Joseph, The Shifts in Hizbullah's Ideology: Religious Ideology, Political Ideology, and Political Program, (Amsterdam University Press, 2006)

Fazaeli, Roja, Islamic Feminisms: Rights and Interpretations Across Generations in Iran (Taylor & Francis, 2016)

Farrior, Stephanie, Equality and Non-Discrimination under International Law, Vol.2, (Ashgate, 2015)

Farrior, Stephanie, Equality and Non-Discrimination under International Law, (Routledge, 2017)

Freeman, Marsha A.; Chinkin, Christine M.; Rudolf, Beate, The UN Convention on the Elimination of All Forms of Discrimination Against Women: A Commentary (OUP Oxford, 2012)

Hellum, Anne; Aasen, Henriette Sinding, Women's Human Rights: CEDAW in International, Regional and National Law (Cambridge University Press, 2013)

Jänterä-Jareborg, Maarit; Tigroudja, Hélène,Women's human rights and the elimination of discrimination (Leiden: Brill Nijhoff, 2016)

Joseph, Sarah; Castan, Melissa, The International Covenant on Civil and Political Rights: cases, materials, and commentary, Third Edition (Oxford Univ. Press, 2013)

Leckie, Scott; Gallagher, Anne, Economic, Social, and Cultural Rights: A Legal Resource Guide, (University of Pennsylvania Press, 2011)

Leeuwen, Fleur van, Women's rights are human rights: the practice of the United Nations Human Rights Committee and the Committee on Economic, Social and Cultural Rights, School of Human Rights Research series / School of Human Rights Research <Utrecht>. - Antwerpen [u.a.] : Intersentia, 1999- 36 (Antwerp [u.a.]: Intersentia, 2010)

Nowak, Manfred, U.N. Covenant on Civil and Political Rights: CCPR Commentary, 2nd, rev. ed. Aufl. (Kehl [u.a.]: Engel, 2005)

Rai, Suman, Law Relating to Protection of Women from Domestic Violence: An Exhaustive Commentary on Protection of Women from Domestic Violence Act, 2005 with Emphasis on Various Studies by UNO, WHO, UNICEF, Amnesty International and Other National and International Organisations on the Topic Along with Australia, Japan, Malaysia, Mauritius, Singapore, South Africa, Sri Lanka, U.K. and Zimbabwe Laws on Domestic Violence (Orient Publishing Company, 2013)

Riedel, Eibe; Giacca, Gilles; Golay, Christophe, Economic, Social, and Cultural Rights in International Law: Contemporary Issues and Challenges (OUP Oxford, 2014)

Ross, Susan Deller, Women's Human Rights: The International and Comparative Law Casebook (University of Pennsylvania Press, 2013)

Saul, Ben; Kinley, David H.; Mowbray, Jacqueline, The International Covenant on Economic, Social and Cultural Rights: Cases, Materials, and commentary (OUP Oxford, 2014)

Sepúlveda, M. Magdalena, The nature of the obligations under the International Covenant on Economic, Social and Cultural Rights, School of Human Rights Research series / School of Human Rights Research <Utrecht>. - Antwerpen [u.a.] : Intersentia, 1999- ; ZDB-ID: 2017500-0 18 (Antwerpen [u.a.]: Intersentia, 2003)

Smith, Rhona K. M, Textbook on International Human Rights (Oxford University Press, 2016) Ssenyonjo, Manisuli, Economic, Social and Cultural Rights in International Law (Bloomsbury Publishing, 2016)

Stark, Barbara, International Family Law: An Introduction, (Ashgate Publishing, Ltd., 2013)

Vandenhole, Wouter Non-Discrimination and Equality in the View of the UN Human Rights Treaty Bodies (Intersentia nv, 2005)

Yahyaoui Krivenko, Ekaterina, Women, Islam and International Law: Within the Context of the Convention on the Elimination of All Forms of Discrimination Against Women (BRILL, 2009)

Ziemele, Ineta; Reservations to human rights treaties and the Vienna convention regime: conflict, harmony or reconciliation, The Raoul Wallenberg Institute human rights library / Raoul Wallenberg Institutet för Mänskliga Rättigheter och Humanitär Rätt. - Leiden [u.a.] : Nijhoff, 1997- ; ZDB-ID: 2026501-3 17 (Leiden [u.a.]: Nijhoff, 2004)

Zwingel, Susanne, Translating international women's rights: the CEDAW Convention in context, Gender and Politics (London: Palgrave Macmillan, 2016)

B) Articles

Abdelkader, Engy, To Judge or Not to Judge: A Comparative Analysis of Islamic Jurisprudential Approaches to Female Judges in the Muslim World (Indonesia, Egypt and Iran), Fordham International Law Journal, Volume 37, Issue 2, 2014

Ahmad, Nausheen, Land Rights for Pakistani (Muslim) Women: Law and Policy, Policy Brief Series, Nr- 23, 2010

Al-Heis, Abdulaziz, Women Participation in Saudi Arabia's Political Arena, Al Jazeera Centre for Studies, 2011

Ansari, Sarfraz Husain, Forced Modernization and Public Policy: A Case Study of Ayub Khan Era (1958-69), Journal of Political Studies, Vol 18, Issue – 1, 2011

Anver, M. Emon; Khaliq, Urfan, Private International Law Private International Law, Islamic Law, and Cross-Border Child Abduction, A Historico-Legal Analysis, Institute Letters, 2016

Ashraf Nemat, Orzala, Comparative Analysis of Family Law in the Context of Islam, The Heinrich Böll Foundation, 2006

Awan, Muhammad Ali, Political Participation of Women in Pakistan, Historical and Political Dynamics Shaping the Structure of Politics for Women, FGI, Frankfurter Forschungszentrum Globaler Islam, 2016

Bary, Ida, Women's Political Participation in Muslim Brotherhood between the Hammer of Ambiguity and the Anvil of Inclusion moderation: (The Case of Egypt and Tunisia), Norwegian University of Life Sciences Faculty of Social Sciences Department of International, Environmental and Development Studies (NORAGRIC), 2015

Brown, Gordon (ed.), The Universal Declaration of Human Rights in the 21st Century: A Living Document in a Changing World. Cambridge, UK: Open Book Publishers, 2016

Campbell, Meghan, "Women's Rights and the Convention on the Elimination of all Forms of Discrimination Against Women: Unlocking the Potential of the Optional Protocol", Nordic Journal of Human Rights 34, Nr. 4 (1. Oktober 2016): 247–71

Childs, Sarah; Lena Krook, Mona, Analyzing Women's Substantive Representation: From Critical Mass to Critical Actors, Journal compilation Government and Opposition Ltd Published by Blackwell Publishing, 2009

Chiongson, Rea Abada; Desai, Deval; Marchiori, Teresa; Woolcock, Michael, The Role of Law and Justice in Achieving Gender Equality, World Bank, World Development Report 2012, "Gender Equality and Development", 2011

Cusack, Simone; Pusey, Lisa, CEDAW and the Rights to Non-Discrimination and Equality, Melbourne Journal of International Law 14, 2013

Dawood, Muhammad; Afridi, Manzoor Khan, Comparison between 1956 and 1962 Constitution of Pakistan, Ma'arif Research Journal, 2016

De Pauw, Marijke, Women's rights: from bad to worse? Assessing the evolution of incompatible reservations to the CEDAW Convention, Merko urios - Gender in European and International Law - Vol. 29/77, 2013

Fortier, Corinne, The Right to Divorce for Women (khul') in Islam: Comparative Practices in Mauritania and Egypt, OALib Journal, 2010

Freeman, Marsha A., RESERVATIONS TO CEDAW: AN ANALYSIS FOR UNICEF, United Nations Children's Fund (UNICEF), Gender, Rights and Civic Engagement Section, Division of Policy and Practice, New York, 2009

Friedhoff, Anna, Bras and Ballots: Comparing Women's Political Participation in Pakistan and Saudi Arabia, OREGON REVIEW OF INTERNATIONAL LAW, 2013

Haas '06, Sherri, Female Parliamentary Representation in Islamic Countries, Res Public - Journal of Undergraduate Research: Vol. 11, 2006

Jyoti Das, Hirak, National Assembly Elections in Kuwait, 2016, Contemporary Review of the Middle East, 2017

Kar, Mehrangiz, Who are the Judges in the Islamic Republic of Iran, LEGATUM INSTITUTE, 2011

Karimi, Behzad, WOMEN'S POLITICAL PARTICIPATION IN THE CONTEMPORARY IRAN: A STUDY OF WESTERN IRAN, IMPACT (International Journal of Research in Applied, Natural and Social Sciences), 2014

Kurzman, Charles; Naqvi, Ijlal, ISLAMIC POLITICAL PARTIES AND PARLIAMENTARY ELECTIONS, United States Institute of Peace, 2009

Naqavi, Ali Reza, The Family Protection ACT of Iran, Islamic Research Institute, International Islamic University, Islamabad, 1967

Nowak, Manfred, Comments on the UN High Commissioner's proposals aimed at strengthening the UN human rights treaty body system, Netherlands quarterly of human rights / Studie- en Informatiecentrum Mensenrechten <Utrecht> 31, Nr. 1 (2013): 3–8

Mapulanga-Hulston, Jackbeth K, Examining the justiciability of economic, social and cultural rights, International journal of human rights, Volum 6, 2002

Mayer, Ann Elizabeth, Reform of Personal Status Laws in North Africa: A Problem of Islamic or Mediterranean laws?, WLUML Occasional Paper No. 8, 1996

Mirshahvalad, Minoo, Can Iranian Women Compensate for Their Absence From the World of Fiqh?, Jura Gentium, ISSN 1826-8269, XIV, 2017, 2

Mohamed Adil, Mohamed Azam, "Custody and Religion of Minors in Malaysia", Islam and Civilisational Renewal (ICR) 8, Nr. 2 (16. August 2017): 272–74

Mohammadzadeh Rahni, Mohammad Reza; Kavousi, Peyman; Fatemeh, Kavousi, Divorce in Iran and Cases in Which the Woman Has the Right to Divorce, Journal of Applied Environmental and Biological Sciences, 2014

Moinifar, Heshmat Sadat, PARTICIPATION OF WOMEN IN IRAN'S POLITY, GEMC journal, 2013

Monforte, Tanya, BROAD STROKES AND BRIGHT LINES: A RECONSIDERATION OF SHARI'A BASED RESERVATIONS, Columbia Journal of Gender and law, 2017

Musawah for equality in the family, THEMATIC REPORT ON MUSLIM FAMILY LAW AND MUSLIM WOMEN'S RIGHTS IN SAUDI ARABIA, 69th CEDAW Session, Geneva, Switzerland, 2018

O'Neil, Tam; Domingo, Pilar, The power to decide, Women, decision-making and gender equality, Overseas Development Institute, 2015

Otto, Dianne, Gender Comment': Why Does the UN Committee on Economic, Social and Cultural Rights Need a General Comment on Women?, Canadian Journal of Women and the Law, 2002

Rolland, Abby M, Muslim Women Political Leaders and Electoral Participation in Muslim-Majority Countries, Gettysburg College's institutional, 2015

Oostland, Rolanda, Non-discrimination and Equality of Women, A comparative analysis of the interpretation by the UN Human Rights Committee and the UN Committee on the Elimination of Discrimination against Women, Oostland, 2006

Shaheed, Farida, Gender, Religion and the Quest for Justice in Pakistan, United Nations Research Institute for Social Development (UNRISD) and HeinrichBöll-Stiftung, 2009

Shqarri, Fjorda, Reservations to Treaties, Prohibited Reservations and some Unsolved Issued Related to Them, Mediterranean Journal of Social Sciences, 2015

Shuaib, F. S., Kamal, M. H., Bustami, T. A., Othman, N. and Sulaiman, M. S, Towards an Apex Sharia Court in Malaysia, Shuaib, F. S.*, Kamal, M. H., Bustami, T. A., Othman, N. and Sulaiman, M. S, SOCIAL SCIENCES & HUMANITIES, 2017

Sokhi-Bulley, Bal, The Optional Protocol to CEDAW: First Steps United Nations and Regional Human Rights Systems: Recent Developments, Human Rights Law Review 6, 2006, 143–59

Sonneveld, Nadia; Lindbekk, Monika, Women Judges in the Muslim World: A Comparative Study of Discourse and Practice, BRILL, 2017

Toperich, Sasha; Mullins, Andy, A New Paradigm: Perspectives on the Changing Mediterranean, Center for Transatlantic Relations, 2014

Tajali, Mona, Islamic Women's Groups and the Quest for Political Representation in Turkey and Iran, The Middle East Journal, 2015

Tajali, Mona, Notions of Female Authority in Modern Shi'i Thought, Religions, Open Access Journal of Theology, 2011

Tajali, Mona, Protesting gender discrimination from within: women's political representation on behalf of Islamic parties, British Journal of Middle Eastern Studies, 2017

Wan Muhammad, Ramizah, WOMAN AND SHARI'AH COURT: A STUDY OF MALAYSIA AND INDONESIA, International Journal of Cross-Cultural Studies, 2015

Weiwei, Li, Equality and Non-Discrimination Under International Human Rights Law, The Norwegian Centre for Human Rights, 2004

Yacoub Al Rabadi, Rania Farah, Legal Reform in Women's Rights: A Comparative Study Between Jordan and Bahrain Concerning Citizenship and Political Participation, Cuvillier, 2012

Zia, Maliha; Butt, Riffat, Pakistan NGO Alternative Report on CEDAW 2005-2009, Aurat Publication and Information Service Foundation (AF), 2012

C) International Documents

Center on Housing Rights and Evictions (COHRE), In Search of Equality: A Survey of Law and Practice related to Women's Inheritance Rights in the Middle East and North Africa (MENA) Region, Geneva, Switzerland, 2006

Commission on Human Rights, Report of the Special Rapporteur on the independence of judges and lawyers, Report on the mission to the Kingdom of Saudi Arabia, E/CN.4/2003/65/Add.3, 2003

Council of Europe, Non-Discrimination: A Human Right, Seminar to mark the entry into force of Protocol No. 12 Strasbourg, 11 October 2005, (Council of Europe Publishing, 2006)

Economic and Social Commission for Western Asia (ESCWA), A Review of the Status of Women and Gender Equality in the Arab Region, 20 Years after the Adoption of the Beijing Declaration and Platform for Action, 2016

Fourth World Conference on Women, Action for Equality, Development and Peace, Beijing 1995

Geneva Forum Series no. 1, Women and the Judiciary, International Commission of Jurists, 2014

Human Rights Council, The Guiding Principles on Extreme Poverty and Human Rights, Resolution 21/11, The Office of the United Nations High Commissioner for Human Rights (OHCHR), 2012

Human Rights Watch, Boxed In: Women and Saudi Arabia's Male Guardianship System, 2016

International Law Association, Committee on Feminism and International law, Final Report on Women's Equality and Nationality in International Law, in Report of the Sixty-Ninth Conference, London Conference, 2000

International Law Commission, The discussion during of Meeting with Human Rights Bodies, International Law Commission, Fifty-ninth session, ILC(LIX)/RT/CRP.1, 26. Juli 2007

International Law Commission, Meeting with Human Rights Bodies, Fifty-Ninth Session, ILC (LIX)/RT/CRP.1, July 26, 2007

Inter-Parliamentary Union (IPU), Women in parliament in 2016, The year in review, 2017

Inter-Parliamentary Union (IPU), Women in parliament in 2017, The year in review, United Kingdom, 2018

Inter-Parliamentary Union and United Nations, The Convention on the Elimination of All Forms of Discrimination Against Women and Its Optional Protocol: Handbook for Parliamentarians (United Nations Publications, 2003)

NYU Global Institute for Advanced Study, Article 7: The Equality and Non- Discrimination Provision. Appendix E to the Report of the Global Citizenship Commission. (Cambridge, UK: Open Book Publishers, 2016)

UNHCR-OHCHR, Meeting Report, Regional Expert Meeting on the Human Rights of Stateless Persons in the Middle East and North Africa, 2010

OECD/CAWTAR, Women in Public Life: Gender, Law and Policy in the Middle East and North Africa, OECD Publishing, Paris, 2014

OECD Global Forum on Public Governance, Women's Leadership in Public Life: Fostering Diversity for Inclusive Growth, OECD Conference Centre, Paris, 2014

OHCHR, Vienna Declaration and Programme of Action, adopted by the World Conference on Human Rights in 1993. A/CONF.157/23

Reunite International Child Abduction Centre, Morocco, Approved by Jean Gabriel Tomaly, 2005

Suhakam's Report on the Status of Women's Rights in Malaysia, SUHAKAM, 2010

The ACE Encyclopaedia: Parties and Candidates, published by ACE Electoral Knowledge Network, 2013

The Equal Rights Trust, Declaration of Principles on Equality: A Contribution to International Human Rights, London, 2008

The Global Initiative for Economic, Social and Cultural Rights and ESCR-Net, The ICESCR at 50: The Significance from a Women's Rights Perspective, 2016

The International Commission of Jurists (ICJ), Egypt's Judiciary: A Tool of Repression: Lack of Effective Guarantees of Independence and Accountability, 2016

The OSCE Office for Democratic Institutions and Human Rights (ODIHR), Handbook on promoting women's participation in political parties, 2014

The United Nations Children's Fund (UNICEF), KUWAIT, MENA Gender Equality Profile Status of Girls and Women in the Middle East and North Africa, 2010

The Woodrow Wilson International Center for Scholars, "Best Practices" Progressive Family Laws in Muslim Countries, 2005

UN. Committee on the Elimination of Discrimination against Women, Compilation of Guidelines on the Form and Content of Reports to be submitted by States Parties to the International Human Rights Treaties, International Human Rights Instruments, HRI/GEN/2/Rev.1/Add.2, 5 May 2003

UN Office of the High Commissioner for Human Rights (OHCHR), Fact Sheet No. 16 (Rev.1), The Committee on Economic, Social and Cultural Rights, May 1996, No. 16 (Rev.1)

United Nations, Guide to Practice on Reservations to Treaties, adopted by the International Law Commission sixty-third session (A/66/10), Yearbook of the International Law Commission, 2011, vol. II, Part Two

United Nations, The Convention on the Elimination of All Forms of Discrimination Against Women and Its Optional Protocol, Inter-Parliamentary Union (IPU), 2003

United Nations Development Programme; National Democratic Institute for International Affairs, Empowering Women for Stronger Political Parties: A Good Practices Guide to Promote Women's Political Participation, 2011

United Nations Development Programme Pakistan: Political and Legislative Participation of Women in Pakistan, Issues and Perspectives, Research Report, Islamabad, 2005

United Nations Division for the Advancement of Women, Convention on the Elimination of All Forms of Discrimination Against Women, the Optional Protocol: Text and Materials (United Nations Publications, 2003)

United Nations, Women and Election, Guide to promoting the participation of women in elections, United Nations Office of the Special Adviser on Gender Issues and Advancement of Women (OSAGI), 2005

Womens UN Report Network, EGM/EPDM/ REPORT, Equal Participation of Women and Men in Decision-Making Processes, with Particular Emphasis on Political Participation and Leadership, United Nations, Division for the Advancement of Women (DAW), 2005

World Bank. 2012, World Development Report 2012: Gender Equality and Development, The International Bank for Reconstruction and Development / The World Bank, 2011

C.1) UN Documents

CEDAW, Communication No. 1/2003, Ms. B.-J. v. Germany. Decision adopted on 14 July 2004, thirty-first session. Excerpt from A/59/38

CEDAW, Communication No. 18/2008, CEDAW/ C/46/D/18/2008

CEDAW, Communication No. 17/2008, CEDAW/C/49/D/17/2008

CEDAW, General Recommendation No. 1: Reporting by States Parties, 1986

CEDAW, General Recommendation No. 21: Equality in marriage and family relations, 1994

CEDAW, General Recommendation No. 25 on Article 4, on Temporary Special Measures, Thirtieth session, 2004

CEDAW, General Recommendation No. 28: on the Core Obligations of States Parties under Article 2 of the CEDAW, 2010

CEDAW, General Recommendation Nr. 29: on article 16 of the Convention on the Elimination of All Forms of Discrimination against Women, CEDAW/C/GC/29, 2013

CEDAW, General Recommendations Nr. 32: on the gender-related dimensions of refugee status, asylum, nationality and statelessness of women, 2014

CCPR, General Comment Nr.4: on Article 3 (Equal Right of Men and Women to the Enjoyment of All Civil and Political Rights) U.N. Doc. HRI/GEN/1/Rev.1, 1981

CCPR, General Comment No. 18: Non-discrimination, Adopted by the Human Rights Committee, 1989

CCPR, General Comment Nr. 24: Issues Relating to Reservations Made upon Ratification or Accession to the Covenant or the Optional Protocols thereto, or in Relation to Declarations under Article 41 of the Covenant, CCPR/C/21/Rev.1/Add.6 1994

CCPR, General Comment No. 25, The right to participate in public affairs, 1996.

CCPR, General Comment No. 28: Article 3 (The Equality of Rights Between Men and Women), 2000

CESCR, General Comment No. 11: Plans of action for primary education, 1999

CESCR, General Comment No. 16: on the Equal Right of Men and Women to the Enjoyment of All Economic, Social and Cultural Rights, UN Doc. E/C.12/2005/4, 2005

CESCR, General Comment No. 20: Non-discrimination in economic, social and cultural rights, 2009

HRC, Concluding observations on the initial report of Bahrain, CCPR/C/BHR/CO/1, November 2018

HRC, Concluding observations on the third report of Kuwait, CCPR/C/KWT/3, 11 August 2016

Human Rights Council, Resolution A/HRC/RES/20/4, Promotion and protection of all human rights, civil, political, economic, social and cultural rights, including the right to development The right to a nationality: women and children, Twentieth session, 2012

Human Rights Council, Report on discrimination against women on nationality related matters, including the impact on children, Report of the Office of the United Nations High Commissioner for Human Rights, Twenty-third session, A/HRC/23/23, 2013

Human Rights Council, Report of the Secretary-General, Human rights and arbitrary deprivation of nationality, Twenty-fifth session A/HRC/25/28, 2013

Human Rights Council, Report of the Special Rapporteur on the independence of judges and lawyers, Gabriela Knaul, Mission to Qatar, A/HRC/29/26/Add.1, 2015

Human Rights Council, Report of the Special Rapporteur on the independence of judges and lawyers, Gabriela Knaul, Mission to the United Arab Emirates, A/HRC/29/26/Add.2, 2015

Human Rights Council, Report of the Working Group on the issue of discrimination against women in law and in practice, A/HRC/29/40, United Nations, 2015

Resolution 66/130, Women and political participation, adopted by the General Assembly, 2011

Resolution 1325, adopted by the United Nations Security Council, on women and peace and security, 2000

C.2) Reports and Concluding Comments of the CEDAW

CEDAW Committee, UN Doc. CEDAW/C/OP.8/PHL/1, 22 April 2015

CEDAW, Consideration of reports submitted by States parties under article 18 of the Convention, 13th session, A/49/38, 1994

CEDAW, Declarations, reservations, objections and notifications of withdrawal of reservations relating to the CEDAW, Sixteenth meeting, CEDAW/SP/2010/2, 2010

CEDAW, Fifteenth meeting, CEDAW/SP/2008/1, 30 July 2008

CEDAW, Report of the Committee on the Elimination of Discrimination Against Women, 10th Session, A/46/38, 1991

CEDAW, Report of the Committee on the Elimination of Discrimination Against Women, 11th Session, A/47/38, 1992

CEDAW, Report of the Committee on the Elimination of Discrimination against Women, 13th Session, A/49/38, 1994

CEDAW, Report of the Committee on the Elimination of Discrimination Against Women, 19th session, A/53/38, 1998

CEDAW, Report of the Committee on the CEDAW, Third session, Volume II, No. 45 (A/39145), 1984

CEDAW, Second periodic report of States parties, Morocco, CEDAW/C/MOR/2, February 2000

CEDAW, Combined initial and second periodic report of Tunisia, Fourteenth session, CEDAW/C/TUN/1-2, 16 January – 3 February 1995

CEDAW, Initial reports of States parties, Jordan, November 1997, CEDAW/C/JOR/1

CEDAW, Report of the Committee on the CEDAW, Third session, Volume II, No. 45 (A/39145), 1984

CEDAW, Consideration Report, Initial report of Algeria, Twentieth session, CEDAW/C/SR.406, 2002

CEDAW, Initial reports of States parties, ALGERIA, CEDAW/C/DZA/, 1 1 September 1998

CEDAW, Initial report of Algeria (continued), CEDAW/C/SR.412, 6 February 2002

CEDAW, Initial report of Algeria, CEDAW/C/SR.407, 1 February 2002

CEDAW, Initial report of Algeria, CEDAW/C/SR.406, 5 February 2002

Consideration of reports, Combined initial and second periodic report of Malaysia, Thirty-fifth session, CEDAW/C/SR.731, 2006

CEDAW, Thirty-second session, Report of the Chairperson of the pre-session working group Second periodic report of Algeria, CEDAW/C/SR.667, 2005

CEDAW, Concluding Comments: Algeria, CEDAW/C/DZA/CC/2, 11 January 2005

CEDAW, Report of the Committee, Third session, Volume II, No. 45 (A/39/45), 26 March 1984

CEDAW, the third report and the combined fourth and fifth periodic reports of Egypt, CEDAW/C/SR.492 and 493

CEDAW, Third and combined fourth and fifth periodic reports of Egypt, CEDAW/C/SR.492, 26 March 2001

CEDAW, Third and combined fourth and fifth periodic reports of Egypt, CEDAW/C/SR.492, 26 March 2001

CEDAW, Third and combined fourth and fifth reports of Egypt, CEDAW/C/SR.493, 27 March 2001

CEDAW, Combined sixth and seventh periodic reports of States parties: Egypt, CEDAW/C/EGY/7, 5 September 2008

CEDAW, Combined initial and second periodic reports of States parties: Malaysia, CEDAW/C/MYS/1-2, 12 April 2004

CEDAW, Consideration of reports, Combined initial and second periodic report of Malaysia, CEDAW/C/SR.731, 20 June 2006

CEDAW, Consideration of reports, Combined initial and second periodic report of Malaysia, CEDAW/C/SR.731, 20 June 2006

CEDAW, Consideration of reports, Combined initial and second periodic report of Malaysia, CEDAW/C/SR.731, 20 June 2006

CEDAW, Combined third to fifth periodic reports of States parties due in 2012: Malaysia, CEDAW/C/MYS/3-5, 17 October 2016

CEDAW, Concluding observations on the combined third to fifth periodic reports of Malaysia, CEDAW/C/MYS/CO/3-5, 14 March 2018

CEDAW, Consideration of reports combined initial and second periodic reports of Saudi Arabia, CEDAW/C/SR.815, 15 February 2008

CEDAW, Combined initial and second periodic reports: Saudi Arabia, CEDAW/C/SAU/2, 29 March 2007

CEDAW, Combined initial and second periodic report of Saudi Arabia, CEDAW/C/SAU/2, 17 January 2008

CEDAW, Concluding comments: Saudi Arabia, CEDAW/C/SAU/CO/2, 8 April 2008

CEDAW, Consideration of reports Combined third and fourth periodic reports of Saudi Arabia, CEDAW/C/SR.1582, 2 March 2018

CEDAW, Concluding observations on the combined third and fourth periodic reports of Saudi Arabia, CEDAW/C/SAU/CO/3-4, 14 March 2018

CEDAW, Combined initial, second and third periodic reports: Pakistan, CEDAW/C/PAK/1-3, 3 August 2005

CEDAW, Combined initial, second and third periodic report of Pakistan, CEDAW/C/SR.781, 19 July 2007

CEDAW, Combined initial, second and third periodic report of Pakistan, CEDAW/C/SR.782, 18 July 2007

CEDAW, Concluding Comments: Pakistan, CEDAW/C/PAK/CO/3, 11 June 2007

CEDAW, Fourth periodic reports of States parties, Pakistan, CEDAW/C/PAK/4, 24 September 2011

CEDAW, Concluding Observations on the fourth periodic report of Pakistan, CEDAW/C/PAK/CO/4, 27 March 2013

CEDAW, Concluding Observations: Algeria, CEDAW/C/DZA/CO/3-4, 23 March 2012

CEDAW, Concluding Comments: Malaysia, CEDAW/C/MYS/CO/2, 31 May 2006

D) Online Sources

A Brief Overview of the Saudi Arabian Legal System - GlobaLex, accessed: http://www.nyulawglobal.org/globalex/Saudi_Arabia.html#_Toc200894588.

Algerians debate female inheritance rights, accessed at: http://www.algeria.com/forums/algeria-en-alg%E9rie/28514-algerians-debate-female-inheritance-rights.html.

Can Iran Have a Female President?, accessed at: https://www.trtworld.com/mea/can-iran-have-a-female-president--6402

CEDAW Reporting, zugegriffen 2. Februar 2017, http://www.un.org/womenwatch/daw/cedaw/reporting.htm.

CEDAW Sessions, accessed at: http://www.un.org/womenwatch/daw/cedaw/reservations-country.htm

Committee on the Elimination of Discrimination against Women, accessed at: http://www.un.org/womenwatch/daw/cedaw/committee.htm.

Family Law in Kuwait, U.S. Embassy in Kuwait (blog), accessed at: https://kw.usembassy.gov/u-s-citizen-services/local-resources-of-u-s-citizens/family-law-kuwait/.

Female Lawyers in Saudi Courts: 'We Are Equal to Male Counterparts', Arab News, 29. December 2016, accessed: http://www.arabnews.com/node/1030991/saudi-arabia.

Freedom House, Women's Rights in the Middle East and North Africa 2010, accessed at: https://freedomhouse.org/report/women039s-rights-middle-east-and-north-africa/womens-rights-middle-east-and-north-africa-2010.

Global Campaign for Equal Nationality Rights, „The Problem", accessed at: http://www.equalnationalityrights.org/the-issue/the-problem.)

Gooch, Liz, The female face of Islamic law in Malaysia, accessed at: https://www.aljazeera.com/indepth/features/2017/08/female-face-islamic-law-malaysia-170802110726630.html.

History of the Document, accessed at: http://www.un.org/en/sections/universal-declaration/history-document/index.html.

Human Rights Watch, CRIME OR CUSTOM?, Violence Against Women in Pakistan, 1999, accessed to: https://www.hrw.org/reports/1999/pakistan/Pakhtml-03.htm#P336_49235.

Hussain, Dr. Abid, THE ISLAMIC LAWS OF INHERITANCE, accessed at: https://www.islam101.com/sociology/inheritance.htm.

Icelandic Human Rights Centre, The Right to Equality and Non-Discrimination, accessed at: http://www.humanrights.is/en/human-rights-education-project/human-rights-concepts-ideas-and-fora/substantive-human-rights/the-right-to-equality-and-non-discrimination.

International Law: Muslim Divorce in Bangladesh", International Law (blog), Prof. Gabriel Sawma, 10. Juli 2013, accessed at: http://gabrielsawma.blogspot.com/2013/07/muslim-divorce-in-bangladesh.html.

International Family Law Firm, JORDAN AND CHILD ABDUCTION, accessed at: http://www.international-divorce.com/ca-jordan.htm

International Justice Resource Center (blog), Overview of the Human Rights Framework, accessed at: http://www.ijrcenter.org/ihr-reading-room/overview-of-the-human-rights-framework/.

International Parental Child Abduction Kuwait, accessed at: http://www.pass-portsusa.com/family/abduction/country/country_503.html.

Iran: Women Call For Rights Ahead Of Presidential Poll", RadioFreeEurope/RadioLiberty, 2005, accessed: https://www.rferl.org/a/1059254.html.

Iranian Parliament Seeks Ruling on Women's Presidential Eligibility, accessed at: http://www.payvand.com/news/04/mar/1120.html.

Islamic Family Law and Justice for Muslim Women, Asia Society, accessed at: https://asiasociety.org/islamic-family-law-and-justice-muslim-women.

Jamileh, Kadivar, An Unofficial Boy's Club, Majalla Magazine (blog), 24. Mai 2013, accessed at: http://eng.majalla.com/2013/05/article55241743/an-unofficial-boys-club.

Jan W. van Deth, What is Political Participation?, Oxford Research Encyclopedia of Politics, 2016, accessed at: http://oxfordre.com/politics/view/10.1093/acrefore/9780190228637.001.0001/acrefore-9780190228637-e-68

Kadivar, Jamileh, An Unofficial Boy's Club, Majalla Magazine (blog), 24. Mai 2013, accessed at: http://eng.majalla.com/2013/05/article55241743/an-unofficial-boys-club.

Kuwait Marriage Law - Kuwaiti Family Law and Divorce, accessed at: https://www.visit-kuwait.com/living/marriage-law.aspx.

Michele Brandt; Jeffrey A. Kaplan, The Tension between Women's Rights and Religious Rights: Reservations to Cedaw by Egypt, Bangladesh and Tunisia, JOURNAL OF LAW & RELIGION, 1995

Miki Caul Kittilson, Gender and Political Behavior, Oxford Research Encyclopedia of Politics, 2016, accessed at: https://doi.org/10.1093/acrefore/9780190228637.013.71.

Messieh, Nancy; Gaber, Suzanne, A Win for Women in Egypt's Courts, Atlantic Council, accessed at: http://www.atlanticcouncil.org/blogs/menasource/a-win-for-women-in-egypt-s-courts.

Nicholas, Sarah, Islam and Women's Rights in Modern Pakistan, SPRING 2016, accessed to: https://history.libraries.wsu.edu/spring2016/2016/01/19/womens-rights/

Official document of the United Nations accessed at: http://legal.un.org/docs/?path=../ilc/texts/instruments/english/draft_articles/1_8_2011.pdf&lang=EF

OHCHR | Core International Instruments, accessed at: https://www.ohchr.org/EN/ProfessionalInterest/Pages/CoreInstruments.aspx.

OHCHR | International Law, accessed at: http://www.ohchr.org/EN/ProfessionalInterest/Pages/InternationalLaw.aspx.

OP CEDAW > What is OP CEDAW? > OP CEDAW Overview : IWRAW Asia Pacific, accessed at: https://www.iwraw-ap.org/op-cedaw/what-is-op-cedaw/op-cedaw-overview/.

OPTIONAL PROTOCOL TO WOMEN'S CONVENTION COMES INTO FORCE, accessed at:http://www.un.org/womenwatch/daw/cedaw/protocol/wom1242.htm.

Pakistan Council for Science & Technology, History of women empowerment in Pakistan, accessed to: "http://www.pcst.org.pk/wst/wst_hwep.php

Pakistan - Oxford Islamic Studies Online, accessed: http://www.oxfordislamicstudies.com/print/opr/t236/e0616.

Qatar, 29. Januar 2017, accessed at: https://freedomhouse.org/report/freedom-world/2017/qatar.

Report of the International Law Commission, Sixty-third session, A/66/10/Add.1, 2011, accessed at http://legal.un.org/ilc/reports/2011/english/addendum.pdf.

Reservations to CEDAW, accessed at: http://www.un.org/womenwatch/daw/cedaw/reservations.htm.

Shahrokni, Nazanin, All the President's Women, 2009, MER253, accessed: https://www.merip.org/mer/mer253/all-presidents-women

Shariah High Court appoints first women judges in Malaysia, http://www.themalaymailonline.com/malaysia/article/the-first-two-women-shariah-high-court-judges-in-malaysia.

Southeast Asian Human Rights Studies Network (SEAHRN) Human Rights, Textbook, accessed at: http://shapesea.com/wp-content/uploads/2016/02/HR-Textbook-Ch-1-Fundamentals-Ed-1.pdf

Rules of Procedure - Annex I To the CEDAW Report A/56/38, accessed http://www.un.org/womenwatch/daw/cedaw/cedawreport-a5638-RulesOfProcedure.htm

Text of the draft guidelines on reservations to treaties provisionally adopted so far by the Commission, A/62/10. 2007. guideline 3.1.6", zugegriffen 5. April 2016, http://legal.un.org/docs/?path=../ilc/documentation/english/ilc_lix_rt_crp1.pdf&lang=EF.

The New Arab, "Tunisia Takes Groundbreaking Steps towards Gender Equality", alaraby, accessed at: https://www.alaraby.co.uk/english/news/2018/1/20/tunisia-takes-groundbreaking-steps-towards-gender-equality.

The United Nations Human Rights Treaty System (An Introduction to the Core Human Rights Treaties and the Treaty Bodies Fact), Office of the United Nations High Commissioner for Human Rights Fact Sheet No. 30/Rev.1 (2012), accessed at: http://www.ohchr.org/Documents/Publications/FactSheet30Rev1.pdf.

Tunisians Divided Over Women's Inheritance Rights, *The North Africa Post* (blog), 18. August 2017, http://northafricapost.com/19367-tunisians-divided-womens-inheritance-rights.html.

Tunisian Women Stand up for Gender Equality in Inheritance, The North Africa Post (blog), 12. März 2018, http://northafricapost.com/22654-tunisian-women-stand-gender-equality-inheritance.html

Tunisia becomes the first Arab nation to approve gender equality in inheritance law, Dhaka Tribune, 25. November 2018, accessed at: https://www.dhakatribune.com/world/africa/2018/11/25/controversial-gender-equality-in-inheritance-law-approved-by-tunisian-cabinet.

UN Commission on Human Rights, Note verbale dated 5 December 1986 from the Permanent Mission of the Netherlands to the United Nations Office at Geneva addressed to the Centre for Human Rights ("Limburg Principles"), 8 January 1987, E/CN.4/1987/17, accessed at: https://www.escr net.org/resources/limburg-principles-implementation-international-covenant-economic-social-and-cultura

United Nations, Treaty Collection, accessed at: https://treaties.un.org/Pages/ViewDetails.aspx?chapter=4&clang=_en&mtdsg_no=IV-4&src=IND#EndDec

United Nations Treaty Collection, accessed at: https://treaties.un.org/Pages/ViewDetails.aspx?src=IND&mtdsg_no=IV-5&chapter=4&clang=_en

Universal Declaration of Human Rights (UDHR) | 1948, Encyclopedia Britannica accessed at: https://www.britannica.com/topic/Universal-Declaration-of-Human-Rights.

Vienna Convention on the Law of Treaties (1969), accessed: http://opil.ouplaw.com/view/10.1093/law:epil/9780199231690/law-9780199231690-e1498.

Yearbook of the International Law Commission, Vol. I. 651st meeting. 25 May 1962. Law of treaties (A/CN.4/144 and Add.l), accessed at: http://legal.un.org/ilc/publications/yearbooks/english/ilc_1962_v1.pdf.

Lightning Source UK Ltd.
Milton Keynes UK
UKHW051344130422
401512UK00018B/220

9 783631 843918